**Penguin Books**

## The Making of Managers

Robert Heller was born in 1932. He began his career in journalism in 1955 with the *Financial Times*, having left Cambridge with a first-class honours degree in history. At the *Financial Times* he was successively Industrial Correspondent, US Correspondent (opening the paper's first post-war office in the United States) and Editor of the Diary, 'Men and Matters'. He left the newspaper in 1963 to edit the business pages of the *Observer*. After a successful relaunch of this section, he left to fulfil his longstanding ambition of launching a major monthly business magazine. *Management Today*, founded in 1966, replaced a publication with a circulation of 27,000, which has now increased to over 100,000. Robert Heller was the magazine's editor from 1966 until 1982 and was editorial director until 1987. *Management Today* is published by the Haymarket Publishing Group of Companies, of which Robert Heller was a director. In his work for Haymarket he was closely associated with many highly successful magazine launches, including those of *Campaign, Accountancy Age, Computing* and *Marketing*.

Among Robert Heller's other journalistic interests are the publications of Sterling Publishing Company plc, of which he is a director, and for which he edits the magazine *Finance*. He has written for most major newspapers and general-interest magazines in the UK and has broadcast widely on radio and television. Robert Heller has given talks or seminars to a vast range of audiences in many parts of the world.

Since publishing his first, bestselling book, *The Naked Manager* (1972), which was translated into six languages, Robert Heller has published many others: *The Common Millionaire, The Naked Investor, The Once and Future Manager, Superman, The Business of Winning, The Business of Success, The New Naked Manager, The Supermanagers, The Pocket Manager*; (with Norris Willatt) *Can You Trust Your Bank?* and *The European Revenge*; *The Naked Market, The Supermarketers, The State of Industry: Can Britain Make It?* and *The Age of the Common Millionaire*. He won the John Player Award for Management Journalism in 1970 and the Blue Circle Award for Journalism in 1980.

He has four children and lives on the edge of Hampstead Heath in Highgate, North London. His interests include collecting modern art, looking at art (modern or not), reading, drinking (wine, preferably old), music, eating (preferably well) and exercise.

# Robert Heller

# The Making of Managers

with an Introduction by
LORD WEINSTOCK

PENGUIN BOOKS

Published by the Penguin Group
27 Wrights Lane, London W8 5TZ, England
Viking Penguin Inc., 40 West 23rd Street, New York, New York 10010, USA
Penguin Books Australia Ltd, Ringwood, Victoria, Australia
Penguin Books Canada Ltd, 2801 John Street, Markham, Ontario, Canada L3R 1B4
Penguin Books (NZ) Ltd, 182–190 Wairau Road, Auckland 10, New Zealand

Penguin Books Ltd, Registered Offices: Harmondsworth, Middlesex, England

This selection first published by Sidgwick and Jackson 1989
Published in Penguin Books 1990

Printed and bound in Great Britain by
Cox & Wyman Ltd, Reading
Filmset in 10 pt Linotron Galliard by
Rowland Phototypesetting Ltd, Bury St Edmunds, Suffolk

0140091351

22/2/91

# Contents

*Acknowledgements* vii

*Introduction* by Lord Weinstock ix

1 *Why successes flop* 1

2 *The management mishmash* 11

3 *The manager of the past* 41

4 *The manager at the crossroads* 51

5 *Motivating the manager* 61

6 *The future of management* 71

7 *The objects of the exercise* 80

8 Plus ça change 93

9 *How to develop drive and overdrive* 106

10 *How to manage the new industries* 122

11 *Damn* la différence 164

12 *Mergers make strange managers* 173

13 *The discontinuous present* 180

14 *Opportunities in changing times* 187

15 *Battle of the bestsellers* 219

16 *If you can't be careful, be good* 230

17 *The well-dressed executive* 242

*Index* 252

# *Acknowledgements*

'Why Successes Flop', 'Battle of the Bestsellers' and 'The Well-dressed Executive' (Chapters 1, 15 and 17) first appeared in *The New Naked Manager*, published in 1972 by Hodder & Stoughton Ltd. They are reproduced here by kind permission of the publisher. 'The Management Mishmash' (Chapter 2) first appeared in *The Naked Investor*, published in 1976 by Weidenfeld & Nicolson Ltd. It is reproduced here by kind permission of the publisher. 'The Manager of the Past', 'The Manager at the Crossroads', 'Motivating the Manager' and 'The Future of Management' (Chapters 3 to 6) were first published by Associated Business Programme in 1976. They are reproduced here by kind permission. 'If You Can't Be Careful, Be Good' (Chapter 16) first appeared in *The Common Millionaire* published in 1974 by Weidenfeld & Nicolson. It is reproduced here by kind permission of the publisher. 'The Objects of the Exercise' and '*Plus ça change*' (Chapters 7 and 8) first appeared in *The Business of Winning* published in 1981 by Sidgwick and Jackson. 'How to Develop Drive and Overdrive' and 'How to Manage the New Industries' (Chapters 9 and 10) first appeared in *The Supermanagers* published in 1985 by Sidgwick and Jackson. 'Damn *la différence*', 'Mergers Make Strange Managers' and 'The Discontinuous Present' (Chapters 11 to 13) first appeared in *The Naked Market* published in 1984 by Sidgwick and Jackson. 'Opportunities in Changing Times' (Chapter 14) first appeared in *The Supermarketers* published in 1987 by Sidgwick and Jackson.

# Introduction

by Lord Weinstock

Britain has produced very few management writers of international reputation, which might seem to reflect the relatively poor performance of British industry since the Second World War. Writers and thinkers based on the United States and Japan, using American and Japanese examples, have carried a conviction that a Briton could hardly expect.

Robert Heller, however, has always refused to accept that Britain's relatively poor performance and failure are inevitable. On the contrary, as a journalist, author, broadcaster and lecturer, Heller has argued that British management is not condemned by some form of original sin, but can, by taking thought and action, achieve results to match the best. This positive emphasis partly explains why his books have proved an exception to the British rule, and have sold widely in many languages, from Norwegian to Japanese.

Heller's career as a journalist began on the *Financial Times* in 1955, and included an obviously formative spell of three years as that newspaper's first full-time correspondent in the post-war United States. Heller was the first business writer of his generation to be fully exposed to American ideas and practice; that experience, constantly renewed, has been crucial in forming his management philosophy.

This American influence was evident when I first met Heller in the early 1960s. He was then Business Editor of the *Observer*, to whose pages he introduced the personalization of business reporting long prevalent in New York. However unwelcome to British managers, the style became universal here, and its central message – that management is a human activity, engaged in by fallible human beings, who must take full responsibility for their own deeds and misdeeds – has permeated Heller's writings.

It was the theme of his first book, *The Naked Manager* (1972), which constituted an attack on the pseudo-scientific management that was briefly the rage in the later 1960s. Heller's attack on the pretensions and mythology of the times was a classic exposé. But its lasting reputation, and the fact that a revised version, *The New Naked Manager*, could appear successfully in 1986, are testimony to the strength of the constructive ideas that underlay the deserved debunking.

Other commentators endeavoured to define the optimum structure and organization for businesses, and to formalize the intricate processes of corporate planning and decision-making. Conclusions derived from psychological studies of human behaviour and motivation were applied to the business world with mixed results. While often providing relevant and helpful insights, these conclusions generally fall far short of a blueprint for success.

This is not surprising when one considers that the interactions between the many people whose actions are decisive in a business constitute a complex, and to some extent unpredictable, process. For a start, people in business, as in other walks of life, do not consistently behave with complete rationality. And irrationality cannot easily be accommodated by management theory.

The process of management continues to defy attempts at homogeneous systematization. But Robert Heller at least lighted on some obvious truths that most of his colleagues missed; Heller argued that the key to success was clear, pragmatic thought, leading to effective action, which in turn had to be closely monitored through meaningful measures of performance. The management principles applied in Britain's General Electric Company were quoted approvingly in this context, which makes it difficult for me to argue against these ideas. But it has always been Heller's practice to draw widely from the examples and cases he has encountered.

His columns for the *Observer* were especially influential in the period up to 1975, a period in which many British managements found their past sins of omission and commission catching up with them. The columns were frequently highly critical, and the criticism was usually well founded and deserved. Their critical edge contributed to the debunking tone of *The Naked Manager*, which derived from the *Observer* column. But the observation of the more permanent characteristics of management, as opposed to the transient, is also acute.

Indeed, reading *The Naked Manager* today, it is remarkable how little of its basic themes has had to be changed. The book was unusually prescient in spotting such important developments as the upward and outward thrust of Japan (then in its formative stage) and the relative decline of American management. But the philosophy of the book – its emphasis on results, its scorn for conventional wisdom, its impatience with cant and its essential understanding of the human element – has an enduring value.

For his next book, Robert Heller turned to other business areas: millionaires, stock-market investments, the European defeat of the American challenge, the banking scandals of a turbulent decade. The less well-known, shorter, but deeply thoughtful book, *The Once and Future Manager*, explored the prospects for all of the main managerial disciplines in turn. Typically, this work was based on a series of interviews (of people drawn from the firm of selection consultants who commissioned it). All Heller's books have been based on reporting, because he knows that the successful management writer must confront facts and that windy speculation will help nobody.

The two books *The Business of Winning* and *The Business of Success* took this idea to its logical conclusion, giving managers useful and usable advice. However, the value of their content was perhaps obscured by their form, especially in the case of the second book. The revised American version, *The Supermanagers*, was rebuilt around the essential characteristics of entrepreneurial success, in how-to-do-it style, and has been Heller's bestselling book to date. The combination of short case histories with succinct exposition of the associated techniques and arguments is very effective.

Heller's second-generation management books move forward from debunking to definition of the business management task, and description of how experience shows it to be best accomplished. Above all, the identification of the entrepreneur with the corporate manager, and the concentration on persuading the manager to think and act like an entrepreneur, are at least as important as his earlier emphasis on stripping away myths and striving to achieve reality.

This entrepreneurial approach leads naturally to the market place. Heller saw early on the enormous significance of the switch from markets of need to markets of desire as rapidly changing technology, shrinking geography and slower world growth generated what can best be described as an explosion of competition. That dominant change in all markets in the last quarter of the twentieth century is the theme of *The Naked Market* and its very much changed American version, *The Supermarketers*.

What distinguishes Heller's works, though, is that while they are effective guides for busy managers, they are also entertaining and readable in a way seldom associated with books about business. He gives us living business histories that can stand comparison with any other accounts of contemporary life, which use the same combination of wit, clarity and pace that were the hallmark of his columns for the *Observer*. Heller, like Peter Drucker, the management thinker he most admires and quotes, thinks of himself as writer first and guru second, if at all, for his touch is light enough to hide from the reader that he is involved in serious study.

But a writer whose dominant theme has been effectiveness must expect himself to be judged on how effective his writings have been. Heller has not spawned any cults, and he has not spawned slogans, like that of management by 'objectives' or 'excellence'. For me, this is a plus, because I share Heller's deep suspicion of cults and respect his refusal to oversimplify. There are no business or management panaceas. But there is a body of accumulated wisdom and experience: the strength of these books is that they have made so much of it available to managers who choose to take notice and apply the lessons.

Heller's work is all about *doing* – after thinking; and then thinking again, as the results of action are demonstrated, as a preface to further decisive, and possibly corrective, action. The undertone of exhortation is unavoidable; one feels that the author, though philosophically patient with human weakness, wishes passionately that managers were less inhibited by it. In particular, one senses a quite deeply felt chagrin, even frustration, that managers do not rush to investigate the potential value of new ideas and methods that offer the chance of substantially improving their businesses, and, if satisfied, to adopt them.

It seems to me that this mental slackness has materially lessened in recent years; the British manager is a good deal less naked than he was, and I cannot think that Heller has been without influence in this development. There is, of course, far to go. Some of that backwardness historically reflects specific British failures and conditions; some reflects mankind's inevitable falling short of perfection. But it is one thing to acknowledge human imperfection in business management, and quite another to tolerate it. The feature that attracts me most strongly to Heller's writing is his persistent refusal to accept any alternative to striving for the best and towards the light. And there is a compelling reason for that attitude.

To quote a famous *Times* editorial, 'It *is* a moral issue.' The first of Heller's Ten Truths of Management, from his first book, says, 'Think before you act, it's not your money.' It is not only that managers are responsible to shareholders: they also have a wider responsibility to the community. Even where, technically speaking, the money *is* theirs (in a wholly private company), the need and the duty to act rationally and unselfishly is not diminished. I agree with Heller that there is no inherent conflict of interest between the proper objectives of a business and those of either shareholders or society. But there can be conflict of interest between the aims of society, which include the needs of the company itself, on one side, and those of greedy and egotistical managers on the other.

Heller's indignation with the corporate malpractices exposed in recent years, especially in the United States, is certainly righteous. He shares with Drucker the concern that abuses of the system will sap its viability. There is evidence, amply documented in these books, that the Japanese, immune for various reasons from some of the temptations of power, have found that their greatest weapon lies less in their own strengths than in the weaknesses of their Western opponents.

It is characteristic of Heller that, in stressing the crucial need for innovation and intelligent modernization, he does not forget the ancient virtues. This comes across very strongly in his views on labour relations, where he has never shown much enthusiasm for the theories of the social science school. The bedrock of good management of people, in his view, is common humanity, common decency; and the most important tool in turning this code into effective practice is common sense. This natural vein surfaces in every Heller argument, whether on financial issues, production management or information technology: adopt the new with energy and zeal, but do so in a pragmatic spirit, and with proper respect for the enduring virtues.

In that little book *The Once and Future Manager* Heller thus concludes by suggesting that 'managers can reflect on the example of the switch in corporate financing, back to Victorian ideals of cash on the nail and in the till, as a pointer to the future.' It was certainly a pointer to the only way to recover from the severe recession that at that time lay ahead of British companies. In relative prosperity, the ideals of conservative finance have again been discarded by too many people in business and in the City. Those who have forgotten the old precepts may well live (or die) to regret it.

Though he has chronicled and explained so many corporate deaths, Heller hates failure and castigates those responsible – not least because of the damage inflicted on the innocent. There may be something romantically idealistic about his conclusion from the book just quoted, but both the ideal and the prognosis are surely unarguable: 'The future holds terrors only for those who are mismanaging the present.'

London
August 1987

# 1  Why successes flop

from *The New Naked Manager*

*The Naked Manager* has a particular place in my heart, not only because it was my first book, but because its iconoclasm still seems to me highly relevant in greatly changed times. The Crash of 1987 has painfully retaught the lessons that idols are erected only to fall, that winning streaks are always broken and, above all, that the enduring economic verities always reassert themselves.

The lessons of 1987 are in large measure a replay of the ones that I formed from observing the collapse of the hot-shot management reputations of the 1960s. But my affection for *The Naked Manager* also springs from its positive affirmation that good management, however nebulous, does exist, and that the goodness can and should be ethical as well as effective – that the power of business, even that of the biggest of the big, to change and improve human life can be exercised with benevolence, decency and (still) effectiveness.

When I came to rewrite the book after a decade and a half of momentous and unforeseeable events (the oil-price shocks, the defeat of union power, the march of the microprocessor, the death of once-great companies by takeover, etc.), two principal thoughts struck me: first, how the economy (like politics) is essentially unpredictable – there is no such thing as a surprise-free future; second, all the same, how little any of the basic philosophy or arguments of the original book required change.

Perhaps the best analogy is with a sea voyage: the route, the weather conditions and the vessel itself may vary enormously, but magnetic north stays in the same place. *The Naked Manager* did seek for stability in an unstable environment, and my hope – perhaps not over fond – is that to some extent it succeeded. At any rate, many of its heterodox ideas later became part of the new orthodoxy, which must prove something.

The naked emperor in Hans Christian Andersen's story was magnificently dressed, not only in the public's mind but in his own. The business executive, ruler of economic empires richer than many nations, has gone one better. The public believes in him, he believes in himself, but his clothing is not simply that of personal prestige and power (though both can be great). The manager is wrapped in a rich and seamless garment, which, going by the name of management, has become a pervasive religion of our time. But management, like the emperor's clothes, does not exist. The prime myth of management is that it does.

Management's non-existence explains why there are so many confused and conflicting attempts to define a pastime that all but monopolizes the waking hours of earnest men, many of them able, creative, and industrious; many of them none of these things. Any definition of management must be right, because almost any definition must fit something so amorphous and shifting. 'Achieving results through other people' is one of the more popular definitions. It applies to the president of General Motors, but it also fits the madam of a brothel. And she is an executive facing real problems of personnel selection, marketing, and accountancy, not to mention her tax and legal arrangements.

The president of GM may not fancy the idea that a madam is in the same business, but she is – the business of business. All executives are in the same line of work, which is that of organizing something or somebody in such a way that somebody else, somehow or other, will pay for it. The job of a big business executive is basically the same as that of a small shopkeeper – turning a (more or less) honest penny. And the executive forgets this (as he often does) at his peril.

Efficient businesses and brilliant executives are those who turn the most pennies, make the most money. The public never bothers about the methods. It accepts the results as evidence of their excellence. And this seems perfectly right and proper. So the good executive is the effective one, and the effective executive is the good one – or is he?

Effectiveness means more than goodness, but not much more. This little difficulty explains how a professor of management can write, 'Effectiveness is best seen as something an executive produces from a situation by managing it appropriately.' Substitute *effectively* for the last word in that mishmash and you have a sentence that means exactly the same, that is, nothing. There is no absolute criterion of managerial achievement. A manager is good and a company efficient only because others consider the results of their work good; their so-called goodness endures only as long as this good opinion holds.

Ivan Kreuger, the European match king, and Samuel Insull, the American utilities magnate, are early figures in a line that stretches to the crack of corporate doom. President after president, honest and less honest, has been turned into a hero figure, sometimes even without benefit of assiduous publicity. Behind the great collapses of companies and reputations – IOS, King Resources, National Student Marketing, Equity Financing, Penn Square, Continental Illinois, and so on – are collapsed heroes, feet of clay, now mostly forgotten names. Among fallen idol companies, some, like Litton, ITT, or Rolls-Royce, would be too conspicuous ever to forget even if they hadn't survived; others slid so far from grace that nobody remembers either their names or the exact astronomical height of their former price/earnings ratios.

In management, wonders nearly always cease. One day, events will surely expose any executive, in all his nakedness, for what he is: a fallible human being trying, with the help of others, who are equally fallible, to cope with circumstances that are constantly changing. In the kingdom of the uncertain, the one-eyed manager makes mistakes. And that is why corporate goodness, even measured on the standard scales, is infrequent. Any study of leading companies will show that few can claim to be good – if you define goodness as doubling profits in real terms in a decade, maintaining return on stockholders' equity over the ten years, and having only one off year.

The average performance of big companies is just that – average. In the United States, half of the largest companies had annual earnings per share growth of less than 7 per cent in the period from 1973 to 1983; and any company that couldn't double its earnings in a grossly inflationary era, in which all manner of juggles for the painless boosting of earnings per share were still available, has no claims to any managerial skills, even low cunning.

Executives are not always to blame for mediocrity. Running large corporations, or middling, or small, is never easy. To run them effectively is always tough, and is sometimes impossible. This explains the management that is excellent in everything except its results – as in aluminium. You won't find a harder-working, keener, better-developed bunch of men anywhere than in companies such as Alcoa and Alcan (heaven knows why, because aluminium is the world's second most boring industry, after cement). Yet the result of all their effort and massed brainpower was an insignificant return on capital, profitless growth, and a terrible proneness to accident. Alcan, possibly the most expert of the groups erecting aluminium smelters in Britain, naturally had the project that went most grievously awry; and the whole industry has shown an uncontrollable urge to plunge into excess capacity.

A former boss of Alcoa once made the immortal remark: 'There is no overcapacity, only underselling' – another of those management sayings that read the same backwards or forwards. Executives are bad judges of their own actions, their own talents, their own stock prices. Every member of the board thinks his company's shares are too cheap, although few are foolish enough to buy them (they don't mind having them free). Whenever a company boasts of its managerial excellence, sell the shares; and if you own the firm, fire the boss.

Bids bring out the worst in executives. They can't judge their own ability fairly, which is understandable. But they can also be awful judges of other managers. When you hear a chief executive say, 'You should not forget that in buying a company we are buying management as a primary asset' (to quote one merger fanatic), run for the hills. Management does not exist, and here's this colossus paying good money for the invisible and evanescent. You can't buy management, but you can very easily buy trouble. Better executives can, and often do, walk out; and sometimes after the reality emerges from the image, the worst ones have to be fired. An American group bought a red-hot British growth company for a tycoon's ransom and discovered subsequently: '(a) it does not have good reporting and control data, (b) the production output per person employed is very poor, (c) it has too many people for the job they are doing, (d) it has never really set good targets, (e) it is much too diversified.' Otherwise, the buy was in pretty good shape.

The optical illusion of goodness arises from the one-idea phenomenon. Sigmund Freud called *The Interpretation of Dreams* his greatest work, noting that inspiration of this order came to a man only once in his lifetime. Companies and chief executives are subject to the same law. A company such as Apple has a large notion about small computers and a couple of brilliant men who can make it work. In the process the company's worth – and their fortunes with it – swells in half a dozen years from peanuts to $1.7 billion in 1982. All this proves, not that the Apple crew are supermanagers, but merely that their one super-idea was good, wonderfully good. The managers will look good as long as the big idea does, but so will all their other ideas, including the foolish ones, until – as happened to Apple when the small-computer market was invaded in overwhelming force by IBM – the profits are poleaxed and new men must be imported to remake the management and the success.

Scepticism in the face of success is an impudent posture. But corporate history must foster the sceptical approach. The eye-opener lies in the way that respectable, established, conservative corporations and their no less clean and decent executives start off in one direction and end up facing the other way, with equal ardour for both postures. Sad examples here are the copper companies, which once threw fortunes into the laps of other people in a doomed and silly effort to keep prices down – and then discovered the virtues of the free market they had sought to destroy.

In corporation land, you learn rapidly that there are some villains but no heroes. I once had to write the profile of an oilman reputed to be the hero–genius behind one of the world's greatest companies. Research showed that, after an incomparable early career battling against the arch-enemy, he had long since sat on the sidelines. In despair, I asked the real boss to say what the hero did. 'Well,' he said, after deep thought, 'he has the office next to mine.' The profile, inevitably, perpetuated the legend. Nobody would have believed the reality, any more than most people would believe that a young family scion, famed (falsely) for internationalizing an introverted Midwestern business, was once so claustrophobic that he held conferences in an open bus. Cured by his shrink, he then became so agoraphobic that he could work only in a windowless room.

Men like him, or the Cunard chairman who never took a ship to America, are the human factors, the real stuff of management – eccentric to the point of lunacy in a few cases, and generally odd enough in multitudinous smaller ways. Time and again, what happens in corporations cannot be explained by economics. It can be understood only by realizing that, naturally enough, men express in their work the same motive forces that drive them in their ordinary lives. Management is an arena for human behaviour at its most naked – under stress, but freed from many restraints of civilization. You can yell and scream at a subordinate in a way that would not be tolerated even by a wife. You can force a man to lose all his assets, though you wouldn't trespass on his lawn. You can tell lies, but if the lies are good enough, they will be applauded as universal truth.

This is the background against which one Harry Figgie can be seen as a real management hero of our times. Figgie, a manager of brilliant reputation, had won high academic respect and an avid stock-market following for his 'nucleus theory of growth', which he applied to Automatic Sprinkler. The nucleus theory proved to be an empty sham. The reality was that in rapid succession Figgie bought a fire-hose-nozzle company whose profits promptly fell from $939,000 to $76,636; a vacuum-cleaner firm whose sales methods were outlawed just before acquisition; and a metal-bending defence contractor that managed to lose $8 million on a $6.3 million Pentagon contract. There are no theories of growth, nuclear or non-nuclear. There are only actions – intelligent, not so bright, and stupid. And the only thread binding the intelligent actions is that they work, as Figgie himself demonstrated after these dismal events. His company has not only changed its name since those days, first to ATO and then to Figgie International Holdings, but has also changed its theories and its spots and can consequently boast one of the better growth records among the *Fortune* 500.

The trouble is that in management nothing succeeds like success – if you define the latter as winning a high, wide, and handsome management reputation. But pride goeth before a flop, as *Business Week* recently discovered, retreading the ground covered by *In Search of Excellence*. It found, under the title, *Oops!*, that 'at least fourteen of the forty-three "excellent" companies' highlighted in that booming bestseller 'have lost their lustre'.

Worse still, several of them shouldn't have been in the book at all; notably Atari, a firm so appallingly mismanaged that it infringed all eight of the book's 'attributes', or rules of management, and very nearly busted its miserable owners, Warner, in the process. But what did the *Business Week* analysis prove? First, that there are no universal rules of success (thus, Hewlett-Packard, which has 'stumbled badly' in the critical microcomputer and superminicomputer markets, obeyed all eight commandments). Second, past success by no means equates with either future triumph or excellent management.

So what else is new? Speaking (or writing) personally, I've stressed both self-evident truths *ad infinitum* (if not *ad nauseam*) for the best part of two decades. But nothing will ever stop managers, especially at times of great uncertainty – like the 1980s – from seeking, and overvaluing, examples of apparent certainty. All the same, the 'Oops' analysis is valuable, maybe more so than the original study. For instance, eight of the fourteen flops didn't stay close to the customer – companies like Avon, Disney, Revlon, Tupperware, and Levi-Strauss, which are practically synonymous with consumer satisfaction.

Take the last named. As long as the worldwide jeans market was booming, Levi's management could afford, paradoxically, to ignore it. 'For so long we were [always] sold out. Our time was prioritized on getting more product, new factories, more raw materials. We were internationally oriented.' As for the customers, 'We let the relationship with our retailers fall into a sad state of disrepair, the company completely missed the powerful [and profitable] trend towards fashion jeans.' Direct, in-the-home sellers Avon and Tupperware similarly failed to spot or react to the blatant consequences of more women going out to work. Disney went on flogging clean and decent entertainment to an increasingly less wholesome market place.

Yet turn the clock back a decade and what proved to be crucial defects were being hailed as heroic virtues. Theories or methods of management can work wonders in individual companies at individual times, but only because they suit the way in which individual managers like to act in individual markets. The methods that Robert Townsend, of *Further Up the Organisation*, used to run Avis were a marvellous way for Robert Townsend to run Avis. But they might paralyse a different company with different men – even Hertz. Yet executives, beset by corporate ailments, reach for a theory formed in a different context as if it were a broad-spectrum antibiotic, a wonder drug. They see their businesses as suffering patients requiring medical treatment, though there is seldom anything wrong with a company that better, or better-directed, executives won't cure. Executives, however, will undergo almost any treatment rather than amputation of themselves.

But self-amputation is far more effective for the stockholders. I know of two companies, one large, one gargantuan, that found themselves with cuckoos in the nest – two tough, aggressive, ruthless entrepreneurs whose drive, hunger for profits, and magical rapport with figures couldn't live with the passive, profitless vagueness on the existing board. Laying their own heads on the block, the older directors voluntarily handed the axe to the new men. In the next few years, both companies grew by such prodigious bounds that some of the superannuated oldies became very wealthy – and they deserved every penny. They followed the golden rule: if you can't do something yourself, find somebody who can – and then let him do it in his own sweet way.

In contrast, many cures that less self-effacing boards may purchase are subject to the same objection as psychoanalysis: they are expensive; they take a lot of time; the patient does all the work, and there's no way of telling that he wouldn't have got better, anyway, with the mere passage of the years. If it takes two years (to take one example from the past) to draw up a new shop-floor management structure in a car company, the problem won't be the same at the end as it was at the beginning. That's why, in the discontinuous present, speed has become of the essence. Today you not only have to fix it, you must fix it fast.

Any improvement, however, can always be looked at two ways. You can pat yourself on the back (as most executives do) for your brilliant advance, or you can kick yourself for the imbecility that made improvement necessary. If the executive doesn't like one view through the telescope, he can turn it around and look through the other end – precisely because management is not a scientific and objective activity but a subjective historical process, full of ifs and buts. Thus Roy Ash, when President of Litton and forced to explain how the management wasn't to blame for errors that wiped out billions in stock-market value, had no trouble at all: 'Operationally, we could have made sure of never facing the problem by never undertaking the venture.' Nothing ventured, nothing lost, in fact. That's like the guilty party in a mid-air collision offering as excuse that if he had never learnt to fly the accident would never have happened.

The literature and history of companies like Litton or ITT bear careful reading by anybody who believes that the emperor–manager is wearing clothes. In this book, although there are no heroes, there are Goodies and Baddies. The Baddies range from leading actors – the bankrupt or all-but-broke giant companies like International Harvester or Continental Illinois – to a strong supporting cast, many of them conglomerates like the two mentioned above, whose badness lies in the damage done by arrogant managers to innocent stockholders.

In the early 1970s, in addition to the Baddies, the Heavies – such as Du Pont, General Electric, I C I, and General Motors – were conspicuous underperformers, companies that were neither very good nor at all poor but whose enormous potential for goodness was constantly frustrated by their own bad habits. Many such Heavies proved *in extremis* in the early 1980s, with G E leading the bunch, that the underperformance was indeed culpable; they changed their awful habits, and that enormous potential came bursting through on to the bottom line.

There are Goodies, too, in my books: men (and there are many of them) who can be trusted with the stockholders' money to the last line on the balance sheet unless and until I am proven wrong: and in two such cases, the gang at IBM and the bosses of Daimler-Benz, to demonstrate the last point, the jury was still out at the end of 1987.

*Think before you act; it's not your money* – the First Truth of Management – is a home truth. But management is a far more homely business than its would-be scientists suggest, more closely allied to cooking than any other human activity. Like cooking, it rests on a degree of organization and on adequate resources. But just as no two chefs run their kitchens the same way, so no two managements are the same, even if they all went to the same business (or cooking) school. You can teach the rudiments of cooking, as of management, but you cannot make a great cook or a great manager.

In both activities, you ignore fundamentals at grave risk – but sometimes succeed. In both, science can be extremely useful but is no substitute for the art itself. In both, inspired amateurs can outdo professionals. In both, perfection is rarely achieved, and failure is more common than the customers realize. In both, practitioners don't need recipes that detail timing down to the last second, ingredients to the last fraction of an ounce, and procedures down to the last flick of the wrist; they need reliable maxims, instructive anecdotes, and no dogmatism. This is a cookbook for managers who want to get their clothes back.

# 2 *The management mishmash*

from *The Naked Investor*

*The Naked Investor*, born out of the Second Great Crash, deserves a new lease of intellectual life in the age of the third Wall Street catastrophe of modern times. In the later years of the long bull market that was finally broken by the hurricane of October 1987, the Second Great Crash was almost entirely forgotten. It was the title of the book's first chapter, which described a débâcle that took longer than the 1987 collapse, but was every bit as horrible.

Indeed, the horrors exceeded those of 1929. To quote: 'where, in December 1968, the Dow-Jones Index would have cost a Swiss gnome 28.4 ounces of gold, by July 1973 the little fellow could have picked up the same bundle for a mere seven ounces . . . That July London share prices were only a fifth down from their all-time peak. Within eighteen months the *Financial Times* Index had collapsed to 146 – a quarter of the historic high reached in 1972, and a decline far more catastrophic in magnitude even than Wall Street's.'

Even the causes strike a late-1980s chord: 'The economic explanations included the endless United States balance of payments deficits, the consequent rise and globular swelling of the Eurodollar bubble, the consequent escalation of inflation . . .' The inflation of the 1980s was of asset prices, instead of those of goods, but the effect was the same: the creation of a bubble that had to burst. The book concluded by observing that 'If the lessons have not been learnt, and the naked investor again tries to reach Utopian financial salvation through the stock market, the Second

Great Crash will not merely be a recrudescence of the First. It will be a trailer for the Third – and the Third might be Last.'

The chapters I've chosen, however, are not those that deal with the myths and the malpractices of the financial market place, which has itself changed radically with globalization and deregulation – although the basic debunking of professional expertise, the 'hedge against inflation' theory and the efficacy of so-called watchdogs, etc., holds as true as ever. But one myth in particular seemed to require a renewed assault: the idea that marvels in the stock market somehow equate with marvellous management. Hence the excerpts: however, all the vices spelt out in this book about the mid-1970s resurfaced in the mid-1980s.

The remedies I thought obvious then were: 'tax reforms that will treat dividend payments on equal terms with interest and end the present discouragement of pay-outs; accountancy reforms that will bar the deceitful game of maximizing reported earnings; legal reforms that will redress the balance of power between manager and investor by removing the defects, such as stock options and the cosy dependence of auditors on management, that currently distort the relationship; regulatory reforms that will make the seller, not the buyer, beware'. The remedies are still obvious: but they are still largely unapplied.

## What price glory?

The shares that made the headlines and the money, for longer or shorter spans of time in the 1960s, had one general characteristic: the purchasers, for however brief an encounter, held in high regard the qualities of the management of the companies concerned. This respect might be not only awarded but even enhanced if the management, to the naked eye, consisted of only one man. Genius in management, like genius in art, but for less good reason, is commonly held to be at its best when undiluted by the presence of others. Those who backed a Ross Perot in computer services, a Charles Bluhdorn in conglomeration, a Bernie Cornfeld in mutual funds did so without knowing or caring about the quality of the minions. It was enough that a maestro was on the podium: he could be trusted to hire a good orchestra, or at least to make it play lucrative symphonies.

In a sense, those who took the maestro's eye view were reverting to the days and attitudes before management came into fashion. Between the wars, business was thought of in terms of men rather than of management. Only after the Second World War did the pioneering work in organization and methods blossom into the modern school (and the many schools) of management.

As the level of organizational expertise rose in the post-war years, as the numbers of men trained in management theory grew and as the output of that theory increased, so the idea gradually gained currency that management was like a company's resources of technology – an identifiable asset that could be added to, compared to the equivalent stores of other companies or assessed as part of the firm's basic strength. The problem is that although a firm's technology can be identified easily enough by the number of its patents, the quality and uniqueness of its products, its pace of innovation and so on, management consists almost entirely of men. They cannot be inspected or judged as easily as a set of blueprints. True, the men have methods – like, say, the famous decentralized organization of General Motors. But the methods are inseparable from the men who use them, and in any event nobody knows how to separate the contribution of methodology from the other strengths of a company: like the sales network bequeathed by corporate ancestors, or the technological strength that, even if inherited in an age of galloping progress, can last out two or three generations of top management.

Still, the statement that an ICI, or a Shell, or a Du Pont, or a Boeing has superior management is safe and obvious enough. The heavy job of holding these complex operations together down the years demands the development of high organizational skills; and the pressure for high skills, together with the grandeur of the corporation and of its jobs, attracts the best quality of organization men – recruits to whom the giant corporation can afford to pay the highest rewards. But investors are not attracted by this proposition – probably with justice. The solid extra management qualities of the giant are offset, often outweighed, by the solidifying effects of bureaucracy and the other constipations of large scale. Only the investor seeking safety will turn to the big blue chip, although his sole security is that the business won't go bankrupt, and will certainly rise (but also fall) with the economic cycle. The investor wanting to sample the joys of dynamic management turns elsewhere.

He isn't seeking quality of management in itself: he is seeking the *results* of 'good' management. From this formulation, it follows naturally that managers are judged solely by their results. Up to a point, this is entirely just. Results are what managers are paid to achieve, and no manager can claim prowess unless it is reflected in performance. But the linkage breaks at the point where results are identified with managerial brilliance. The analogy is with two men throwing unloaded dice. A gambler backing one of the throwers wants his man to come up with the winning number more times, but he wouldn't conclude that the winner is actually more physically skilled at throwing dice. The success of managements similarly may have little to do with innate skills: luck and timing play as large a part as brilliance, and science a smaller role than hunch.

Since giant corporations, by virtue or vice of their very size, could not produce the results the gamblers were seeking, the latter turned to the second, third and fourth ranks; and wherever they found performance, the performance-seekers also located managerial brilliance. In some cases this error did actual harm, where a man or a group possessed of mediocre ability fell in love with a false image and proceeded to ruin a perfectly respectable business with their subsequent excesses: for example, the sound paper business of Boise Cascade was turned into one of the dizziest and most disastrous seekers after conglomerate glory.

But the main result was to accentuate both the positive and the negative. The myth of management expertise pushed the price of the shares higher still in the phase of ascendancy; then, with the discovery of gross failures in financial control, or fatal product obsolescence, or some other unsuspected ailment, the devaluation in the down phase was all the sharper for the exaggeration in the days of glory.

The rise and fall of management heroes was also a constant feature of the fifties, following the tidal movements of business itself. But the sixties produced a brilliant refinement of the illogic that identified excellence of results with wonders of management. By then the science of management had been reinforced, not just by each year's output of business-school graduates, many of whom swelled the ranks of consultants whose stock in trade was scientific management, but also by the public-relations effort on behalf of great national programmes in aerospace.

The technology of landing men on the moon was breathtaking, and outsiders assumed that equally stunning scientific applications of management underlay the technological achievement. Just as everybody wrongly believed that the miracles of space hardware would be readily transferred into civilian product lines, with incalculable benefits, so many assumed, equally wrongly, that new scientific management skills developed in organizations like the National Aeronautics and Space Administration could be applied with equal impact to civilian firms. The theory bobbed up in the argument of defence contractors that their specific skills in military programmes were not limitations but golden opportunities. The theory also played a more subtle role in the emergence of companies whose main offering was simply management. Their promoters said, not just in effect but specifically, that since outstanding performance stemmed from superb management, a company manned entirely by scientifically trained and superbly competent managers was bound to perform superbly, to land men on the corporate moon, even though mission control had not made up its mind in which business or businesses the performance would be achieved.

Their business wasn't business – it was management. And the object of management was not to manufacture goods, or to market them, or to provide services: it was to produce earnings per share, and to multiply them so rapidly that the share price would quite inevitably perform with the exact precision of the first flight to the moon. Not only that, but because the company was oriented entirely to management and earnings growth, the forward motion could be expected to be perpetual.

The super-managers were not attached to any one business or market, and would know when and how to switch when prospects dimmed. If troubles arose in any part of the diversified empire, they constituted a readymade consultancy team, able to arrive as rapidly as any fire brigade to put out a conflagration. Every article of this faith was a lie – notably the assumption that management can be separated from specific markets and businesses, the idea that educated skills can be universally applied, the notion that a permanent corporation can be built on shifting sands. But the most dangerous error, because it ramified beyond the conglomerates into the ranks of traditional business, was the identification of management with financial results – specifically earnings per share.

The collapse of the conglomerates was itself a powerful cause rather than an effect of the Second Great Crash: the uncovering of their big lie antedated the worst of the stock-market collapse. But the impact on managers in traditional businesses of the new theory of management had more pervasive effects. First, pride alone inspired them to prove (if they could) that they were just as skilled at managing as the sweetest young thing in conglomerates. Second, they accepted the criteria the latter had laid down: they agreed that maximizing capital gains for the stockholder was the true task of management. Third, they adopted the methods of the conglomerators – the search was on for diversification, for high-growth industries, for financially oriented central direction.

The disease infected staid, solid old Middle West companies like Honeywell, which reversed Horace Greeley's celebrated advice and went east – grafting on to itself a horrendously expensive computer operation which transformed the whole nature of the corporation, without contributing much in most years save an unsustainable elevation of the price/earnings ratio into the upper forties. At Honeywell the objective of the corporation became something its founder, a single-minded salesman who used to sit in a buggy at the end of the road supervising the troops as they peddled his heating controls, would not remotely have understood: a 15 per cent rise in earnings per share, year in and year out. If there was a rationale in this objective, it was that a 15 per cent growth company would surely always command a substantial price/earnings ratio, which would with equal certainty produce a handsome share price and capital appreciation. Its irrationality lies in the fact that, while management has many identifiable functions, none of them (outside the specialized area of the corporate finances) has any direct, immediate connection with this newer-fangled financial goal.

Given that, as we know, the connection between earnings perform-ance and the stock price, while direct, is wholly indeterminate, there is no way in which the earnings-conscious management can guarantee the results on which it sets its collective heart.

A strong or good management can achieve a variety of concrete objectives. It can avoid or eliminate no-hope, loss-making situ-ations; on the other hand it will develop to the maximum attainable potential the sound businesses in which the company is engaged; it avoids investments (diversifications or otherwise) that overstretch its resources of money and management; it stays alert to changes in its markets that demand changes in products and practices; it looks for opportunities within its competence that will return large and early amounts on shareholders' funds; it ensures that its subordin-ates and replacements are of the necessary calibre; it keeps the company's products and processes up to date – and so on, right down a long list of visible and attainable objectives. Other things being equal, all or any of these attainments will very probably have the effect of improving the company's earnings. The exceptions to this rule, however, are of extreme importance – for instance, when a company is forced to bunch heavy investment into one year, so that earnings necessarily take a beating. At crucial moments like this the pursuit of earnings as the prime objective of the company ceases to make sense, and may impose dangerous nonsense, like the various formulae that company after company adopted to keep current expenditure on research and development out of the accounts.

Investors, even if they noticed such devices, probably didn't care. After all, if the object was to elevate earnings, how could any means that achieved that end, even a stroke of pure accountancy, be anything but divine? Similarly, shutting down a loss-maker, if it demanded a large write-off, might seem infinitely less appealing than simply allowing the losses to continue and hoping that they could be stemmed, or (by some miracle) turned into profits. Time and again the imperative of a fixed target for earnings growth was translated into an unrealistic figure for divisions that were in the above leaky boat and also for others that in contrast were well-found vessels.

Within the corporation, too, the attainable object took second place to the unattainable, and managements down the line were lumbered with targets they either could not meet or (worse still) could meet only by forms of cheating. In some conglomerate operations a new form of business cycle became apparent. The new man arriving for the normal three-year stint as chief divisional executive would find a mess – a sharply declining profit trend, which resulted largely from inadequate investment in the previous reign. In his first year the new man remedied the deficiencies and took the losses in profit on his predecessor's departed chin. The second year showed the inevitable sharp upturn, earning the incumbent praise and pay all round. But progress could be maintained in the third year only if investment and other supporting expenditure were cut back, which meant, of course, that after the new man had been promoted, or had moved out of the conglomerate altogether, to take a striking new job, his successor found himself in exactly the same mess in his turn.

Another damaging process was classically illustrated by a celebrated case in which a profit forecast, instrumental in averting an unwelcome raid on the company, was missed by a grotesque margin. The company was organized into divisions, each with its own subsidiaries – this now standard form of organization is the most pervasive contribution of the new post-war school of management. When the forecast was drawn up each subsidiary boss added 20 per cent to his original budgeted profit. The division added all the forecasts together and, not to be outdone, added its 20 per cent on top. And the central management added 20 per cent on top of that. This geometrical progression guaranteed total disaster – by the time the original one-fifth boost had been subjected to this treatment, the group had transmogrified it into a 72.8 per cent target.

The efforts to make the manifold contributions of a welter of divisions and subdivisions, not to mention their individual managers, add up to a given earnings target of 15 per cent or whatever often had much the same asinine character. Moreover, there was an inherent absurdity in the insistence on a particular time span – and a short one of twelve months at that. If an investor is making a short-term bet, then it might make sense from his viewpoint to crowd all possible profits into (and defer all possible expenditures out of) the year immediately ahead. But most investors, especially the big institutions, have much longer time horizons: in 1965 an insurance company might have been predominantly interested in the outcome in 1985, when its policy-holders would cash in their chips. Sacrificing the long run for the short is maniacal seen from this angle, since by the nature of things the process must come to an end: the deferred expenditures will catch up with the overstated profits, and the result is a Penn Central or a Rolls-Royce.

The real manager, as opposed to the counterfeit variety, has no option but to manage for the long term. A good company (the kind in which most investors would prefer to place their money) is a long-running attraction, which means that management decisions taken in any one year must be weighed against the long-term as well as the short-run interests of the corporation. In any event, many of the projects essential to a company's development take a long time to mature: longer than the three years of a conglomerate job-changer, at any rate. Earnings matter to the real manager, partly as a measure of his real attainments, partly because they finance his future corporate growth. As ends in themselves, however, the financial targets are meaningless.

Another trap lay waiting for the manager seduced by the new blandishments. The emphasis of modern management, as practised by the conglomerates and their imitators, lay in the future, which the old-style manager, of course, also had to consider. But if the company was going to be valued solely on its future growth, the tendency was to forget to some extent about its present perform-ance. At one and the same time managers were cooking the books to show the highest possible earnings figure for the period just past, while ignoring the evidence that showed that in the current period (or over a long string of current periods) their performance, measured in absolute rather than relative terms, was inferior.

An emphasis on future growth rates, in any event, meant that present levels of performance were no longer relevant. Suppose that two identical companies with stockholders' equity of £100 million start off from the same base date, the one earning £10 million and the other £20 million, but the first growing by 15 per cent annually and the second by 10 per cent. Even if those relative growth rates are guaranteed to remain constant, which cannot be promised by God or man, after ten years the first company would be generating £40·5 million of profits and the latter £51·8 million. Thus at all points in their decade of progress, the second firm would have been markedly more efficient. The first firm would have been able to congratulate itself solely on moving from relatively hopeless to comparatively moderate.

Possibly the greatest error and the most hard-lined management trap of all lay in the concept of glory itself. Business is a splendid occupation, a worthy way of spending a career, and the foundation of the modern economy, east and west of the formerly Iron Curtain. But like all occupations, from sport to politics, literature to public administration, it throws up few genuine heroes. Other occupations, however, seldom carry within them the means of their own apotheosis: sportsmen, at least initially, are turned into gods by their fans and their successes, not by the efforts of public-relations departments – and especially not by PR operations paid for by the fans. By convoluted logic, the business managers who employed these trumpeters, hired with shareholders' funds, to sound the virtues of their bosses even persuaded themselves that it was really for the good of the shareholders. After all, if the publicity pushed up the share price, wasn't that what the holders wanted?

Real management is an inglorious activity, compounded of equal parts of caution and dash, of unremitting attention to detail as well as ability to stand back and survey the panorama, of awareness of the public reaction to the company's deeds and of indifference to transient manifestations of that reaction – like, for main instance, the price/earnings ratio of the equity. Once the man puts the transient manifestation first and foremost, he is doomed: each and every action, from an otiose purchase of another company to an over-optimistic forecast about a new business venture, can be justified by the putative beneficial effect it will have on the company's standing in the stock market.

But the path of cause and effect in the market follows no known route. Nor is the short-term boost ever translated into the long-term gain. Managers who chased the share price were pursuing a chimera; and investors who chased managements dedicated to financial growth were equally hot in pursuit of a will-o'-the-wisp. Good management is something you recognize only when you've got it, and which may never be reflected – if you are lucky – in a supreme price/earnings ratio.

## The cult of earnings

Although earnings per share had so little to do with management, their cult was embraced most fervently by two distinct groups of managers, yet for one and the same reason. Executives in the larger corporations in the United States, and the founder–managers of new, thrusting companies in both Britain and the United States, were the most fanatical devotees. This wasn't because of a common conviction that the new growth cult was the be-all and end-all of business activity, although the seductions of fashion did play a part. Far more persuasive was the seduction of money. So long as the cult held sway, managers who lived by the cult, for the cult and of the cult would reap maximum personal rewards.

The mechanism operated in the United States mainly through the stock option or through the founder's shareholding in the case of the entrepreneurial companies. Whether or not it was good for stockholders, workers or the company itself to maximize earnings per share, it was unquestionably good for those with a vested interest in the share price: good, that is, for as long as investors were prepared to pay fanciful premiums for rapid growth in the magical numeral. The fortunes made by stock option fat-cats were large enough to match even a founder–manager's takings.

Even in the awful conditions of 1974, four executives in United States companies reporting one-year option gains cashed in to the extent of $500,000 of pre-tax personal profits. The year before, according to McKinsey figures, five salted million-dollar option gains away in their personal gold mines. True, the number exercising options had fallen by 1974 – down a third on 1973 and 55 per cent on 1972, leaving a mere 165 executives with their fingers in the gravy. Shareholders were expected to acquiesce joyfully in such convenient arrangements (and many did) on the old routine of sauce for gander equals sauce for goose. The more the stock price soared, the more the options were worth. But since the shareholders' worth was expanding in step, who cared? The lack of a direct relationship between the reward to the manager and the results of the company bothered nobody, especially those who were pocketing the rewards. Since we know that there was no direct link, either, between the movement of share prices and the movement of the earnings per share figure, we also know that a perfect circle of nonsense was created. Within the circle many managers waxed fat (and stayed fat, if they remembered to sell their option shares before the crash), while shareholders were set up for the big let-down.

Many hundreds of executives shared the disillusion, however – not because they were caught with devalued paper fortunes (although many were), but because they altogether missed their chance to seize the fortunes. As share prices descended to the nadir, the value of stock options swiftly evaporated. This was deeply unwelcome in the executive suite, whose inhabitants promptly awarded themselves 'stock appreciation rights'. These allowed their happy owners to reap a rich harvest from any rise in the companies' shares while sparing them from the inconvenience (not to mention the risk) of having to purchase the things.

What must have stung those landed with worthless options of an older, less sophisticated and more painful variety was that their devaluation often occurred regardless of the results of the company. Many large United States corporations went on raising reported profits throughout the Second Great Crash, yet their shares suffered revisions scarcely less drastic than those of companies all but annihilated in the economic vice. Whatever the impact on the suffering executives, however, it's doubtful whether any up-and-coming contenders for the executive suite and its manifold joys were at all deterred by the experience of the un-fortunates, mostly because no better engine than the option for the painless creation of personal fortunes has ever been devised, or is likely to be invented.

That is one of the main arguments against the cult of earnings. The stock option provides managers with a built-in personal incentive to boost the earnings per share figure by any means within their power. The stockholder of the 1960s thus became the victim of the same process as had so smoothly defrauded his forefathers almost a century back, when the villains were robber barons intent on forcing up the price of their stock preparatory to offloading the inflated currency on the gullible public.

The advent of professional management in the territories once ruled by the likes of J. P. Morgan and Jay Gould was supposed to have much the same effect as the replacement of corrupt hereditary monarchs by elected democrats. In both cases, however, the public was sorely deceived. Corruption has many forms, and you don't actually have to own a company, or inherit political power, to abuse your position.

In simple cases of fraud, in simpler days gone by, the technique was to promise a dividend which the company could in no way pay. When it defaulted, the investors were left holding the baby. But this technique, even had it not been outlawed, would have had relatively little utility in an age when tax considerations put shareholders off their dividend feed. When growth companies were eagerly sought after, despite paying out only a minute fraction of their earnings, the cash dividend had plainly disappeared from the equation. Some measure, yardstick or talisman had to take its place, and that something could only be the figure for earnings per share.

The magic number was slow in arriving on the British scene. The investors of days before 1964 had to exist under an antiquated system which mixed up personal income tax and company taxation. It fell to the Labour Government elected in that year to give the final push to the divorce of share prices from cash returns, to the almost infinite joy of a generation of share promoters, some of them only recently born. The motive of the socialists was to stimulate the plough-back of funds into investment: the old system did not discriminate between profits paid out in dividends and profits retained in the company. Under corporation tax, money retained carried a lower impost than money handed over to the shareholders. Thus the company could in theory invest the shareholder's money, even at the same rate of return, more effectively than the shareholder himself – because the personal income tax didn't have to be deducted before making the investment.

Even before this change, which gave the earnings cult a mighty shove forward, the British had been partial to something called the earnings yield. This is simply the reciprocal of the price/earnings ratio. That is, if earnings per share are 20 and the price of the shares is 100, the earnings yield is 20 per cent, and the price/earnings ratio is 5; 5 times 20 equals 100 – and thus the reciprocal relationship is demonstrated.

But the earnings yield, unlike the price/earnings ratio, can be related directly to the dividend. Thus, if the above company was paying out 10 per cent per share in dividend, the City of London at that time would say that it had a 10 per cent dividend yield, twice covered (which, of course, equals 20 per cent). A twice-covered dividend is obviously much more attractive than one with single cover, but only because it is that much more unlikely to be cut.

In this way, the earnings yield keeps in touch with the reality of dividend payments. But the price/earnings ratio, even though it is the reciprocal of the yield, is expressed in a different numerical form: a percentage and a multiple do not relate as readily in the normal non-mathematical mind as two percentages. Moreover, the earnings yield is not dynamic, quite the reverse. A red-hot stock, earning 20 per cent a share and priced at 800, has an earnings yield of 2·5 per cent, which sounds terribly small (as, indeed, it is). But that same stock has a price/earnings ratio of 40, which sounds fantastically high (as, indeed, it is). But anybody would prefer a fantastically high figure to a terribly small one: the ratio is simply a far more alluring method of stating the same mathematical fact.

Thus London ended up on the same bandwagon as New York. The emphasis on earnings per share introduced a wholly new element into the game. Growth had always been the game's name, since, as we know, shareholders believed that higher profits year by year would be translated more or less automatically into higher share prices. But the overall profits figure can't be readily translated into terms that apply to the individual shareholder – in the same way as a dividend payment can, for example. Divide the net earnings between each share, however, and you derive a figure that looks much the same as a dividend payment – only the company doesn't actually have to pay over the money. Moreover, it's a figure with much more elasticity than a profits total.

The classic equation is that of the £10 million company with a million shares in issue and a 20 times multiple that buys another £10 million, million-share firm with only a 10 times multiple. The profits thus double, but the earnings per share of the first company will rise by a third. That might seem a poor exchange, until the implications are considered.

The two companies before merger had a million shares and £10 million of profits apiece. Therefore putting them together, at first glance, should in no way improve the lot of the shareholders concerned. The amount of earnings available for distribution as dividend, or as anything else, hasn't increased by one red cent. Looked at from this angle, the conjuring up of a one-third rise in earnings per share is a feat worthy of any magician who ever sawed a woman in half. The trick is worked by in effect withdrawing half a million shares from circulation and from the corporate sums. The highly valued company exchanges the above number of shares for twice as many of the underdog's. Exactly the same effect could be achieved if a quarter of the top company's shareholders were persuaded to tear up their stock and forget all about it. The amount of earnings will not be changed as a result, but the number of pieces of paper to which those profits are attached will be sharply reduced. Since the earnings per share figure is achieved by dividing net profits by the shares in issue, there must be a rise – and in this case a real one, since a quarter of the investors no longer have any entitlement to the loot.

But does the same truth apply in the merger case? Suppose that both firms paid out £5 million in dividends, retaining the remainder for necessary investment in the business. After the merger, the same investment is required: so £10 million is available to be distributed among 1·5 million shares, instead of among a couple of million as before. But it's not as simple as that. The investors in the taken-over company will have to accept a sharp drop in income if they go along with the above arrangement. They have only their half-million shares now; and their one-third share of £10 million, or £3·3 million, is £1·7 million less than they were entitled to before. In fact they would never agree to a merger on those terms. But to match their previous pay-out, the combined company would need to pay £15 million in dividends – which means either investing £5 million less or borrowing the money from some other source, paying interest on the loan and incurring lower profits as a result.

So the woman hasn't really been sawn in half. The realities must assert themselves sooner or later, and the apparent sharp improvement in the well-being of a company that has improved earnings per share by cutting the number of shares in the sum is like all conjuror's tricks: once you know how the trick is worked, the mystery and the entertainment value disappear.

Not that the earnings per share figure is useless to the straight and good manager. Any deal or financing arrangement that reduces the figure is immediately suspect and needs to be carefully scrutinized to ensure that pigs are not being bought in pokes. But this control is essentially negative, a financial discipline applied to managerial plans and ambitions. It's a very different matter from making the enhancement of that figure the sum of those devices and desires.

The number of shares can be altered in several ways other than mergers: the neatest trick, always available in the United States though it used to be barred under British law, is to repurchase the company's stock in the market for cash. Between 1968 and 1973 United States corporations splashed out many millions on buying back their own stock (a total whose proportions can be gauged by noting that it was equivalent to *half* of all new funds raised by non-financial corporations). As shares slid and staggered downwards in the Second Great Crash this stratagem had become increasingly attractive as a means of trying to stem the tide. Once again, no results in real terms followed the move. But the retired shares no longer ranked for dividends, or for allocations of earnings, and the directors had thus accomplished the trick of raising the magic figure without lifting a finger. It was scant consolation for an investor who had bought at a multiple of 20 and was nursing a fall of three-quarters in his capital to be presented with this mathematical gift. What the boards concerned were doing was to make the best of an exceedingly bad job.

Many companies lacked the cash, even if they had the will, to use this device. As the market slump was followed, in the usual pattern, by a genuine business recession, the squeeze on companies' cash flow intensified all over the world. Good managements had always kept close control of cash as an instinctive part of their housekeeping and supervisory roles. But stagflation, the combination of low or no growth with double-digit price increases, turned the normally desirable into the acutely necessary.

Almost overnight, profit ceased to be the name of the game: the game's new name was cash. No firm ever went bust through earning insufficient profit. But nearly every bankruptcy is the result of a critical shortage of liquidity. It's a distinction that managements of large companies tended to forget until the recession of the 1970s brought it painfully to their notice.

The most remarkable impact came in the arcane world of corporate accounting. Since cash is an indispensable control of managerial excellence, excellent managers would presumably do everything in their power to keep money within the company – for instance, by paying as little tax as possible as late as possible. But the presumption ignores the influence of the earnings cult and its devotees. Managements were pulled in two opposite directions. On one side, sound business principles tugged them towards minimizing profits and maximizing cash retentions. On the other end of the rope, the lure of the stock market (and of their own stock options) lugged them towards overstating profits and reducing cash retentions by the amount of additional tax that then had to be handed over to the government.

In the United States this beneficence was entirely optional in one unique respect. The Internal Revenue Service, while not generally given to generosity, allows United States companies to opt for FIFO or LIFO when accounting for stock. These heavenly twins, respectively first-in-first-out and last-in-first-out, have profoundly different effects on company finances, and the effects become more profound the more rapidly inflation advances. A company in love with FIFO assumes that the stocks used in making the latest product to leave its assembly lines were the earliest purchases left in the warehouse. If the prices of its raw materials and components have risen since the earliest purchase, it follows that the resulting profit will be the highest it could report (not *make*, mark you, merely report). On the other or LIFO hand, if the company assumes that the latest purchases are the first consumed, the profit will be reduced by the amount of the higher price of the stock. A company using a hundred units of stock in a year, starting with a hundred purchased for a dollar each

( = $100); buying a hundred more for $2 apiece during the year ( = $200); and selling its output of a hundred units for $300, can show a profit, after incurring other costs, of $100 or nothing, depending on which accounting method it uses.

Now if a company has made $100 of profit, you would expect to find the money somewhere about the house. But in the case above, the company has shelled out $300 in the year and received only $300 back. The sole improvement in its circumstances is that instead of $100 in stock, it now has $200. But the profit locked up within that stock can't be realized until the stock is sold as product – and, even then, only at a price very much higher than $3 apiece.

Actually the situation is a good deal worse, because the $100 of supposed profit attracted corporation tax, which meant that the firm had to find $50 of real cash (which it hadn't generated, remember) in order to keep the tax wolves from the door. All elementary stuff: yet, it wasn't the simpletons of United States business who fooled themselves with FIFO, nor even the whip-smart boys who were intent on lashing the share prices of their conglomerates into a lather, but most of the larger corporations in the United States.

The truth was that in earlier years all the reddest-blooded US businessmen preferred to show the biggest possible profit to encourage the stock market; in recent circumstances, when the market wouldn't have been moved by the Second Coming, these same corporations have preferred conserving their cash to paying higher taxes. In many cases (following the usual procedure) managers were deceiving themselves as much as the shareholders. Like the latter, boards of directors thought that the illusory earnings they were reporting truly existed. The chairman of Arthur Andersen, one of the biggest international accountancy firms, put it as follows to *Business Week*: 'The high-flying era of the 1960s was in many cases a misallocation of capital. It appeared to a public not fully informed that certain companies were growth opportunities. But then the sales started to slow up and you started to have other costs. It turned out that these weren't really economic profits at all.' Note the fine remoteness of the language: 'It appeared to a public not fully informed' is one of those passive locutions which suggests that some impersonal force has been responsible both for creating the appearance and for the lack of full information. In fact the responsibility for informing (or not informing) lay as much with the western world's accountants as with anybody else.

Throughout the high-flying era, however, the auditing firms showed remarkable readiness to patch up rickety aircraft and send them sputtering back into the high skies. Accounting conventions have so great a degree of elasticity that two sets of auditors operating on different assumptions could quite legitimately come up with utterly different sets of earnings from the same data on costs and sales – in fact, even the definition of a sale is a matter of opinion and disagreement.

Thus even the statement of total earnings could not be understood by the public unless it was also fully informed on the conventions that had been applied. Even if all the relevant information had been supplied in the footnotes, the subtlety of a financial Jesuit was often required to apply the necessary correction to the published accounts and come up with an alternative number. Since most members of the public (like most members of the New York Stock Exchange, as it happens) lacked either the time or the talent for the exercise, they were bound to fall back on the hope that what was good enough for Arthur Andersen, or Price Waterhouse, or Touche Ross was good enough for them.

Now if the earnings figure is elastic, and the total of shares in issue can also be manipulated, it follows that the arithmetical product of dividing the one by the other is a number of singularly low reliability. Certainly, investors cannot rely on that product to demonstrate either that the real value of the business has increased, or that its ability to pay a higher dividend has been enhanced, or even that its financial future is secure. If the earnings per share plummet, true, that is a bad omen. But in many cases the augury comes too late: the oracle pronounces *after* the damage has been done.

The reason is elementary. Overstatement of earnings is concealed by rising sales. The company is in effect borrowing from next year's profits, which can be maintained so long as the true earnings are advancing year by year. But when the true profits dip, the reported figures must bear the brunt of the earlier borrowings from profits as well as the losses from the present calamities.

Yet this was the flimsy foundation on which many a stock-market boom has rested. The earnings per share figure was hypothetical; the ratio that linked that number to the price of the stock in the market was evanescent; and yet managers, as previously noted, fixed their targets in terms of percentage growth on that figure as if by doing so they were fulfilling their duty to both the shareholders and themselves.

If earnings per share meant anything, it was as a measure of the company's ability to pay the cash dividends that shareholders preferred to shun. Yet the figure measured nothing of the sort. To quote again from *Business Week*, this time from James W. McSwiney, chairman of a conglomerate, Mead Corporation, 'Financial accounting tends to emphasize reported earnings. The name of the game [there's that phrase again], however, is cash on hand and the future availability of cash.' Mead, in fact, could be taken as a paradigm of the high-flying years: a sober and conservative paper company that embraced diversification and modern management ideas as its strategy for taking its place among the ranks of those few firms that would enter the New Jerusalem. Mead played the big company game (to be examined below) to the hilt. It even invented a system of matrixes, built round RONA (Return On Net Assets), to govern its crucial investment decisions. And yet in 1974 the total return to Mead's investors, in dividends and the price movement of the shares, came to an annual decline over a decade of 1·01 per cent. This ranked Mead at 304th among the 500 top companies listed by *Fortune*, from which it may be correctly deduced that around half of the above companies, even without allowing for inflation, had yielded a nil return to investors over a full decade.

Yet Mead, for one, had raised earnings per share by a noble 12·4 per cent compound over the same period. Not only was the pursuit of earnings per share growth illusory, in that it meant nothing and proved less. It was open to a worse condemnation still: to use McSwiney's phrase yet again, it wasn't even the name of the game.

## It's only money

Virtue is usually made of necessity. Big companies, all the way from Mead to General Motors, attract most of the attention in the investment world, despite their conspicuous dullness, less because of their looming power on the economic scene, national and international, than because, if the stock market is considered as a casino, large companies supply the overwhelming majority of the chips. If the game is to be one for many players, or, to use the pompous title, a property-owning democracy, all of us – and not just the fund-managing professionals – have no option but to play with big company chips. They are the only ones in large enough supply to go round. Indeed the ratio between the Goliaths and the Davids is among the more awesome discrepancies in world finance.

The market capitalization of a London-based multinational like Shell was £2000 million in the autumn of 1975 – and that accounted for only 40 per cent of the Anglo-Dutch group's total majestic assets. Over in Wall Street, US Steel, by no means either gee or whiz, cashed in at the same time at $500 million more. Between these Everests of commerce lies many a mighty peak: to buy International Nickel would have cost £1,500 million; Kaiser Aluminium £385.6 million; Rank Organization £281 million. Against these, the middling companies of the Anglo-Saxon world hardly weighed much. Out of the 200 largest public companies in Britain in June 1975, only 43 had market capitalizations of more than £100 million. Moreover, if the investor's interest was confined to the fastest-growing or most profitable companies (and why not?), few apples of his eye would then have weighed in above £30 million.

Of course, saying that it would cost £2000 million to buy Shell is a manner of speaking, a grand euphemism. London newspapers are fond of reporting that so many millions have been wiped off the value of a company's shares because of some natural calamity (like forgetting to count the inventory, or the celebrated fracas at the Rank Organization, when the chairman and chief executive had a difference of opinion over policy and personal matters). But the loss is purely on paper, which is just as true of the market capitalization: it is a paper calculation. The market can value only what is actually on the market. Even in a loosely held company, only a small proportion of the shares will be available or potentially available at any time, and a major chunk of the equity may be tied up as securely as a Christmas parcel.

This isn't necessarily because some founding family is clasping the shares to its bosom for ever more. A large, inert body of shareholders always exists: institutions and individuals who for some reason, or no reason, regard their holdings as precious heirlooms, never to be distributed. The motivation is the same as that which generates abysmal loyalty to delinquent boards of directors: self-identification coupled with ignorance. The most remarkable demonstration of the latter attribute came in the troubled Britain of 1975.

After the British Leyland car giant had collapsed into the arms of the government, more money had to be funnelled into the sickened-unto-death corporation by its new overlords. This was accomplished by an issue of new shares, which naturally had to be offered to those individuals who, since they had rejected the government's far from princely offer of 10p per share, still held part of the equity. Since the new shares were priced at 200p, however, only a certifiable lunatic, or a socialist minister, would take them up, and so the shareholders were advised again and again. Yet a goodly number positively insisted on shovelling good money after bad – paying their 200p for shares they could then buy in the market for 80p.

In a market where such misguided minds can survive, the attachment of holders to hollow shares is no surprise. But the free proportion of big company equities is certainly greater than in the case of the middling-to-small variety, where the chances of proportionately large holdings being stuck firmly with families and friends must be greater. Moreover, the presence of institutions, who are somewhat less likely to take permanent, unreasoning shines to a stock, is much more marked among the big battalions. From the supply and demand point of view, therefore, the shareholder should be on their side: especially since Mammon, if not God, is on that side as well – the received view at all times in the second half of the twentieth century has been that the large corporations, however undynamic in stock-market performance, would inherit the economic earth.

The rationale is encapsulated in the ideas of economies of scale. Over time the race has gone, in market after market, to the competitors who can spread their costs over the largest and longest product runs; or, at the retail end, to those who can buy and distribute in the greatest quantities. Not only are there scale economies in production and distribution, but management, if theory means anything, should reap a similar benefit. One brilliant man handling £100 million of sales should earn at least ten times the profit of an equally clever executive with only £10 million of turnover to exploit. And the extra financial muscle bulging in the first fellow's biceps, in terms of both cash flow and borrowing power, will turn an edge into an overwhelming and irreversible advantage.

But theory means only as much as practice will allow. Many industries may well have a minimum size below which the dis-economies are so great that competition becomes impossible. But it doesn't follow, even in theory, if theory is re-examined, that economies of scale are subject to no ceiling at all.

In management, this phenomenon is well established and well understood. Above a certain size – some say 200, some 500, some 1000 – factory employment passes beyond the ability of one ace to exercise effective control and direction. No matter how excellent he may be, the task has expanded beyond his span. The larger the company gets, the more layers of management have to be inserted between top and bottom, which means often enough that the ace at the summit, far from reaping economies of management scale for his own talents, isn't engaged in any activity that could truly be called managing.

But if the economies of mass management are a chimera, few people, even today, have queried those of mass production, although in one of the world's most conspicuous markets – motor cars – the middling, not to say relatively piddling, firms like Peugeot, BMW and Volvo have consistently confounded the giants like General Motors, Ford, Volkswagen and Fiat, whose million-car runs should have carried all before them – in theory. In fact a paper delivered in 1972 by two Shell International Chemical experts at a conference in Bratislava not only queries the benefits of massive scale, it demolishes them. The experts argued that every giant chemical maker in the world (and few such firms are not gigantic) built plants well above the optimum size (partly because they ignored costs and considerations that would have spoilt the proleviathan sums). Since all the giants were building these 'monuments to megalomania' simultaneously, they also guaranteed a condition of oversupply that savaged their prices and profits beyond short-term repair. Of course, they stayed in business. But this saving grace of the great company is its underlying weakness: the *diseconomy* of scale in the matter of wealth. The diseconomies of scale are many and varied. In ethylene plants (the particular baby of the Bratislavites) they include disproportionately high commissioning and ancillary plant costs, overproduction of unwanted 'co-products', higher penalties for sub-capacity working. But the wealth diseconomy is especially pernicious because it enables companies to absorb horrendous difficulties like the above, and almost to pretend that they have never happened.

From the manager's angle, that is a consoling ability. But for the caring investor, the cushioning of mistakes, the making of losses and the sterile commitment of capital add up to a running disaster. The price of the great company's absorption powers is that the return on capital, the source of all goodness, remains stuck in the nether regions.

Merely consider the case of Du Pont. Sales in 1974 came to $6,910 million, or $18.9 million for every working and weekend day. Even after all costs, interest and taxes had been lopped off, the company had $910.4 million left in net profits and so-called depreciation, or $2.5 million a day. If the company's comptrollers could contrive to delay payment of expenses ('costs of goods sold and other operating charges') for a day after receipt of income, its directors would have $13.9 million more to play with round the world. A week's delay adds up to no less than $97.3 million on the 1974 figures.

Nor are Du Pont's figures especially gigantic. Royal Dutch-Shell's British half (with its 40 per cent of sales) sold as much in pounds in 1974 as Du Pont did in dollars. For a company of Shell's size, losing £8.6 million in three years in partnership with the

United States Armour giant in a forlorn effort to gain £20 million of fertilizer sales is a breeze. Even dropping £85 million, with equal futility, in nuclear energy (another Shell misfortune) isn't enough to spoil the boardroom luncheons.

The cash-flow factor means that there is no practical limit to the grandiose nature of the plans directors of large companies can form. Most such dignitaries will throw up their hands in horror at this juncture: to them life is a constant procession of schemes for which the capital can't be found, of having to appropriate limited funds between clamouring claimants – especially in the tight money conditions that accompanied the great fight against inflation and threatened to last into the 1980s. But the horrified ones overlook two points: in the first place, minor expenditures, even up into the millions, proceed without let or hindrance; and in the second place, the capital shortage arises partly because grandiose new plants have been piled upon the relative failure of equally superb monuments to past megalomania. Thus it wasn't surprising that Lockheed was strapped for cash for new projects as a result of the entirely predictable, and predicted, drain on its resources generated by the bloodsucking Tristar airliner. Yet even though the Tristar was beyond Lockheed's financial powers, it was still able to proceed – foolishly, for sure, but as inevitably as death or taxes, just as Chrysler was able to go on supporting its money-losing British subsidiary while its own equity capital was being eaten up.

A high return on capital not only generates all goodness, as noted above, but is the source of all future capital – self-generated or borrowed from outside. The besetting illusions of big boards include the idea that money borrowed doesn't come from the company itself. Their self-deceptive thought is that the money meanders into some wondrous asset, where it rests in perpetuity. So long as the investment generates an after-depreciation return which is higher than the interest paid on the borrowed money, and is sufficient to repay the capital, the company must win. They forget the catch that the asset must be replaced for far more than the depreciation money; and often equally negligently overlook the inconvenient fact when the investment actually returns less than the interest cost. A twenty-year borrowing at 10 per cent, in any event, requires the generation of cash equal to 300 per cent of the sum borrowed merely to take care of the interest and capital on the loan. Since the capital repayment has to be made post-tax, that means a total return of 20 per cent a year, and very few large companies have ever managed that much for more than one glorious summer out of five.

But low returns on the capital they have already invested never stop managements of the mighty corporations from investing still more, be it in mammoth plants worthy of Bratislava-type scorn or mergers which, time after time, will go the way of much corporate flesh: into relative failure. This is more likely with big company mergers than with those further down the pecking order – another paradox.

In that evanescent theory, again, the large company should have the resources of men and money, plus the know-how, to make its mergers work. In practice, big company mergers take as long to succeed as elephants to gestate, except that, in the latter case, something always comes out of the process. Big company buys come unstuck in part mostly when they are friendly, agreed affairs: giants don't like to be seen committing rape and, as we noted previously, resented and resisted mergers far outscore those concluded in an atmosphere of sweetness and light.

From mergers to marketing, however, money is only as much of an objective as the entrenched management cares to make it. At least investment spending is subject to all manner of controls, often culminating in mandatory board approval for all expenditure above a certain low limit. For some arcane reason, money invested is considered more holy than money spent on current account. Thus at the very moment when a board is gravely deliberating whether to spend £250,000 on an extension to one of its plants, some unsupervised fellow may well be committing the company to an overspend of £2.5 million on a current item like materials. No doubt the board of Rowntree-Mackintosh, which was looking somewhere else while one of its senior men took a plunge in cocoa (that unluckiest of commodities) that eventually cost the shareholders £32 million, scrutinized every penny of the money invested in its chocolate and sweets machinery.

When they do approve investments or other spending that turns out to be woefully ill-advised, managers are only sometimes guilty of simple error or profligacy. In most cases, the spring of their motivation lies in the survival of the corporation. It was the sight of its defence business going out of the window that inspired the management of Lockheed to seek civil salvation – and financial damnation – in the Tristar. It was the knowledge that one day mounting competition and market saturation would reduce the profitability of traditional lines that led so many managements, from RCA to Xerox, into the hopefully rich, actually ruinous, world of computers. Many studies have come to the same finding: that the perpetuation of the company, far more than any pecuniary motive, is what serves as the foundation of the managerial life and the true corporate philosophy of most major groups.

But perpetuation is of singularly low interest to the investor. He wants the company to survive only to the extent that he can cash in his chips whenever he wants: he doesn't want to be stuck with a 10p burnt offering, like those unfortunate owners of British Leyland. From his point of view, the managerial idea of survival is no use – because survival is so easily contrived. So long as the management can maintain an adequate cash flow (which in any company of vast turnover is a simple trick for people of remotely competent stature) the corporation can survive even with inadequate profitability.

The shareholders might be better served if the business were trimmed down to its profitable elements, or sold off completely. Some textbook examples of the conflict of interests came with the proposed nationalization of the British steel industry. Of all businesses to escape from, steel has been high on the exit list for most of the post-war period. Yet the two largest engineering conglomerates that owned steel works, Guest Keen & Nettlefold and Tube Investments, hotly resisted this disinvestment. Naturally the fell deed at once raised their return on capital to a degree that no effort of their managements could have achieved, in steel or anything else.

The evidence shows, moreover, that shareholders in trust-busted enterprises, like the former components of the Standard Oil Trust, fared much more lavishly after break-up than they did before, or could have expected to do if John D. Rockefeller's robber barony had remained intact. And it's hard to believe, for another example, that an integrated I. G. Farben chemical empire could have outperformed the three component parts into which it was split by the unintentional kindness of the Allies.

The picture is fully supported by the reports on the dismal showing of big companies in the annual ten-year league tables published by *Fortune* and *Management Today* on their respective sides of the Atlantic. While the point is true that smaller firms dominate the lists in part because ten years ago they were of insignificant size, that is another way of expressing the equal truth that the diseconomies of scale apply to growth potential as well. Nor can the mathematical advantages of beginning from near zero be easily distinguished from the inborn managerial assets that go with tininess. If money is tight, it tends to be tightly used. This general rule has many exceptions, like one little company of my acquaintance that was worrying its head off over a ten-year prospect while its cash was disappearing at a ten-month gallop; or Venesta, the good plywood firm that splintered itself totally by diversifying (two of its stabs being separate disasters in the reprographic field) until it was earning only a third of its one-time all-plywood profits.

The smaller company has one other attraction for the share selector: at least the management's track record, if any, is visible. Nobody can even take a stab at judging the management calibre of the General Motors board. Even if (and the proposition is dubious) the chairman and the president do run the company, their stay is so short, and knowledge about their work beforehand so scanty, that the question isn't worth attempting. Who, after all, will reach for his chequebook on being informed that one Richard G. Gerstenberg, aged sixty-three, of whom he has heard nothing either good or bad, has been elected to the GM chair? In the occasional years when a leviathan turns in bumper earnings, they cannot be attributed to any one man or any group of men; the reigning group, anyway, is by the laws of averages and the business cycle likely to have presided over at least one year of doom. And even when the track record is discernible, there is no guarantee that the past provides any guide to the future. Heroes of business and their corporate vehicles are, like man himself, born only to die.

Take as one case in a thousand exemplars the story of Playboy Enterprises, Inc. On the strength of a marvellous record, Playboy went public in 1971, with the populace snapping up a quarter of the shares for $23.50. Nobody suspected that the once-phenomenal ability of Hugh M. Hefner, he of the round bed and bunny jet, in magazine publishing was coupled with a striking inability in every other field, including the running of clubs and hotels. Had Hefner proceeded with his plan to become private by buying back the shares, which had dropped to $3, the deal would have rubbed in the new robbery. A man who sells goods for $23.50, and buys them back, say, for $5, has made a profit of $18.50 from the transaction.

If the investing public can go wrong judging a Hefner, whose works and ways are out in the comparative open, it hasn't a hope when it comes to one of the amorphous neo-conglomerate managements that dominate shareholding lists of the world. Nor can the investor now repose much faith in the traditional strengths of size. The Bratislava concept has begun to permeate the consciousness of big company managers: in an age when small steel plants can be highly profitable, and large ones return minuscule yields, the penetration of management minds by the virtues of smallness is proceeding apace. This sounded especially true in an era when shortage of capital had begun to loom among the largest single preoccupations on the economic scene. If the economists' calculations had been correct, industry would have needed almost three times as much capital in the 1975–84 decade as in the previous ten years; there was not the faintest sign of where such mighty sums could be found – and yet the decade ended with capital in super-abundance.

The capital starvation of large companies, like the recurrent reports of the death of western civilization, was greatly exaggerated. But from many angles the big company seems a less safe refuge for investment money than in the past. This raises an almost insoluble paradox. If the smallest companies include the best buys, yet there are not enough to go round, what is the investor, institutional or private, to do with his money? Was the ridiculous run-up in the price of alleged growth stocks in the 1960s in part the reflection of too much money retreating from AT & T or ICI and plunging into too small a supply of the lesser-sized alternatives?

The situation could perhaps be resolved if the big companies

were to revert to the old gilt-edged, blue-chip status of which AT
& T was once the prime example. Such an investment would be
cash-rich: its managers would concentrate on paying bigger and
bigger dividends in perfect safety year after year; they would
distribute capital surpluses back to the shareholders; and growth in
earnings per share would be as meaningless to their managements
as the Koran. Above all, they would watch the spending of the
shareholders' money with unremitting attention. To many big
company managements, seven-digit sums have become only
money. But to the investor, it's only money – his or her money –
that counts.

# 3 The manager of the past

from *The Once and Future Manager*

As a self-appointed foe of visionary philosophizing about either management or the future, I should perhaps have refused the commission offered by Per Berndtson to write this book. Per Berndtson was one of the first of the multinational headhunters: multinational in both his staff and his clients, who were led by ITT. My dilemma was resolved by basing the book on reports from Per's consultants in the field (who greatly amused me by conforming strictly to national stereotypes during the interviews).

The results, reread after a decade, didn't make me regret my rare resort to the crystal ball. No doubt it's because management, rooted in the laws of human nature and economics, can't change so much as the technologies of product and process – where forecasts have tended to go sadly awry. The relative consistency of management works for both good and ill: it's easier to discern the developments of good practice, but the obstacles to these developments – mostly, the inherent human conservatism – remain much the same.

In choosing excerpts, I decided to begin with a historical account that both sets the scene for present times and establishes where movement has been minimal: where 'plus ça change, plus c'est la même chose'. Western management, however, is still at the crossroads described in the second excerpt: of the three possible solutions I suggested, the third, 'a far more marked breakdown of hierarchical management than has yet occurred', emerged as the correct assumption: but in the vast majority of companies, its full flowering is still awaited.

That has a very obvious bearing on the crucial matter of motivation, on which millions of words have been spilled. I have not added greatly to their number: and I don't think there is much that needs to be added today to my text. The same, I hope, applies to my vision of the future of management. It's a comforting vision – especially for me, since I have found no reason, after a decade, to change even one of my sentiments.

The world of 1966 was a simpler place, for managers as for everybody else. In the United States, which then bestrode the western economy like a colossus, the Kennedy–Johnson boom was still going strong, and the domestic devastation to be unleashed by the Vietnam War was still in the future. It was the high tide of the American corporation, and the rest of the world of management took its coloration from the American example.

Even then, there were palpable soft spots. The great steel and aluminium companies were failing to return appreciable amounts on capital. Detroit was showing up poorly in competition with foreign imports, above all the Volkswagen Beetle. The railways, with few exceptions, were becoming permanently weak sisters of the economic society. But still and all, the United States was a Great Society – and the greatness was not confined to the old and long established.

The old-line companies, such as General Electric, or Du Pont, or RCA, attracted enormous respect, often as much for their management skills as for their products, profits or technology. But the pace was set by newcomers: nothing before had been seen in the business world to match the trinity of International Business Machines, Xerox and Polaroid. IBM was a pre-war company that had achieved its post-war breakthrough with a revolutionary new product, one that loomed over the whole management world in 1965. The computer was not just a product, it was a way of life – more, it held the key to vast and wonderfully promising change.

Yet even these companies, and others like them, failed to sum up the quintessence of the age. The hero company was probably an extraordinary Californian creation called Litton Industries. Litton, which had risen from nothing to join the two dozen or so biggest companies in the United States, exemplified all the certainties that age of management took for granted. In fact, image and reality were not, as Litton proved later on, the same thing. But what was important for management round the world was the legend rather than the fact, and the legend held that Litton was a *management* company.

While it boasted excellent products and high technology, Litton's vital ingredient was supposedly the management that brought the products to life and that had unique skills at turning technology into commercial properties. Also, the company was financially acute, and financial controls and sophistication were the handmaidens of the overriding objective of making the corporation hum with diversified activity. Diversified was the key word, not because, like troubled aluminium companies, the corporation needed defensive strategies, but because aggression demanded the seizing of new territories.

Nor did this present any problems, because the company's special management skills were capable – almost by definition – of handling any industry, any market, any problem. The aim of this well-knit enterprise, moreover, was clear: growth in earnings per share, which in turn would support a further advance in a share price that had performed astoundingly since Tex Thornton, a refugee from Ford, had established the company and made his big breakthrough in inertial guidance systems for military planes. That dependence on defence might sound warning bells for lesser companies, but not for Litton, since it provided the chance to shift technology from the frontiers of government-financed technology to the hinterland of immensely profitable civil developments. Thus everything hung together. The corporation was both systematic and adventurous, controlled but dynamic, creative but organized.

The untrue image pictures the realities of men's thoughts. It was an age when nobody felt that there were serious limitations to the powers of management. The United States had only recently embarked on a mission to place men on the moon – and a society whose managers could envisage and execute a task of such terrifying difficulty and scale could plainly work out how to run a railroad. The omnicompetence of a Litton therefore fitted the prevailing mood. No fewer than eight United States companies were convinced that they could successfully exploit the new technological wonders of the computer, and a few firms in Europe had exactly the same idea. Most of them proved to be devastatingly wrong, but none of them would have believed it in 1966. The marketing revolution had taught managers how to penetrate new markets and to develop products to fit market needs. The evolution of financial controls had made even technology susceptible to management. What the corporation wanted to achieve, it could achieve.

To European companies, looking not only across the Atlantic, but also at the increasing number of American invaders in Europe itself, it seemed clear that the only way ahead was to imitate the Americans. Only by becoming more American could they hope to match the achievements of American business. A trickle of American methods, management teachers, consultants and theories became a flood. In Britain, where economic anxieties were most acute, two brand-new business schools on the American model were started with money raised from government and industry, even though the country, by the standards of the Continent, was already unusually rich in management schools. But Britain had no institution of prestige even remotely comparable to the Harvard Business School – and this was seriously seen as a major impediment to the country's economic growth, even as one of the main reasons for its relative decline.

The dominant thought in management strategy was that the future belonged to the multinationals, principally to the American company in Europe – an idea that inspired many Europeans to believe that, unless they too could form cross-frontier mergers, to derive the same benefits as the Americans, they were doomed. The whole Common Market, then only five years old, was predicated on much the same grounds. The firms of western Europe needed continental markets if they were to match the innate strength generated by the huge, homogeneous United States. To thinking European managers, this view was as axiomatic as the faith in technology.

From the viewpoint of 1976, however, it was clear that a decade before, when men and managers felt they were at the dawn of a new age of technological breakthrough, they were actually witnessing the tail end of just such an era. Nuclear power, the new electronics, the jet engine – the great inventions had been made; as it happened, the next decade was not to see their like. It followed that the battle against American competition, which had been seen largely as a struggle to recapture the ground lost by technological inferiority, developed a wholly different nature. The pursuit of technological equality could be taken for granted: time would take care of that. What came to dominate managerial thinking were anxieties common to managements on both sides of the Atlantic, to which no country had the answer.

In hindsight, 1966 was a watershed year in many respects. Two decades of American political and economic hegemony were reaching their zenith, and were shortly to be replaced by decline. Two decades of producer domination, kept going artificially by the Korean and Cold Wars, had ended. Two decades of financial stability built on the rock of the US dollar were over, though few men recognized the fact. Two decades of astonishingly stable political and industrial relations in most of the industrialized countries of the West were also about to come under severe strain. All these changes were bound to have profound impacts on managers and the companies they served. Thus the 1966–76 decade became an era of reappraisal, sometimes agonizing, always difficult.

These twisting strands were bound together by the end of an economic dream. The two post-war decades saw an unprecedented general prosperity. For nearly the whole period rates of unemployment were extraordinarily low in the West: lower than low, since large numbers of foreign workers had to be imported into every country in Europe, including Britain, to fill the need for labour. No government foresaw the day when this continual prosperity could not be taken for granted. No management reckoned on a moment when it would face, not just a temporary fluctuation, but a severe and general downturn. The failure of this dream, while the extent of the slump was not in the least remarkable, certainly not by the standards of the 1930s, set off the engines of doubt and destruction.

The changes of fashion as managers wrestled with these new

developments, simply because they were the swings and round-abouts of style, have not been given the importance they deserve as symbols of substance. Why, for example, was the manager of 1966 so hopeful of the computer as a management tool? What, apart from desire for personal enrichment, explained the rise of the conglomerate? What economic, as opposed to corporate, forces impelled the move to multinationalism? These tidal waves had by no means exhausted their impetus by 1976. Beneath the changing surface, managers were still primarily engrossed with the same problems; the ways of tackling them varied – but the challenges and difficulties stayed broadly similar.

The computer, to start with, offered the chance of reducing to simpler and more manageable proportions what had become far more complex and, in the strictest sense, unmanageable. In 1945 even the world's largest companies were relatively simple affairs, and the simplicity lasted in many cases all the way to 1966. For most of that period, for instance, the largest German car manufacturer, Volkswagen, was effectively a one-product company.

That was an extreme example. But the 1976 complexities of a company like America's General Electric, with 120 different businesses, nearly all of them large enough to outrank the biggest American firms of 1945, undoubtedly developed faster than the management skills needed to control them. No doubt, that is why General Electric was continually among the management pioneers, casting about for new methods that would help to tame the monster created by endless economic expansion.

Such techniques, born out of the imperative of complex compound growth, gave the conglomerates the tools they sometimes used more as advertisements than as management aids. But the conglomerates, too, stepped into a yawning breach. The unequal advance of different business sectors and different companies had left a large number of firms stranded: private companies with no clear management succession or business future, public companies that had lost their way, the undercapitalized and the under-exploited. Management resources, in every sense, were in short supply – partly because the giant corporations, quite inevitably, were sucking in so much of the available human material. The conglomerates were a means of stretching these scarce resources over wider spans of corporate territory: and, interestingly enough, even though they had mostly failed or disappointed financially, in 1976 the conglomerates were largely intact, despite a fair number of disposals and spin-offs. For all their silliness, they filled a need, and that need, again created by the widening and differentiation of markets, will never disappear.

Very similar forces drove the large companies, first in America, then in Britain and Europe, to diversify multinationally. The rise of sophisticated consumer and industrial markets all over the West created a demand for products in every country from every source, and corporations in this era followed not the flag, but the trade. Where they sought to impose new tastes on unprepared markets, like some of the American companies in Europe, spectacular failure often resulted. But the unprecedented rise in world trade in manufactures was inevitably accompanied by an equally spectacular increase in international business – and in international business success. A late starter in the race like Du Pont would have been unable to justify European output of the bulk chemicals which earned its American bread and butter. But by 1966 Europe offered sophisticated enough markets to take speciality chemical products in highly economic quantities. This internationalization, however, brought an extra dimension to the complexities of management.

Problems always feed on each other. Thus the problem of multinational control and consistency created a new kind of confrontation with unions – and even spawned the new challenge of the multinational union. Throughout the decade, the management of diversity, in all its own diverse forms, was a besetting concern of managements big and small. The one-product companies added other products; the one-man bands were forced to hire other and more professional managerial players; the one-country firms started venturing abroad.

In some cases they might be responding to theory and fad, like the 'synergy' idea, a falsely scientific attempt to demonstrate that two and two make five, which inspired a great deal of foolish merger-making. But the mergers, however inane individually, also expressed current necessities: they did seem to offer a solution to perplexing questions of resources and corporate directions. If you couldn't afford to build a new business, you could always, thanks to the invention of the joint-stock company, buy one for paper, which seemed to cost nothing at all.

That was an illusion, and it was one to which young, theoretically trained managers were especially prone. At the end of the war, and right up to 1966, business was largely in the hands of men who had been through some hard schools: the pre-war depression, the wartime battles of armies or factory production, the post-war reconstruction (especially taxing on the devastated Continent). Some of these men achieved extraordinary feats: in cars alone, the saving of Ford Motor by Ernest R. Breech, or the construction of Volkswagen by Heinz Nordhoff, are classics of management, in any language.

But by 1966 these regimes of powerful, often dictatorial figures were coming to an end in company after company. Death came to some great innovators and builders, like Lord Marks, the prime architect of Europe's most distinguished retail chain, Marks & Spencer. But the main cause of the changing of the guard was retirement. Obligatory retirement ages have played a more powerful part in the development of professional management than commonly realized – and one after the other men who reached their own sixties in the decade of the 1960s left the limelight for the shadows of history. Men born in 1900 or thereabouts were in their thirties when Hitler and Roosevelt came to power; in their forties when the Second World War broke out and Pearl Harbor was bombed; and they began to approach retirement as the great switch to a buyer's market was completed. Their background, training and personalities were bound to be strikingly different from those of a man born in 1932, who would not have been a combatant in the war, would never have known the Depression and, in 1966, was approaching his managerial prime and claiming his management opportunity.

A decade further on, the torch had passed inexorably to men of this generation, overwhelmingly in the reaches of upper-middle management, increasingly at the topmost level. The first younger men to break the mould, such as Pierre Dreyfus of Renault, or Arnold Weinstock of GEC, or Harold Geneen of ITT, or Giovanni Agnelli of Fiat, were now either clearly middle-aged or else in the retirement belt themselves. Younger men still had unquestionably been spoilt by the easy and seemingly continuous success of the first half of the decade, which had encouraged the belief that the financial games played at business school were the real thing.

But a little misfortune, in the shape of the worldwide recession in general, and the collapse of a number of star companies and prestige projects in particular, had by 1976 greatly improved their psychological conditioning. Wise old managers often say that the making of an excellent manager requires at least one failure in business, at least one mess to retrieve. By that token, the economic setbacks of the first half of the 1970s should have made many good managers considerably better.

The underlying economic and management problem of handling diversity and scale, within a context of limited resources and of constantly evolving tastes and technological demands, remained – and perhaps tackling this problem is a young man's game. But the babies of the 1930s and their wartime successors were still in 1976 by and large operating in a management world they did not create. The mould of management was set long ago, long before 1966, long before 1945 for that matter.

It was between the wars that the giants of world business were created or completed – General Motors, General Electric, Royal-Dutch Shell, Unilever, Daimler-Benz, Fiat, the Japanese trading empires. They had drawn heavily on military analogies to construct their organizations – quite understandably, since the military offered the only large-scale model and comprehensive organizational theory then around.

Whether or not the military-style line-and-staff hierarchy was the best way to run companies in the last quarter of the twentieth century, that was the style with which the new generation of managers was stuck, not just in big companies, but right down the scale: both by their size and their example, the big companies inevitably set the tone. But by 1976 the big companies were loosening up. Informality became more fashionable than formality. The small company's ways, far from being an object of derision, now became appealing for their very simplicity, directness and creativeness.

Part of this throwback belonged to the worldwide nostalgic

movement of the troubled 1970s. But much of it reflected a true feeling that maybe the problems that dominated 1966 and still persisted in stronger form in 1976 had been approached in the wrong way, with big battalions and heavy artillery (to use the military language), when sharp-shooting and small raiding parties would have been more effective. The years from 1976 saw the first stirrings as the younger managers sought to build their own possibly Brave, partially New, World.

# 4 The manager at the crossroads

from *The Once and Future Manager*

The discontinuity in the world of management in the mid-1970s came as a shock to managers right across the western world. It was as if continuity had been a familiar and comforting aspect of their lives, and those of their predecessors. Yet management and business have always been subject to discontinuities of varying kinds.

Like any human activity, industry and commerce are affected both by the deep changes in the tides of human affairs and by the relatively minor storms and disturbances on the surface of society. In addition, management has an inner life of its own, and management, again like any other activity, is subject both to evolution and revolution. Thus if management seemed different in 1976, this was no more than had always been so. Management always is different.

Companies, too, are living organisms. Although the continuities of companies are often fully as impressive as their breaks with the past, the company, like the family, changes from generation to generation. Take the chemical industry alone: the Du Pont of 1976, the Imperial Chemical Industries, the Bayer, the Tojo Rayon, the Rhône Poulenc, the Montecatini, the CIBA-Geigy – all of these had changed radically both in their structure and in their culture compared with twenty years previously, let alone thirty or forty.

Technology had transformed product lines and processes; restructuring had eliminated some activities, greatly expanded others; social relationships between managers, and between managers and men, had been altered profoundly; markets, both geographically and in product terms, were often completely different. In any industry, much the same observations could be made. The only constant in managerial life is change.

Yet the change that confronted management appeared to be, and in a sense was, qualitatively different. The evolutionary element seemed to be much less, the revolutionary one far greater. The trigger for these changes wasn't anything specifically within management's control – it lay in a world economic situation that, for a variety of avoidable reasons, had got out of hand.

For the first time in post-war history, the industrialized countries inflated in step, ran into simultaneous and similar crises as a result, cut back at the same time in a desperate effort to curb hyperinflation, and succeeded, more or less in step, but at the price of enduring their first combined recession. The men who truly ran the economy – the managers of the world – could do nothing about this cycle of breakages except pick up the pieces. But the shock of the crash was inevitably hard.

Its extent can be appreciated by summing up the problems the managers of 1976 faced and that their fathers would have worried about either not at all or to nothing like the same extent. The first and greatest concern was inflation. Post-war full employment and welfare-state policies had condemned most economies to a steady but mild inflation year by year; the erosion of the currencies was rarely sharp enough to cause immediate worries, although it should have excited more long-term anxiety than it did.

But double-digit inflation introduced a new element of danger with which managements were totally unprepared to cope. Since the old answers no longer worked, men naturally sought for new ones, and inflation accounting, a change in financial reporting designed to reflect the impact of hyperinflation, was duly given enormous impetus.

The second untoward development had been gathering speed for some time: the growing encroachment of government in corporate affairs, an invasion that gathered force from all the other specific tendencies of the time, including inflation. For instance, the government in Britain took an active interest in inflation accounting – as a government was bound to do, given the new system's inescapable effect on revenues from corporation tax. But the added involvement of all governments, including the Common Market Commission in Brussels and the Republican Federal Government in Washington, also reflected the general spread of collectivist ideas and ideals.

Even governments of rightist persuasion were prepared to contemplate a degree of interference in business that would have seemed barely thinkable to governments of the Left a decade or two previously. Thus the French government intervened to keep open a watch factory that had been occupied by its workers. The American Government under Richard Nixon introduced price and profit controls. The British Conservative Government under Edward Heath, not to be outdone, built on the Nixon ideas to create a truly Draconian system of control over corporate income and personal earnings.

Where social democratic governments were in the ascendancy, even less obstacle existed to the idea that the state was in duty bound to regulate economic life and to lay down rules and restrictions backed by the force of law. Whether the issue was multinationals or the rights of dismissed workers, the state would not simply hold the ring: it would enter the fight on the side of the masses, which in effect meant against the management.

The increased role of the state in industry and commerce had first been spurred by its own advance to become the dominant customer for goods and services in many spheres, not simply defence. Companies in the forefront of this nexus (what President Eisenhower called the military–industrial complex) had developed elaborate knowledge of a new form of management called 'government relations'. Now this branch of corporate affairs has acquired new and added importance: the state, claiming to speak for the community, has become a critical management dimension in its own right.

Much of the force behind this development has come from the pressures and supposed pressures of the working masses. The industrial proletariat of the West has changed out of all recognition since Karl Marx first analysed its exploitation. Its steady rise in prosperity, to standards that would have been considered middle class only a short time ago, might have been expected to result in more stability, both in national politics and in the factory.

Instead, the 1960s saw violent outbreaks of unrest in every country on the Continent and (if the black riots in America are considered as working-class uprisings) the United States as well. The troubles that beset General Motors at its new Lordstown plant in Ohio were taken as another clear indication that the social mould had cracked. In many cases, the riots and unrest could be traced directly to disappointed economic expectations. But behind this disappointment also lay disaffection – and that was ultimately far more worrying.

Serious thinkers have been led to assert that all over the industrialized world the workers are in revolt. While this is plainly an exaggeration, it does seem clear that the old adage, 'man does not live by bread alone', develops greater force as prosperity advances. Politicians, who depend on the mass vote, and who, because of the need to cut back inflation, were unable to offer the usual inducements of more jobs and higher pay, turned to the subject of disaffection in part as a substitute, in part out of genuine anxiety about the future of industrial society.

Managers, confronted with less manageable situations in many plants and with an overwhelming unanimity on the subject of the need for greater industrial democracy, turned to a number of new nostrums, mostly deriving from the new ideas (or at least new formulations) of behavioural science. 'Job enrichment' and 'group technology' entered the language. Again, the new threat produced a new response, and the sense of violent discontinuity became still more marked.

While the unions in many cases did not lead the uprising of worker dissatisfaction, they have been quick to exploit the advantage. Industrial life since the war can be seen (although the picture is misleading) as a war between organized labour and organized management. The battle has mostly been fought over the age-old issue of dividing the added value: how much shall go to profits, how much to labour in the form of increased wages.

But organized labour has come to feel that it will always be at a disadvantage in this conflict so long as management has total control of the levers of decision. By moving production from one country to another, closing a plant here, opening another there, and in many similar ways, managements, in this simplistic view, can attempt to win back on the swings anything they have lost on the roundabouts. So the unions then sought to win back in the political arena what they feel they have lost at the bargaining table.

Governments anxious about worker unrest, winning votes and maintaining union support were too easy to convince that their strongly interventionist powers should, in effect, be turned to strengthening the power of the unions in industry. This isn't quite the same as strengthening the power of the workers, although that, too, is happening at grass-roots level and represents real changes in the composition, education and motivation of the working classes.

The unions, however, are a power bloc, an estate of every realm, quite apart from their representational role. The increase in their power against management's was an especially difficult problem of change for the managers, who lack any equivalent power base of their own. Just as behavioural science offered the apparent escape route from worker reactions, so the various devices for involving union representatives in the process of management decision-making looked like the only way out: if management could avoid sharing power, it must learn how to do so.

Finally, managers have to worry, as their fathers did not, about the impact of their companies on the environment or, more specifically, the impact on the companies of agitation about the corporate environmental influence. In its broadest sense, this takes in the consumerism movement, which at one point threatened to make almost every business decision a bear trap for the manager. The movement has had some signal effects – in the very tough rules in the United States on fuel emission, for instance, or in the resistance to new nuclear plants or the construction of pipelines across the open country.

These objections will continue to impose major, but probably justified restraints on industry; the extreme of reaction to this new anxiety, however, was the 'social audit', designed to measure a firm's contributions to society. But the audit missed its moment. By 1976 it was noticeable that consumerism had lost some of its steam as mass anxiety turned from the nature of economic activity to its scale: in other words, from pollution to jobs.

Exactly the same phenomenon explains why the labour riots, which coincided with a period when rises in living standards failed to come up to expectations, were on the whole not repeated during the period of recession and inflation, when living standards actually fell. Workers were far more anxious about having a job than about any other aspect of their employment, and their mood and behaviour changed accordingly.

This only rubs in the point at the start of this chapter. Management is always different, and the conditions have changed again since the managements of the West seemed to be staging a kind of Custer's Last Stand against the incursion of the heathen hordes. Like every other nostrum ever put forward as the solution to management's problems, in fact, the new remedies contained a measure of applicability and a measure of irrelevance, of both sense and nonsense.

Inflation accounting is an obvious and non-controversial example. Inflation matters critically to the manager because it gives a false impression of the two yardsticks by which he has been trained to live – growth and profit. In other words, at a time when the value of money has fallen by half, a company that has doubled its sales and profits has recorded no real increase.

If its physical sales have risen, in fact, the company's financial position may worsen seriously, when it has to support a larger volume of business on a reduced cash flow – and the consequences became painfully apparent to companies large and small as double-digit inflation ate into their resources and forced them into the hands of their bankers. But inflation accounting will not remedy the cash-flow problem. The method will still use depreciating currency – but in a different way.

By revaluing stocks and plant, the various methods of the new accounting cut profits (and taxes, which is an even better idea). Many leading American companies greatly improved their cash flow through lower taxes, at the expense of reporting lower profits, by switching from the First-In-First-Out method of accounting for stocks to Last-In-First-Out – a wise precaution at a time when the last stocks were costing so much more than the first.

In Britain companies won tax concessions worth billions of pounds by a rough-and-ready method that had a similar effect. But this was simply the reverse of the 'creative accounting' the conglomerates had used in their heydays to boost artificially their reported earnings per share. Inflation accounting, by the same token, is designed to show not higher, but lower, profits and thus comes no nearer to portraying reality – the kind of reality the management accounting systems installed in the more efficient companies throw up as a matter of course.

The reality is cash, a truth recognized in the sudden switch from 'profit is the name of the game' to the discovery by manager after manager in the 1970s that what he was really playing for was cash. By suddenly hymning the virtue of having enough cash in the till at the end of the day, managers were returning to the disciplines of a much earlier time, to rules of conduct that had become sophisticated beyond reason by being dressed up in new clothes; disguises such as discounted cash flow, the favoured technique of investment appraisal in the mid-1960s.

DCF, the formalization of the notion that a bird (or pound, or dollar) was worth more in the hand than in the bush, again had the combination of sense and nonsense found in all management nostrums. It pressed home the concept of the time value of money; it took tax flows into account; it tended to encourage investment. But it also presented a spurious accuracy (the return in year four will be 20.74 per cent), and did not answer the vital question: when do I get my money back?

What DCF shared with the remedies of the mid-1970s (inflation accounting, government relations, behavioural science, participation, social audit) was the quality of response to basic change. DCF was adopted and (like all brave new ideas) translated into everyday technology, because at the time of adoption resources were becoming more scarce while options were growing more numerous.

This was still an underlying problem in the 1970s, obscured by the sharpness of the conditions to which it helped give rise. Resources had simply become inadequate to satisfy all the demands made on them, even in the richest countries on the industrialized earth. Advanced methods of investment appraisal had been devised in a vain effort to allocate scarce financial resources; but in the 1970s energy and materials, often in embarrassing abundance in the 1960s, were added (misleadingly, as the 1980s were to prove) to the list of long-term scarcities.

The managers of Detroit, for instance, had long resisted introducing small cars because of the impact on profits that were already inadequate in relation to the huge scale of their investments. In the 1970s they were forced to abandon the struggle because of the impact of the new shortages (the troubles at the Lordstown plant, by no means parenthetically, arose mainly out of Chevrolet's determined attempt to get enough production of the compact Vega to make the economics tolerable).

Since markets are self-correcting (which is their prime virtue) the pressures of scarcity in energy and materials eased almost as fast as they had arisen – but not before managements had been given an unpleasant shock that will influence purchasing, design and planning policies for many years to come. But the insufficiency of profits, originally a nagging deficit, worse in some countries than others, was turned into a raging toothache by the inflation of the 1970s. In real-money terms, the profits of manufacturing industry around the world have shrunk, even though the demands on profits, to finance badly needed modernization and expansion, have increased disproportionately as inflation has forced up the price of capital goods.

Thus, although cash control is the name of part of the game, the goal has to be profit as well – and scoring was not easy in a world in which the popularity of profit-making was not considerable. Critics on the Left, for instance, were still railing against the profits of multinationals in years when by any orthodox standard many of the colossi were making grossly inadequate returns.

Defenders of the vitality of the capitalist system, however, can take much heart from the way in which managers did cut their coats according to suddenly restricted cloth. New programmes for cash control and conservation achieved instant success: sweeping rationalizations, such as the total switch of Volkswagen's production mix in one hectic year, were pushed through in formidably hard circumstances at maximum speed.

The corporate failures were few, and confined to weak sisters, most of whom had committed sins of financial rather than industrial management. Governments proved much slower than industry to respond to pressures of this kind, but they too had an electrifying shock in the 1970s – one that makes it most unlikely that they will ever again collectively indulge their propensity to finance a disproportionate rise in public spending by an uncontrolled resort to deficit financing.

But long-term restraints in inflationary government policies, while good for business in one sense, are less good in another. They imply that economic growth will be slower than in bygone decades – although any expansion at all will bring enormous relief to many managers who feared that the world had gone permanently ex-growth. If this were to prove true, then most of the ideas developed in management in the past decade would indeed have to be thrown out of the window.

But a shortage of resources, identified above as an underlying problem of the industrialized West, implies a surplus of demand. That demand may not be as heavily concentrated in consumer goods as in the past: but there is in any event a long-term trend away from consumption of goods and towards services. Marketing experts have long recognized that higher prosperity means that saturation points are reached more rapidly; and to that extent the mixture is as before – private consumption will still rise, given the chance, but patterns of consumption will still change.

The combination of these changes with greater restraint on government economic policies may lead to a permanent degree of subcapacity working in many industries. The onus on their managers will shift heavily to minimization of cost by every course open, ranging from lower utilization of labour to greater utilization of the most modern plant. Productivity is a matter of achieving the highest saleable output for the lowest possible input; the political pressures mentioned earlier in this chapter, such as those that severely restrict the dismissal of labour in most Common Market countries, do not make it easy to reduce inputs. But that, too, was a challenge facing managers at the crossroads of 1976: how to do more with less.

The biggest challenge, however, lay within themselves. The five major worries from which their mogul forefathers were free all impinged on managers with a peculiarly personal pain. Inflation eroded their earnings, governments interfered with their plans, workers would not obey, the unions were using heavier political muscle to embarrass management, the social climate had swung against managers, and even management achievements hailed on one side (such as building nuclear power stations) were assailed on the other. Small wonder that many managers appeared to grow discouraged, to lose motivation, to give up the game as lost.

Restoring self-confidence in management can be accomplished by many routes, none as effective as economic recovery. But however strongly the tides of confidence come flooding back, management in 1976, after years of playing about with concepts such as organization development and management by objectives, had still to bring to bear on itself the same scrutiny and eagerness to experiment that the behavioural scientists had encouraged at the lower level of work.

There were no clear signposts at the 1976 junction. But the way forward must be pointing to some kind of new managerial order. Some thought it might be unionized management as a counter-weight to organized labour; others that it might be the final advent of the long-heralded and often-delayed computerization of basic management systems. Given good fortune, it might be a far more marked breakdown of hierarchical management than has yet occurred.

Whatever the outcome, management's destiny still lies in its own hands to a greater extent than the pessimists suppose. Every action produces an equal and opposite reaction: the changes leading up to the 1976 crisis seemed so sudden and sharp that the reaction was bound to be equally rapid – and will probably make nonsense of many a prediction of gloom and doom. More than ever in 1976, western man needed executives and administrators who could make sense of the world economy. Whenever there is an overwhelming need the only people who can supply it (in this case the corps of managers) cannot possibly be starting from a weak position.

# 5 *Motivating the manager*

from *The Once and Future Manager*

Attract, retain and motivate, the Holy Trinity of executive selection and remuneration, include more than their fair share of subjective assumptions. Attraction, however, has a measurable dimension: if a company cannot find managers to fill its executive jobs, then plainly something is wrong with the organization or its conditions of employment or both. The same is true of retention: unless a company deliberately pursues a high managerial turnover, heavy fall-out, quite apart from being expensive, indicates again that something is rotten in the State of Denmark.

The most difficult member of the Trinity, however, is motivation. For all the high interest and increased spending on human relations at this elevated executive level, the links between cause and effect are improperly understood, and much of the practical work has been done more in hope than in certainty.

Many companies that have taken the new ideas on human relations most seriously are also highly successful. But this does not prove a causative link between the two aspects. It could be that the same qualities that lead a company to take the motivation of its management (and men) to heart are the identical characteristics that explain equal thoroughness in other more fundamental aspects of business: and this thorough professionalism, not any one manifestation of it, is what lays the golden eggs.

Nevertheless, it was established long ago by the Hawthorne experiments that the company with a caring atmosphere should derive beneficial results from the experimentally proven facts; such as, first, that any change affects motivation; second, that the interest of the organization in its members and their work, not the specific change itself, is the key motivating factor; and, third, that a process of diminishing returns sets in – that the benefits of change are eroded over time, unless a new stimulus is applied.

Even if motivational reforms have unmistakably played some part in a company's revival or continued advance, the problem is not only to isolate the contributory factor, but also to establish that the particular motivational approach was the best that could have been used. The old truth that there is no instant replay for history applies: what is done can sometimes be undone, but it cannot be repeated in identical circumstances.

The stick and the carrot, for example, can be equally effective motivators in the appropriate hands and place. But the motivational movement is not at all interested in such crudities. To the advocates of reform, there is both good and bad motivation, and the stick – the threat of firing or demotion or simply violent upbraiding – is bad, no matter how successful the results.

Thus there is plainly a strong ethical foundation to the motivational movement. The advocates of the various approaches, which can be summed up under the heading Theory $\Upsilon$ (formulated by Douglas McGregor), justify their policies on the grounds that they will improve efficiency and productivity. But they also believe in these policies as part of their general view of mankind and human relations. It is right to be kind, supportive, and understanding with employees; it is wrong to be harsh, demanding and ruthless. It is very hard to see the pendulum swinging back towards the authoritarian Theory $X$. The $\Upsilon$ approach is here to stay and spread, and the problem facing managers is to prove that it really can be applied with no important loss in economic progress.

The origins of interest in motivation, of course, were on the factory floor rather than in the executive suite. The assumption has always been (and probably still is in most companies) that since managers are highly paid, relatively speaking, and fill important and promotable jobs, they will be self-motivating. No quality is more sought after in a manager than the self-starting drive that takes a man to the top.

But the highly motivated manager is in the minority. There is a lumpenproletariat of management and always will be. Moreover, the signs are that proletarian attitudes are increasing among managers. The tendency to join or form unions was only one piece of evidence that the old motivating bonds are weakening, and that managers have to be approached with the same care and the same techniques as the workers studied in the Hawthorne experiments.

It cannot be said that the years since Hawthorne have produced much originality of thought. Much of the contribution of behavioural science has come, in fact, from blinding glimpses of the obvious. It is hard to think of two more trite aphorisms than, say, 'You don't hire the thumb, you hire the whole man', or 'Money isn't everything'. Who, after all, ever believed anything else? But the mutinies in industrialized society in the 1960s and 1970s did reflect general disaffection with authority, and the managerial middle class has by no means been immune from the disaffected sentiments of the masses.

In fact, the media, predominantly middle class in authorship and control, as are the political machines, have played a critical part in spreading the new Theory $Y$ gospels about the correct forms of conduct in a modern industrial society. The danger of over-emphasis cannot be ignored. Some people may be totally disaffected with authority: all people may be somewhat less willing to accept authority than they were, but the silent majority unquestionably does like both authority and work – the idea of mass alienation from work is by and large the invention of middle-class intellectuals who have never done manual labour in their lives and have very little understanding of those who do.

Still, the biggest question hanging over the motivational front is whether men can be motivated any more within the old hierarchical framework, which is the dominant form of all organizations. At the very least, hierarchy is not enough (not that it ever was – any successful hierarchy depended for its success on vital ingredients, such as personal identification with an autocratic founder, which had nothing to do with the chain of command).

Is a substitute needed? That depends on whether the troubles in the decade to 1976 sprang or are seen to have sprung mainly from the breakdown of authority. Just as the waves of strikes were mostly about money, inflation, security and specific disputes, just as absenteeism is the disease of affluence, just as productivity problems are a function of total output and total investment, so the worries about motivating managers cannot be ascribed to any one cause. No really clear line connects the anxieties with hierarchical breakdown. That being so, results can hardly be expected from changes in organization and attitudes alone. Yet any company that is serious about management and motivation alike must look for results. By 1976 the better motivational experts were realizing and stressing the importance of spending time and money only on new human-relations initiatives that were actually seen to work in economic terms.

One catch in this area is that many of the obvious means of making people feel happier are so obvious that they are now taken for granted. Unquestionably, making an unpleasant environment light, airy, clean and comfortable will yield results. So will modifying a payment system to suit individual preferences. So will raising the level of information and consultation (of which managers are deprived fully as often as shop-floor workers). But even if the introduction of these improvements raises productivity by an appreciable degree (which is by no means certain), mere maintenance of what has come to be accepted as the norm, however excellent, is most unlikely to spur prodigies of performances.

If performance levels are unsatisfactory, in any event, what then? Does the company backtrack, or lavish still more Tender Loving Care on the delinquent (TLC is the name which Texas Instruments, one of several new growth companies, mostly in the clean, fast-rising technological industries, gave to its employee relations programme). To be fair, the same problem arises with the stick. Do you whip a manager harder if he doesn't perform?

The answer in both cases is that humane treatment or inhumane treatment should not be confused with the results of an organization. Good treatment is what human beings deserve, and now expect so strongly that the question of what treatment they should receive is largely academic. Getting performance is a far more complex problem, to which the social scientists have postulated some interesting answers. The latter have been so difficult to apply in sizeable corporations, however, that predictions about the future shape of the organization of work are extremely hazardous.

As it is, as many experiments have been abandoned or quietly tucked away as are now still in train.

In some respects, companies are being asked to turn back the clock. On the grounds that the working atmosphere demotivates, managements are being told to encourage individuality, to shun repetitive work, to allow each to make his contribution. A pre-Ford philosophy in the mass production factory is being matched by a pre-Sloan philosophy in the executive suite. (It is interesting how the automobile has shaped our managements as well as our cities.) Where the modern emphasis has been on central control, and for a long time on centralization, now the talk is of breaking corporations down into smaller identifiable units – just like the good old days. In management, too, free-and-easy exchanges of views among experts are to become the new norm – again, just like the good old days of most companies that grew from small beginnings.

The temptation has already emerged to regard these approaches as the universal answer. Future generations of managers are no more likely than their predecessors to resist the appeal of panaceas. When you are drowning in current problems, the temptation to grab, not at a straw, but a whole floating bale of hay is wellnigh irresistible. But the process breeds disappointment, by definition, and will do so again.

Already there has been more abuse than use of behavioural science. The scientist has to seek common denominators – what motivates most men. He must do so in order to make usable generalizations. But the manager is always in a specific situation, for which specific courses of action must be taken. This applies to the treatment of large bodies of workers; it applies even more so to the individual manager. One man's motivating meat may be another man's demotivating poison. For every man who sees a target-setting system as a challenge to go forth and multiply, another will regard and use the system as a safe refuge from real pressure.

The same must be true of companies as a whole, though for different reasons. Individuals differ in their psychological characteristics, which makes it difficult to apply a common stimulus to every psyche. Companies differ in their sociology, their markets, their business conditions, their prevailing ethic, and the balance of needs continuously changes. The example of some companies taking out incentive systems in the States while others were putting them in is a classic demonstration. It is, moreover, perfectly logical. The motivation, like everything else about a company, must fit the need.

The behavioural movement has done one small disservice in encouraging managers to take their eyes off money when thinking about motivation. Money may not be everything, but for the majority of managers it is still the most potent tool in the motivational armoury – and objective-setting derives most of its potency from being associated with financial rewards. This makes it important to recognize that the proliferation and pervasion of financial incentive schemes, particularly in the United States, may be counter-productive.

Managers have gone to considerable lengths to ensure that they get their capital gains through schemes that are as near foolproof and as little linked to genuine performance as possible. Like an automatic bonus, such schemes accomplish nothing but the enrichment of the manager. It no more follows that an enriched manager is a high-performing one than it is true that a well-contented factory hand works harder. Companies will have to do some hard thinking to make financial incentives both more substantial in relation to excellent performance and more punitive when performance is either mediocre or bad.

Apart from these considerations of effectiveness, a social climate in which envy now strikes a loud and discordant note may simply not tolerate get-rich-easy schemes in future. Yet it seems inevitable, to the extent that different national tax laws allow, that the American approach to compensation will cross the Atlantic, and that more managers will become accustomed to getting their pay in at least three parts: basic salary, then the two 'motivating' components of bonus and capital stake.

But motivation is too small a word to cover even monetary relationships, let alone the whole range of motives, from ambition to fear, greed to dignity, that are involved in attitudes towards executive work. To rephrase the remark about not using just people's thumbs, you do not use just people's motivation, you use all of them. The motivational patterns of the coming years will take this wholeness more into account. The change can already be seen in the passing of the 'company man'. Few executives would sing today, as did a character in the musical comedy *How to Succeed in Business Without Really Trying*, that 'the company way is by me OK'.

This once powerful style of motivation, identifying the individual manager, like some member of a knightly order, with total faith in, and commitment to, his organization, has gone out of style. The need to belong, and to admire what he belongs to, will still be there, and will still be effective. But it will play a smaller part in the motivational mix, partly because of social change, and partly because of painful experiences in the last decade, when major companies have had not one but two or sometimes three massive redundancies in management ranks. Managers who have seen what insecurity meant to their friends are less likely to love a company if it turns, as did the mighty Royal-Dutch Shell, from being friendly old 'Joe Shell', always good for a bit of overmanning, into a mass maker of redundant managers.

The implication is that organizational motivation must be more closely geared to the individual's personal drives. No longer will he be satisfied to think that he works for the best of all possible companies in the best of all possible industries. More than ever, he will seek self-realization. The company will not be the objective of his being: his work within the company will be the source of satisfaction.

As such, work will rank more closely with outside interests. 'You don't hire the thumb, you hire the whole man' takes on a new meaning: that organizations now have to be concerned with what kind of people their managers are outside the office, how aware they are of general social, political and economic developments, how open they are to new ideas and influences. The company way, in other words, may no longer be OK even for the company.

If individuals are going to need more individual treatment, that still leaves unresolved the question of how to motivate the collective, the company itself. Books on management have tended to play down the importance of corporate ethos, largely, no doubt, because it is so difficult to identify, still less to regulate and foster. Yet any observer knows that personality can pervade an enormous organization, and that this corporate character plays a very real, often crucial part in determining results. This is one source of poor corporate adaptation. The ethos is harder to change than circumstances, and rapid or severe change in conditions can leave the corporation, like a marketing man wrongly put into production, floundering out of its depth.

In these painful circumstances, the standard response has been for the company to discover, or rediscover, financial motivation. Making a profit becomes the spiritual guideline of management and, in many cases, this orientation works marvellously well. It has the advantage of simplicity and the asset of measurement. But the past decade has shown comprehensively that money motivation is not enough, that companies that assert that their purpose is not to make cars, or cranes, or paper, or whatever, but only to make money seldom do especially well at either activity.

The truth is that managers are rarely comfortable with financial motivation only – even if they pretend to be. Moreover, it is probably undesirable that they should have purely, or impurely, financial motives. The product or service, the integrity and the social contribution of the company are all too important to be relegated to secondary factors.

Management's awareness of this truth has led to some eccentric goings on in recent years. The fact that social contribution has become more specifically vital has been allowed to confuse managers' minds about their real purpose. The aim of a chemical company is not to avoid polluting the planet. It is to produce and market chemicals without, as a by-product, making life unpleasant or dangerous for the neighbours or the planet. There is a danger, in fact, that the social factors will be used as an excuse to shirk economic duties, and the temptation is very obvious at a time when real profits in any event have become hard to earn.

In the next decade, when the capital needs of the private business sector alone will make huge demands on all national resources, profit (or an economic return) must come back into the centre of the stage. Motivation for the manager will have to be linked to this necessity of the company. The logical conclusion is that managers who can achieve the best economic returns for the firms, within their social and political constraints, should rise to the top of the new pecking order, no matter who they are – meaning that positions can no longer be reserved for seniority alone.

The greatest managerial motivation of all, without any doubt, both for the manager personally and for the organization, is the manager's ability to make his way to where his work can be most effective and most productive. Not only do companies need such managers, people who can create profitable enterprises, but they also need heretics. The outsider, the maverick, is always the source of the new orthodoxy, and big organizations, by excluding the heretic in general, and the young heretic in particular, have forced new ideas to emerge into the business world outside big company frontiers.

In the climate of the 1980s, when effort needs to be far more carefully measured, the orthodoxy of experience will be a luxury in economic and motivational terms. Thus, pressures from all sides point to a motivational mode based on breaking down the established hierarchical pattern and on giving managers, not necessarily their heads, but more organizational and personal freedom.

Why should the chairman or chief executive always be the highest-paid employee? Why should decentralization become pseudo-decentralization? Why should the top line jobs go to the middle-aged (or aged), while the energetic young work in staff functions? If a major contribution to the company merits especially high pay, logic says that the money should be made available. If a manager wants to run a business successfully his own way, he should not be made to run it as someone else sees fit. The demanding line jobs are better given to younger men: often the older man has the experience and the stability needed for effective staff work. Whenever logic is denied, motivation is weakened, and all the behavioural devices in the books will not overcome the demotivation.

The explanation is often that housekeeping is confused with managing. The former, the administrative side of management, depends on formal order. Managing quite evidently does not. The task of the 1980s is to set the creative side of business free from the administrative without sacrificing the essential tidinesses.

The difficulties are not so much organizational as psychological. The men whose motivation gets in the way are those in power.

They have to surrender authority, to hand over privileges, and to earn their respect rather than receive it as of right. It is a great deal to ask of men nearing the end of careers in which they have climbed long and hard up the ladder. They can always justify their permanence for many reasons, and they will receive support; especially as their reasons and their interests will be identified with preservation of the corporation, which is still the strongest collective motivation there is. It may also ultimately be the most demotivating force of all.

# 6 *The future of management*

from *The Once and Future Manager*

The crucial fact about management, never to be forgotten, is that it is a human activity, no different in that respect from the theatre, or war, or government. Although, like these activities, it makes use of physical resources and scientific laws, management is ultimately determined by the interplay of human forces.

Our knowledge of these forces is both voluminous and fragmentary. We know how people behave (or rather have behaved) in a vast variety of circumstances and combinations. But this knowledge does not even begin to exhaust the possible combinations. Moreover, the knowledge accumulated from the past tells little about the shape of the future in general – let alone in specific terms.

Thus, all that can be said about management is that certain indicators do appear to point in a given direction, and that it is very difficult to see how these trends can be reversed; although it is wise to remember that in the decade to 1976 some basic assumptions were utterly destroyed, such as the belief that profit was the only name of the game, or the utter certainty that the duty of managers to manage equalled a right to determine every aspect of corporate life. Any prophet of the 1980s is sure to miss certain other trends, some further overthrows of seemingly eternal truths. What happens in politics happens in management; an age which has seen all political parties (except the communists, of course) shift to the Left, and then back to the Right, should not be surprised at signs of discontinuity in management.

Yet the continuity shown in the years since 1966 is the most striking unelaborated fact about the corporate world. Despite the convulsions that have disturbed the world economy, very few of the great economic organizations (and just as few of the middle-sized companies) had disappeared from the scene by 1980. In some cases, like those of Krupp or Burmah Oil or Lockheed, survival had been achieved only with government assistance. But even such relatively new creations as Litton Industries, prime candidates for the axe, kept their heads, however tenuously, until, in the merger wave of the mid-1980s, conglomerate after conglomerate was bought and eviscerated. As for the giant, long-established corporations, from General Motors downwards – in all countries most soldiered through thick and thin without noticeably losing stride (although, admittedly, their pace was seldom especially rapid) again until the acquisition wave struck.

Contrast this with the fate of the wonder-companies. None of the startling new corporations that made headlines nationally or round the world in the 1960s were much in the news by 1975–6. In the years to come, one or two may emerge from the ashes of burnt reputations, and new wonders flash across the corporate heavens. But the age of the corporate marvel-makers largely belongs to the past. It was the deal-makers of the 1980s who were to inherit their clothes.

The covers of *Business Week* as the 1970s drew onwards were dominated, not by whiz-kids, but by the solid corporate citizens who were engaged in the methodical task of restoring order out of chaos. The discontinuity paraded by such as the ace conglomerators had lost its attraction. Experience suddenly seemed more important than glamour and panache, cash in the bank more vital than a high price–earnings multiple. Although the 1970s trend towards sobriety did not continue, it carried a lesson: that managers' eyes tend to focus on what is changing, when by definition what is unchanging accounts for far more of the managerial life.

Much the same observation could be made of society as a whole. When the divorce rate rises, people naturally see and remark the change. Yet most married couples remain married; that will stay more significant than the statistic that more people are getting divorced until, that is, the time comes when the relative stability of marriage ceases to exist. Companies are the mirror of society, of which they form a critically important part: the purveyors of goods, the suppliers of services. Thus, to discover where management is heading, the first necessity is to find out which way society is going. That is a question to which nobody, certainly no good manager, would give a categorical answer. But there are some clues: one of the most important being that, so far at least, the economic imperatives have by no means weakened.

Men and women will still vote with their money if given the chance. To test this proposition, it was merely necessary to ask in 1978 whether a political party in power would have a greater or lesser chance of retaining office if real incomes were low at the time of the election, or whether emigration of British capital from Great Britain would fall or rise if British citizens were allowed to remove it from the islands without let or hindrance, instead of being limited to a pittance under the full penalty of the law. The answer to both questions was provided emphatically by Mrs Thatcher after 1979.

The social unrest of the 1960s and 1970s, widely interpreted by intellectuals as evidence of cultural alienation from the money society, cannot be understood without appreciating the underlying economic forces: principally resentment at lack of expected monetary rewards. If these economic imperatives continue to hold true, then one vital dimension of management has been delineated clearly.

Nor is the demand for more conscious attention to men and women at work truly a difference in kind. After all, the demand that we should give 'as much respect to men as we give to machines' is hardly new: the Luddites would have understood it perfectly. What is new is the way in which the sentiment is articulated. The treatment and condition of people at work has become the business of society and the media, not because workers are being positively maltreated, but because of the negative fact that they have not been treated well enough.

There is no harm in the consequent pressure. But succeeding years are not likely to demonstrate that humanitarian policies are an end in themselves. Organizations exist principally for the satisfying of needs external to the organization and must and will be measured by their success or failure on this criterion.

An interesting illustration of the truth and its implications came from a worker at the Lip watch factory in France, taken over by the workers, and then, after an outside rescue, put under the control of a left-wing executive from the world of advertising. Under his leadership, the Lip business at first recovered substantially; but the worker quoted described the saviour as 'the most dangerous kind of boss, because he makes you forget the injustice of capitalism'.

Capitalism actually has nothing to do with the case. The 'dangerous' boss was removed when the Lip factory relapsed into serious financial trouble, because yet again economic (not capitalist) reality had asserted itself. Unless and until Lip managed to make watches that would sell in sufficient quantity at prices that covered its costs of production (and much more besides) the factory had no future under any system of ownership, co-operative or capitalist.

In the end, economic reality always wins. Resources cannot be overspent in one sector of the economy (by subsidizing an uneconomic railway system, for example) without depriving some other sector of the money and manpower concerned. It used to be thought, as recently as 1965, that the richer a society became, the more it could afford such diseconomies. But the evidence from the United States, the wealthiest society the world has ever seen, now flatly contradicts this view.

The Americans could not afford the luxury of eight companies making main-frame computers; or two companies making wide-bodied medium-haul airliners; or to finance both a massive defence budget and a vast foreign investment programme. The richer a society becomes, the heavier the cost of meeting what are seen as basic needs in the highly developed economy. The painful choices faced by backward, less industrialized nations are repeated at a new and higher level. To run into the awful problems faced by a city like New York, which almost led to civic bankruptcy, a country must first have the prodigious wealth to build it.

If economic reality does not depend on the means of social ownership, then methods of organization are irrelevant as well. It will not be easy to achieve the appropriate career patterns for the modern economy, from the viewpoint of both the manager and the organization, if traditional western ideas of hierarchy and seniority are allowed to remain dominant. But the transition to types of non-pyramidal organization, for which there is very little analogy, except in the wholly different culture of the East, will be accomplished only with difficulty and over time.

The complications arise in part out of nature. Seniority, the cement of the corporate hierarchy, expresses the necessity of ageing. Even if the organization decides that the managing director should be thirty, he cannot always be that age. So compromise is inevitable, but even compromise will demand drastic changes to the authority of position and status.

Changes are taking place fast, in any event. The authority of consent is replacing that of command in every department of business (as of all human) life, from the factory floor to the boardroom. It does not imply a lesser authority; rather, a greater one, since an agreed and supported decision attracts more loyalty and respect than an imposed and resented policy. The tide of change has been shown to be running against authoritarianism everywhere; so a change as simple as that to flexible working hours (typically much more widespread in Europe than in the United States) is symptomatic of the switch from discipline to self-discipline.

But it will take a major effort to change authoritarian (and still more dictatorial) habits. Manners are easier to alter, but it does not follow that a company where people no longer call superiors 'sir' or each other 'Herr Doktor', or where workers no longer have to clock in, has genuinely shifted its control ethos from order-and-obey to advise-and-consent.

That the shift is coming, there can be no doubt. A change in manners or style always anticipates a change in substance. This particular switch, however, will have to be learnt; it will be far more difficult for many managements than the changeover from a production-oriented to a marketing-oriented approach with which the decade began – a change that posed little threat to the psychological make-up and conditioning of managers.

Abandoning old hierarchical styles is another matter entirely, roughly akin in difficulty to persuading politicians to accept that, in brutal fact, their decisions do not shape the world. Not only do ideas have to change – so does practice. The manager's job in the 1960s and 1970s became too much a desk job in many cases; there were those who really did think that computer terminals would turn the desk into the bridge of the corporate battleship. We know better today; the managerial captain cannot stay out of the engine-room; he has to keep in touch with the action.

The authority of consent demands contact. The manager should preferably start his career on the factory floor or in some equivalent focus of real-life action; he must stay in touch with that action throughout his subsequent career, and life at the top must provide better mechanisms for keeping contact than the ceremonial visit of the Great White Chief to the odd tribe of Indians. The slow dropping of caste distinctions between worker and manager (managers, after all, are only workers with higher pay) should assist in maintaining contact. But the time, in sheer manager hours, needed for staying in touch with the business will not be available unless managers find more efficient ways of delegating, using their time, arriving at decisions – all in the knowledge that time is the only resource they personally deploy, since the other resources all belong to the company.

Factory-floor contact will also be enhanced by the likely swing back towards production. The imperative need to raise the technical standard of factories, moreover, has been greatly increased by the levelling up of international comparisons. The days when American firms automatically had the edge – and a wide edge at that – in any important production technology have long since gone. The Europeans stole their march over the US steel companies with the basic oxygen process long ago; the Japanese are second to none in automotive production and clearly superior in much else. Given the great increase in international traffic in manufactured goods, any company whose production methods fall behind is now certain to be crucified in the market place, and sooner rather than later.

Yet to say that companies must now become production oriented, or human-relations oriented, or socially oriented, is itself to speak the language of a bygone age. The realization is sinking in that, as the best managers and management thinkers have always known, the company is a total resource. The old–new concept recognizes that each aspect of the corporation, each asset, inter-relates and interacts with the others.

The tremendous burst of enthusiasm for concentrating on human resources, while entirely explicable in the troubled circumstances of the time, could in the end be only a sterile repetition of past errors. There were, are and always will be problems with human beings, individually and in the mass. But events after the oil price rises of 1973–4 rubbed in the painful truth that the problem is also one of non-human resources; of a society in which, taking one year with another, there is never enough to go round, either in the developed world or in the entire globe, developed and underdeveloped countries alike.

The more that companies are thought of in this total sense, the clearer it becomes that there is no such thing ultimately as marketing – or production, or finance, or personnel. None of these functions, or any others, have any meaning whatsoever save in the context of the others. Paradoxically, the lines between functions will become simultaneously blurred and sharpened: sharpened in the sense that increased specialist knowledge and competence will become more essential, blurred in the sense that the old luxury of working in isolation from the rest of the business will not be tenable, if a company wants to be effective.

Genuine multi-disciplinary training will be needed to enable managers to make the best of this more interchangeable environment. This is not because the finance man will now be expected to earn his spurs in marketing, but because he must be able to understand the marketing man's thoughts and actions, just as the good marketing man learnt some years ago to measure his actions (not always accurately or intelligently in practice) in terms of cash sales and profits, rather than in unit volume.

This presupposes that effectiveness, of the kind that might just as well be measured in money, will remain a touchstone of the corporation, the performance that is expected of it by the community. Just as the most left-wing opponent of capitalism would argue, the corporation is a human organization that has resources at its disposal that have to be applied for the benefit of the community, and the definition applies all the way from the corner shop in London, the delicatessen in New York, or the newspaper stand in Bonn, to the leviathans of big business: General Motors, ICI, Toyota, Daimler-Benz, Pechiney, Fiat, Hoffman La Roche and all the rest. The question is only how communal benefit is to be defined.

The tendency in the mid-1970s, with their severe employment problems, unprecedented in the post-war era, was to place the emphasis on provision of jobs – any jobs. But are human resources inefficiently used any more commendable than wasted supplies of energy?

The answer is too obvious to be worth stating. Yet there is a difficulty with which management has wrestled intermittently since the end of the Second World War: the fact that there is no absolute measure of effectiveness. In what now seems a remote past, the assumption was that high profits equated with high efficiency. But that was before many developments (above all, the exposure of fraudulent 'creative' accounting methods and the period of hyperinflation) revealed that profits are sometimes almost entirely meaningless.

Unfortunately, no other measures are much superior. Even an apparently better concept, such as added value, depends on assessment and allocation of costs. All that can be said is that the search for single measures of effectiveness leads only to nullity. Like the company itself, effectiveness is multi-dimensional; nor does any evidence of success have much meaning outside the context of a competitive market.

Among these multi-dimensions, profit is still a crucial measure, no matter how much it has been abused since 1965. The concept will have to advance a long way beyond the traditional American concentration on 'the bottom line'. Managers now know that the bottom line isn't where the cash is kept, for example. But the margin between true total costs and true total receipts measures the ability of a business to create the new resources without which it cannot perform its prime social duty, which is to carry out the economic function on which the community depends.

The 'social audit', which purports to take a wider view of the company, in fact takes a narrow one. It implies that a company that exercises only its economic function properly has not – inevitably and simultaneously – performed other, non-economic roles as well. This is plainly nonsense, and will be seen as nonsense.

Non-financial yardsticks of a different kind may well become more important: measures of physical efficiency, manpower utilization, market share, and so on. But in the end all these dimensions must add up to a corporation whose cash and surplus generation are rich enough to keep it in an expanding way of business (which embraces the too long overlooked question of giving shareholders a tolerable return in the shape of income). If the physical functions are well performed, the monetary flows will respond, and that is what true profit is: the reward, not the objective, of efficiency.

That is only common sense, a phrase that is coming back into its own in management. Its opposite, after all, is rare nonsense, which aberrations like synergy, free-form management, management information systems and brainstorming turned out to be. The manager post-1976 was better off than his 1966 predecessor in this respect at least – enough nonsenses had been exposed to clear the prepared mind.

Panaceas will reappear, but not the same ones. Marketing, computers, decentralization, recentralization have all had their days, not to be repeated. The mood of the late 1970s was to think less of the cures, more of the ailments, the new and burdensome constraints on the manager: those of the environment, of employee protection, of governments. But even in this vexed new field, managers can reflect on the example of the switch in corporate financing, back to Victorian ideals of cash on the nail and in the till, as a pointer to the future. Companies that make good products, pay good wages and treat people well, at declining real costs per unit, cannot go wrong. The future holds terrors only for those who are mismanaging the present.

# 7 The objects of the exercise

from *The Business of Winning*

The shift over the 1970s from theorizing about management, from precept to practice, was much to my taste: and it's no coincidence that the series of books that began with *The Business of Success* was dominated by the desire to find better ways, more effective methods, between which the manager could pick and choose. The theme of the book was 'back to basics', a message that has never been more relevant, and which became, in the American edition, one of the world's longest acronyms:

**B**ehave towards others as you would wish them to behave towards you.

**A**ssess each business and business opportunity with all the objective facts and logic you can muster.

**C**oncentrate on what you do well.

**K**eep the company flat – so that authority is spread over many people instead of being piled up at the apex of some unnecessary pyramid.

**T**hink as simply and directly as possible about what you're doing and why.

**O**wn up to your failings and shortcomings – because only then will you be able to improve on them.

**B**udget your time and tighten up the organization whenever you can – because success tends to breed slackness.

**A**sk questions ceaselessly about your performance, your markets, your objectives.

**S**ave costs – not just because economizing is an easy way to make money, but because doing the most with the least is the name of the game.

**I**mprove basic efficiency – all the time.

**C**ash in – because unless you do make money, you can't do anything else.

**S**hare the benefits of success widely among all those who helped to achieve it.

The first excerpt contains the essential thinking behind the basics. The second expands on the theme mentioned in my introduction to the excerpts from *The Once and Future Manager*: the eternal management impediments. The chapter on the whole sounds an optimistic note, which is another reason for its inclusion. The truly modern company is better in many ways than its predecessors, and managers (who are inevitably the creatures of their environment) are better because of the corporate improvements.

Where you draw the line between the institution and the people who give that institution its only life is as tricky a question as where brain stops and mind begins. But anyone who believes, as I do, in human progress, would expect corporations to share in and in some respects lead that progress. And the greater awareness of corporate original sin, as delineated here, is certainly playing an important role in the advance.

A few years ago I wrote a book called *The Naked Manager*. It was meant to be an exposé. I wanted to prove that the hero manager of those days, who preached and pretended to practise a new, supposedly scientific brand of management, had no clothes. Today that idea is generally accepted, not because of what I wrote, but because events have proved just how naked those heroes of the sixties actually were.

But managers today owe the nudists a great debt. Their failure has pointed the way to success, while stripping away the veils that blurred the vision of many intelligent and excellent people. Today, managers are within closer reach of the promises that their pre-decessors held out so falsely. The modern manager does have all the equipment and opportunity he needs to make the modern company work – even the company whose huge size and stretch seem to make the job impossible.

The way forward turns out to lie in going back. It's necessary to rediscover the truths of the old-fashioned way of running a busi-ness before the new methods and technologies – which do have a part to play – can prove their worth. The merits of old business virtues were discovered under the duress of cash crises, collapsing markets and inflationary squeezes. But one of the best old truths of business is that the lessons of adversity last longest and teach most.

This book is about that effective one–two combination of the old and the new, used for the only purpose that makes the work of a manager ultimately worth while – to win. Winning doesn't mean trampling over some adversary. It means doing *better*: better than the competition, better than your own past performance, better than the challenge of people, economics and events might have led you to expect. Like it or not, the manager is always in competition; but the competition that matters most is with himself, with his own stubborn inability to perform as well as his talents, energy and chances make possible.

The problem for many managers is that they work for large companies that have lost the habit of winning, and where winners haven't been encouraged. Both the organization and its executives are like flies in amber: trapped by the past and the present in attitudes they can't change. These outfits come dangerously close to existing only to be. The idea of a real objective, call it winning or anything else, has been lost.

In managing to win, the first object of the exercise is to *have* an object. It has been well said that, if you don't know where you're going, and don't know how to get there, any arrival will be strictly by chance.

Take car companies that thought they existed solely to make big cars, or steel-makers who believed only in manufacturing steel. The first lot had no right to complain when small foreign cars captured a vast and valuable chunk of their market. As for the steel men, the evolution of the world economy away from their beloved metal has left most of them stranded like overturned giant turtles.

The fate of any individual executive who opposes such con-ditioned corporate reflexes is rarely happy. When one great manu-facturing firm, chasing multinational dreams down the road of a giant merger, plunged into financial disaster, the sole member of the executive élite to leave was the plan's only opponent. Ghosts are no more welcome at funerals than at weddings. But the funeral for companies like this is their own. In today's world, when avoiding failure may produce it, the search for success is the only real option.

> *Competitive management requires two types of good idea: the insight and the outsight.*

There's still plenty of room for managerial time-servers. The corporation man who imitates the Vicar of Bray, changing his position with each change of regime, is hard to stop. If he is serving his time in a time-serving company, the two have a great chance of being deadbeats together. It's not just that challenge and oppor-tunity are more exciting than staying put. Seeking to win is an insurance policy against corporate and personal obsolescence: and that's more of a threat today than ever.

This isn't because of supposed acceleration in the pace of technological change, although technology surely has something to do with the lessened security of the executive. But it's not clear that today's changes will do as much to create or revolutionize whole industries as did the inventions of the post-war era that spawned the jetliner, antibiotics, the computer, the supertanker, the semiconductor and other fantastic, far-reaching innovations.

These leaps forward were often translated more rapidly into marketable products than has happened, say, with large-scale integrated circuits – the now infamous silicon chip. The manager has less need to worry about the threat of new technologies than over the break-up of the old, safe, corporate life-style. Many of the ideas in this book are being applied with remarkable success by corporate managements all over the world – that's how I came to notice and establish the validity of these ideas. These managements have chosen to win – and anybody who hasn't made that choice will face a harder and harder challenge from those who have.

Choosing a vigorous and competitive policy gets neither you nor the company anywhere if the commitment is mostly in words. To win doesn't just mean staking the corporation's money, and perhaps its future, on the lure of brave, bright, new horizons. Illusions about dynamism lay behind many of the awful corporate disasters of our times – illusions that trapped companies as far apart as the red-hot, highly professional Xerox, which dropped a $300 million bundle in computers, and a corporate cold turkey like Britain's Burmah Oil, which destroyed itself by gadding about in diversions from car parts to supertankers.

In these two cases (and in all such cases) there was a basic failure of thought. Competitive management requires two types of good ideas: the insight and the 'outsight'. The insight is much more difficult than it sounds – it's the idea about oneself, about what a company and its managers really do well, about how what they are doing can be improved. The outsight, which sounds difficult, but can be surprisingly easy to obtain, is the vision and understanding of the world beyond the company's own or present frontiers – the feeling for the present and future events that must shape the company's destiny.

The Xerox failure was predominantly one of *outsight*. The company simply did not gauge accurately how the computer market was likely to develop, or what role, if any, computers needed to play in its own affairs. Had Xerox been right on these points, had it really required a computer capability of the kind it bought so expensively, then the associated failure of insight (the inability of Xerox's managers to see that they weren't equipped to handle expensive acquisitions in strange businesses) would eventually have been overcome.

In Burmah Oil, the essential failure was of insight. Its managers couldn't see that they weren't the kind of businessmen they had set their hearts (and the company's millions) on becoming. Had they been, then the blunders made in buying and managing their enormous volume of corporate purchases would have been less grave. Apart from anything else, they wouldn't have bought so much so expensively. It was that enormity, not just failure of outsight about the tanker market, that laid Burmah low.

Customarily the modern business devotes a great many costly man hours to seeking more and better outsights. It spends little or no time searching for insights. Yet very often the need for outsights can be kept within limits at the very beginning. For example, if a company decides that it can win without any need for major diversification outside its existing activities, then it may not need to form any vision, accurate or otherwise, about the future development of, say, microelectronics. The winning manager never forgets that the further an outsight moves from the present, the more inaccurate it is likely to be: he thus avoids the trap into which the Harvard futurologist, David Bell, fell head-first – predicting a 'surprise-free economy' for the rest of the century, six years before the start of the Yom Kippur war.

Generating good insights and outsights can never be the object of the management exercise. No idea in business is any use until it is translated into action: effective action – the kind that wins satisfactory results. 'Satisfactory' is usually an unsatisfactorily vague word, but not in this instance. Very precisely, no result is ultimately worth having unless the outcome includes a mint of money, a deeply satisfying pot of gold.

Under any name, money has to be the goal. Managers have always, of course, known this. They are now more immediately aware of the truth than they were. Time was, not so long ago, when profits (another, not very precise, name for the game) were so unfashionable that some managers almost apologized for making any. More recently, when adequate earnings in large companies have been few and far between, there's been real reason for apologies. That's because money is the only possible general measure of success in creating new resources out of old ones; and that phrase in turn sums up the whole process and urgency of economic growth.

A company that loses money, or fails to generate enough to replace its ageing plant properly, is consuming capital, eating up resources. A company that makes money in abundance is creating the new resources the use of which, either within the business or outside, will develop other resources still. The making of money and managerial success go hand in hand with each other – and with managing to win.

> *The winning manager needs the immigrant's ability to*
> *see with new eyes – and his determination to succeed*
> *against odds.*

Even people of supposedly stern anti-capitalist principles (like Labour politicians in Britain) have a sneaking fondness for the men for whom success and money go hand in hand, the entrepreneurs. Though the personal judgement of the fanciers is often bad, the general principle behind the politicians' fancies is right. The economic rewards of the winning entrepreneur stem from the initial quality of the insight/outsight perception. When it's said that such businessmen spotted a gap in the market, the cliché really means that people at large wanted important products or services; and that these entrepreneurs were able to supply what was wanted at a cost lower than the price the market was happy to pay.

Very often, the man who spots such a gap is an outsider: sometimes the rankest of all outsiders – an immigrant.

The generation of powerful insights about yourself, and outsights concerning the world beyond, is easier if your mind is not cluttered with preconceptions, built up over years of experience in a particular industry or country. That's why a manager seeking to improve his insights is well advised to pretend as follows: (1) I know nothing about the company; (2) I need to have everything explained to me; (3) I take nothing for granted.

Occasionally, towering fortunes have been built on a single perception. Such a phenomenon was the realization of individual entrepreneurs that, in a post-war world hungry for bulk cargoes, notably oil, a ship was a licence to print money. Not only would shipyards, often backed by governments, fall over themselves to win orders by offering cut-throat prices and generous credit – but, when it comes to approaching banks, a leased ship is among the easiest assets to finance. Not only is a ship security in itself, but a long-term charter – to an oil company, say – both guarantees the cash to pay the interest and doubles the security. Any of the established shipping companies could have spotted such possibilities. None did – not because they were stupid (though some were) but simply because they had far too much of one non-winning quality, Establishment, and far too little of a winning one, Motivation.

The immigrant has none of the first and a lot of the second. To succeed in a strange society isn't so much a challenge as a necessity if you've arrived with no position in the society, and often with no money. The winning manager needs the immigrant's ability to see with new eyes and also his determination to succeed against odds. You don't have to be an immigrant – but it helps.

Take the case, recounted in *Fortune* magazine, of Samuel Regensbrief. Almost nobody in America would recognize the name of the country's largest maker of dishwashers. Regensbrief, a baker's son, had come to the USA from Vienna at the age of four. He first made his living as an efficiency expert – what is now known as a management consultant. Regensbrief got into appliances by saving the hide of a refrigerator firm; when that merged with Philco, he became a company man, but moved out, richer by millions of Philco stock, when his employer merged with Ford.

A stone's throw from Philco's Connersville site, where Regensbrief was looking after the construction of a new plant, was a deadbeat dishwasher operation, with 6 per cent of the market and only one real asset: its largest customer, Sears Roebuck. But that contract was in danger, which explained the low price – $2.6 million – that the owner, Avco, accepted from Regensbrief some twenty years ago. The buyer was totally innocent in dishwashers. But his outsight was correct: that with penetration of only 10 per cent of households, these appliances had wonderful market potential – if their price could be brought down.

For an old efficiency expert, that didn't look like much of a problem. But Regensbrief's major insight, when he looked into his acquisition, was that its dishwashers – like everybody else's – were loaded from the *top*. The obvious inconvenience could be avoided, provided the design was watertight, by loading from the *front*: and that was the proposition with which Regensbrief hung on to the Sears account. According to *Fortune*, 'Other manufacturers scoffed when they heard of Regensbrief's brainstorm. "Everybody thought we'd be a dead duck," he recalled. "But you just can't be a me-too and succeed in business."' In 1979 his company, Design and Manufacturing, had 40 per cent of the US market and claimed to undercut General Electric (the also-ran, at 25 per cent) by a fifth in price – thus demonstrating that victory doesn't always go to the big battalions.

Such achievements make fine reading for outsiders seeking to muscle in. But what about the corporate insider? Is he condemned to lose? To be defeated by the forces of inertia in the company? Not if the company can see itself as a dialectical process, in which the truth, or the true way, is established by stating a thesis; countering with an antithesis, and arriving at a synthesis.

What the company is right now, what it does and how it does it – these constitute the thesis. The alternative activities and methods it might adopt are the antithesis. Their combination, the corporate synthesis, should provide the essential blend of stability and progress. It's obvious that the element that may well not be present, and that must be injected if it isn't, is the antithesis, the voice of questioning, criticism, argument and dissent.

Where the emphasis should go varies from time to time as circumstances change. But the company will always gravitate towards stability, or stasis, given the chance. The tendency isn't unhealthy in itself. The economic world needs continuity no less than the political one. So it's in a way comforting that, of the ten non-oil companies that *Fortune* magazine ranked top in sales in 1969 (General Motors, Ford, GE – the very same company outdishwashed by Regensbrief – IBM, Chrysler, ITT, Western Electric, US Steel, Westinghouse and LTV), only the last two had left the list in 1977. Their replacements were Tenneco and Du Pont, which are not exactly bright young newcomers.

Stability and survival are the *sine qua non* of management. But if they become the objects of the exercise, the game is lost. To survive is no great trick. To use the stable strength of the corporation to make new competitive advances is far harder and far less often achieved. That's why, to make full use of the potential of the new – the really new – management, the large corporation, like management itself, may have to turn backwards towards its own past (possibly one formed by an outsider, even an immigrant). It may have to seek ways of returning to the smaller, more compact organizational forms that firms which are managing to win have found increasingly applicable in today's conditions. If you can't beat the Regensbriefs, it makes sense to join them.

> *What matters is not how large you are, but how effectively you mobilize your strengths at the point of impact.*

It may help to be an outsider: but the corporation man can also outdo other corporation men by following the correct outsider techniques. Even a big firm can find both opportunities and times when it has to buck the odds. A Japanese company called Sakura proved this in the market for colour film. Local sales were dominated by Fuji, which, since it was named after the mountain the Japanese worship and photograph incessantly, had the humdrum Sakura in an apparently hopeless position. The Sakura people (insight) came to the conclusion that they had no hope of beating Fuji by any method of marketing known to man. But from this depressing insight came a deeply constructive thought, or question. Was there any other way in which Sakura could compete more effectively?

The company spotted (outsight) that people buying 20-exposure film always tried to squeeze in extra frames. In contrast, buyers of 36 exposures commonly wasted a few. So Sakura launched a 24-frame film. It proved so successful that the company's market share doubled – and it began to compensate for its lack of holy mountains by a reputation for technological innovation – even though the 24-frame film had involved no technical effort at all (and, for that matter, very little cost).

The Sakura story has deeper implications still, which will appear a little later in the context of why odds only appear to be over-whelming. The choice of a Japanese example is significant, because that whole nation appears to have behaved in the world economy like an outsider, an immigrant at large. Having nothing after the war, never having loomed large in any of the markets they proceeded to tackle, from civil shipbuilding to pocket radios, the

Japanese have consistently shown original thought. They have been forced to do so because their starting technology has been borrowed, with very few exceptions.

Outdoing your competition while using its own inventions demands assets far greater and rarer than cheap labour. The Japanese manager has consistently spotted opportunities in products and markets that were under the noses of big, rich, fully established western competitors. Sometimes the chances were in technology – like the extreme improvements Honda made in motorcycle engines. Sometimes the opportunity lay in market exploitation – like the widening of 35 mm photography from an expensive specialist hobby into a mass market. Sometimes the brilliance lay in creating a wholly new market – like the adaptation of the transistor to create mass sound. Sometimes the chance was taken by painstaking imitation of a competitor's success in circumstances that were geographically more favourable to the Japanese firm – like Toyota's invasion of California in the best VW style.

The firms consistently taken on and defeated by the Japanese had enormous technological and financial power, coupled with apparent strangleholds on their markets. One by one, these giants have toppled – Leitz and Zeiss in cameras, Norton and Vespa in bikes, every single US radio manufacturer. Very few firms have felt safe in face of this ferocious competition from the East.

The precise opportunities taken are significant: but less so than this consistent theme of searching for openings and then pushing through the breach in the Siegfried Line in steadily increasing force – until the small aggressor becomes the dominant power.

The success of Japanese companies in several of the best markets flies in the face of much conventional wisdom. The fashionable school of corporate strategy holds that the firm with the largest market share has the highest profitability; that the race goes, not to the swift, but to the rich; that the rich get richer, because of the economies of scale that only they can obtain; and that market after market will consequently end by being dominated by a tiny number of gigantic firms.

Up to a point, every one of these notions is correct. But the point at which they cease to be correct is crucial. The larger firm presents a larger target at which to aim. Not only that, but the cost of defence against a new competitor may be so much greater than the latter's cost of attacking that the defence may not seem worth the price.

Sakura's successful attack on Fuji is an overwhelming proof. By selling its 24-frame film at the same price as Fuji's orthodox 20-frame product, Sakura posed a painful problem for the stronger firm. Fuji could have retaliated by cutting prices, but that would have been twice as costly as Sakura's certain response – which would have been to match the cuts, yen for yen. Fuji, moreover, would have gained nothing from the exercise: it would have ended, at best, with the same share and much lower profits.

Or Fuji could market a 24-frame film itself. But this response would take time, during which Sakura would be able to establish its 'new' product in the market place. Again, any extra sales Sakura made would be additional business, while any sales Fuji made would merely replace its 20-frame products. Thus Fuji was faced, either way, with unwanted and, from its point of view, unnecessary expense, magnified by the sheer size of its market share; an expense forced on it by an apparently much weaker opponent. In the end, Fuji was compelled to meet Sakura's competition by introducing a 24-framer, but the damage had been done – and it was Sakura that came out on top in this particular encounter (though not in general, Japanese giants like Fuji being notoriously difficult to displace).

Effective competition is not prevented by the opponent's size – it's facilitated, if you can hit him where it hurts. One of those places is certainly the very tender spot where he must incur considerable loss of profit for no compensating gain.

He who starts small in a giant's market, moreover, can win highly satisfactory growth in the early years, even though the total market share remains small. A barely noticeable loss of share for the giant (and it probably won't be noticed if the whole market is growing) can add up to highly profitable volume for the newcomer. In addition to these economic advantages of being small, the invader has the priceless psychological asset of his large opponent's built-in inertia. In part, this inertia is economic, too: the cost and difficulty of modifying a product line selling millions of units are a powerful obstacle to the kind of change that, anyway, large established organizations are always reluctant to make – despite their protestations.

Size, of course, is relative. The ABC television network was no small fry, with a turnover of $1.6 billion when the sales of CBS were a clear billion larger still, and those of RCA, the parent of the NBC network, were $3 billion higher than those of CBS. Yet the two larger networks were once comprehensively and humiliatingly pushed into second and third place in the ratings competition by the smaller battalion – whose chances of winning at the start would have been dismissed as negligible by anybody in or out of the know.

What really matters is not how large you are across the board, but how effectively you mobilize your strengths at the point of impact. For those who master these lessons, managing to win is possible in even worse circumstances than ABC's.

# 8 Plus ça change

from *The Business of Winning*

In a way, 'scientific management' should have been perfectly possible. The science of war, after all, has been intensively developed, and it's not just marketing that gives managing its resemblance to military work. The manager, too, has to administer and lead large forces, to muster (and master) formidable technical equipment, to plan campaigns in which an opponent must be outwitted, or outmanoeuvred, or overpowered.

The winning manager, like the general staff, can and does apply 'science' (that is, knowledge and technique) to help in all these matters. But that can never be how he wins. The same, of course, is true of war. The actions, reactions and interactions of human beings determine the battle, to the extent that material and manpower leave the outcome to chance. But even at El Alamein, where Montgomery assembled an immensely superior weight of arms, his impact on the morale and training of the troops was undoubtedly an essential factor in the victory.

Management is about such human factors, the intangibles and the changing tides of individual men and women and of mankind in the mass. Uncertainty is the name of the game. Thus, reason's main task in management is to limit the zones of uncertainty as far as possible, to reduce risk to tolerable dimensions, to allow scope for changes when the unpredicted (not, note, the unpredictable) happens – as it always will.

It's because of this dominant human factor that management is so full of paradox. One that troubles many writers, including Peter Drucker, is the paramount role of the paramount man. Not only is it wrong in theory for an organization to depend on some Caesar, but in practice the dependence often proves dangerous. The excesses the Emperor commits can be bad enough. Worse still, he customarily bequeaths a legacy of inferior successors. So the correct response seems to be: No Great Men. Except that the ban would mean: No (or few) Great Businesses.

The paradox can be resolved only by accepting that human nature includes, among its quirks, the desire to respond to the personal qualities of someone we recognize as our superior. That's why one man gets better work from the same people who under-perform for another boss. Moreover, the advantages of having a single source of authority and dynamism are considerable. The disadvantages arise from the human nature of the boss himself – from his subconscious (which secretly tries to protect him by appointing acolytes and successors who are inferior to the Great Man); and from his conscious wish to impose himself on every-thing and everybody.

Self-awareness is the only defence, and it can work. Some great founder–proprietors do leave well-worked-out and protected suc-cessions, taking as much pride in their people as their products. But this difficult achievement is, by definition, a rare one. Most mana-gers are not founder–proprietors, nor Great Men, nor anything like it. They may try to behave that way – and that is one of the eternal faults of human nature that prevent the run-of-the-mill professional manager from delivering the exceptional performance that is within his reach.

*Use of managers should conform to the value analysis ideal of Least Input for Most Output.*

The barriers to human perfection are many and varied. But any list of eternal management impediments would have to in-clude: the abuse of time, the managerial lie, the misrepresentation of risk, the overpayment of managers by managers, the misunder-standing of motivation, the false assumption that somebody else's business can ever be like one's own.

The passage of the years has made little difference to the items on this catalogue, and maybe it never will. Managers waste time, which is in limited supply and not replaceable, because it's so hard to concentrate all their time on what is truly essential. They fib (or worse) about the facts, because the latter are less palatable than the manager's fictions. They portray themselves as 'risk-takers' because it sounds romantic and glorifies their actually often humdrum role. They go on and on about motivation without facing up to the truth that corporate hierarchies are demotivating in essence, and that any venturesome young man would rather run a business that is truly his own than some operation where an older (but not necessarily wiser) man can call the shots.

If a manager (or a set of managers) can only break out of these traps, that alone will propel him much of the distance towards success. Take time. How many executives pause to think whether some project they have just launched is worth the expenditure of executive time required? Because every company above a certain size can always afford somebody to do something, the firm easily silts up with permanent and temporary assignments that are not worth the trouble – and specifically not worth the time. The time logs that determined managers use to regulate their own days are also important to the company. Its use of its managers should conform to the value analysis ideal of LIMO – Least Input for Most Output.

But the same process that silts up the executive's personal day tends to clog up the corporation. Committees meet for no purpose with members who couldn't contribute to the objective even if there was one; and external commitments, often of a quasi-social nature, also eat into time. I greatly approved the tongue-in-cheek idea of an author who suggested in *Management Today* that companies should use executives near retirement for these ceremonial purposes – men who know enough to alert the active management if anything important does, by accident, come up, but who otherwise earn *their* bread by allowing other managers to earn bread for the company.

The idea is unlikely to catch on, though, so long as managers hanker and hunger for the prestige that goes with outside bodies and internal committee membership. It's a sound rule that no fully paid manager should have any daytime commitments outside the company that pays him. His job should be strenuous and exciting enough to absorb him completely. If it isn't, something is amiss. Top men with a plethora of outside entanglements will claim that these jobs help the company. Almost invariably, those men lie. It won't be their only lie, of course – in fact, it sometimes seems impossible to get a manager to tell the truth, the whole truth, or anything like the truth about his corporate affairs.

More often than not, to be fair, this is because they don't know the truth themselves. Men will, for example, boast about profits or market share to others who, because of their own business knowledge, can spot the lie at once. But the liar has probably deceived himself: he doesn't want to face the fact that the business makes a pitiful profit or has a pathetic market share. It follows that he will be defeated – if he hasn't been already.

Far better to be like Philip Caldwell, during his climb to the succession to Henry Ford II. Confronted with the task of competing against the all-conquering trucks of Chevrolet, Caldwell sat down with his colleagues to list every attribute that might influence the decision of a truck buyer and rigorously compared the Ford and Chevrolet offerings on each criterion. (As I recall, the Ford came out ahead on only two items, and one of those was the windscreen wipers.)

Now, Caldwell's unforgiving search for truth was made far easier by the fact that he was an outsider, thrust into the truck division to save a losing day. It's a pitiful aspect of human nature that it so often takes new brooms, not to sweep clean, but to raise any dust at all. Anything that any turnaround artist has ever achieved could in theory have been accomplished by the men *in situ* – but they would have needed the very quality, objectivity, whose absence helped to make them failures.

The best cure for this deficiency is an experience of real sharp-end contact and real adversity. I've never met a manager with factory-floor experience who didn't value that grounding above all, and I've never met one who has stared disaster in the face whose survival hasn't shaped his attitudes for the rest of a successful business life.

One such hardened-in-adversity manager likes to say that management is about taking the risk out of business – and his trade, women's fashion, is as 'risky' as they come. But it's most important to be clear-minded about that word. The degree of risk is a measure of the possibility of being wrong. In some trades – like high fashion – it's much easier to be wrong than in others. But there's nothing particularly virile about sticking out one's neck. Older managers who encourage their juniors, if only by lip service, to take risks are wrong: they really mean that their juniors should be 'enterprising' – and that is a very different matter.

The whole concept of risk developed from mercantile trade. You sent a ship forth from Boston or Portsmouth to pick up a cargo of spices, knowing that, if it didn't sink *en route*, your investment would be repaid many times over. There was no risk in the venture, the project: only in its execution. The vast majority of commercial failures are plans that would have flopped no matter how well they had been carried out.

When failures occur, too, the more senior the manager, the less risk he runs of dismissal or demotion, even of any serious impact on his personal fortunes. Look at the highest salaries in any country, especially the USA, and it's hard to make any correlation between reward and achievement. Mostly, men rise to the top through age, and continue to fix matters so that, arrived at the summit, they get the biggest share of the boodle – paid, moreover, in as painless a way as possible.

How much the chairman or even the chief executive of a major company is worth to the shareholders is a question nobody asks – though there are cases where the boardroom remuneration is a fair, or unfair, proportion of the after-tax profits. But plainly a system of hierarchical rewards tends to encourage time-serving and to weaken the positive motivation, the venturesome drive, that the senior men claim to want. So they turn to devices that promise to inject motivation, like fixes of cocaine, and are regularly disappointed.

The solution can lie only in the motivation of the whole company, in the way in which it is structured, and in the amount of true responsibility and early reward given to people who do their jobs successfully. What they run can never be a business like their own – because it isn't their money, a fact they should never be allowed to forget, and won't, if they are really good. But an individual manager's operation should be, quite clearly, *his* business, to run in *his* style: provided only that he runs it well.

> *No matter what relation the price paid by the immediate user bears to the full cost of the product, somebody, somewhere, somehow, is bearing that full cost.*

The 1970s were a good testing and training ground for the new breed of managers, not least because the idea of discrete business units with full operational responsibility had started to percolate through the corporate establishments. But the relative harshness of the economic environment also helped to provide a more rigorous training ground – although, in truth, the world economy suffered nothing like so severe a setback as would have been supposed from reading the media.

But you can't avoid severe shock when the younger citizens of an affluent West, never having experienced world recession, actually have to endure a year of real decline in output, followed by distinctly slower growth than before. For some citizens – such as the managers of West Germany – the initial shock was so traumatic that they surrendered to daytime nightmares about everlasting zero growth. They were totally mistaken, of course. What happened was no cataclysm, like the seismic disaster of the 1930s, but the impact of unprecedented inflation on a world economy that was, in any case, due for certain serious adjustments.

Oil falls under both definitions. Inflation in the West (a classic monetary inflation produced by overexpansion of the money supply in several countries at once, and in the extra-national Eurocurrency market) reduced the real price of oil. The producers reacted in the usual manner at a time when political developments – the Yom Kippur War – unfortunately emphasized both the power of the Middle East producers and the excessive vulnerability of the West to any interruption of Arab supplies. Had world growth continued at its previous clip, the oil crisis would still have arrived, and sooner rather than later. Coming as it did in the middle of galloping world inflation, the switch from cheap glut to expensive scarcity (one of the adjustments that were bound to come) very likely did have the equivalent effect, as *Fortune* magazine once calculated, of taking two machines in every hundred in the West out of production.

If managers can take any comfort from this uncomfortable experience, it lies in the supreme value of knowing that in economics there are forces that cannot be withstood. Governments might and did suppose that they could sustain growth by printing money. But as the value of that money inevitably declined, so the impact of inflation on savings, on interest rates, on earnings and on prices created the very recessionary effects that governments had tried to avoid. Managers, too, were forced to react as inflation and weak markets threatened to undermine some of the mighty corporations that make up the world's great economic powers.

That so few actually did crumble is some compliment to their managers, as well as to the better public, or governmental, defences of private firms. But the time of test by recession – which was not over yet, given the West's continuing propensity for double-digit inflation – did not paralyse consumer and industrial markets. Many went on growing – and growing abundantly. Nor is there any reason to suppose that growth and the exciting development of new markets will ever stop.

Those markets, however, will always be governed by 'the rule of full cost'. This means that, no matter what relation the price paid by the immediate user bears to the full cost of the product, somebody, somewhere, somehow, is bearing that cost. If the full cost exceeds the true market price (that is, the price people are ready to pay out of their own pockets), then ultimately the product or service is doomed. Even if it survives, it will deteriorate. Rail systems in countries where the roads and the air are fully developed are a striking case: the full cost per passenger mile, with public subsidies thrown in, is enormous, and fully explains the contraction and worsening of the West's train systems.

Among managers, the fact that everything has a cost should have been swallowed with their mother's milk. But the stress on 'profit centres' (an attempt to apply the 'business like one's own' theory at large) tended to move emphasis away from *cost* – cost being another word for 'use of resources'. In a context of scarce resources, it's more important than ever for managers to minimize their costs while maximizing their revenues; or, if they have no revenues (like an internal service department) to prove, first, that any cost at all is justified and, second, that the actual level of costs is the right one.

The value of 'zero-based budgeting' (whose popularity may ultimately be President Carter's sole fairly beneficial contribution to the economies of the West) is to systematize this process of challenge: the attack on overheads, which dates back to the beginnings of business. But the attack on production costs is even more vital, since (on the full-cost theory) the lower the true cost of production, the greater the chance of finding successful markets.

A glance at the phenomenon of microelectronics rubs in the point. As production costs have tumbled, the industry has developed from making specialist components for the few to mass output of silicon chips for the millions. If pocket calculators still cost as much as $395, as they did in 1971, sales would be a fraction of their volume today, when the price is tiny – and the machine is actually better. It's a law of economics rather than the advance of technology that explains the development: the rule that, with every cumulative doubling of output, the cost drops by 30 per cent.

By no coincidence, the high-technology firms, including the chip-makers, proved immune to the fall in returns on capital that has plagued most industries in the 1970s. The average US electronics firm had a profit margin of 5.8 per cent towards the end of the decade, compared with 3.7 per cent ten years before – not in spite of, but because of the barely credible deflation of their prices in an inflationary age. Investment in lower production costs and higher performance is a sure way to win: just as failure to match the investment of others is a guarantee of defeat.

Of course, everybody fails, no matter how fine their investment policies, if the whole market goes awry. When demand collapses for ineluctable economic reasons (as in shipbuilding in the 1970s) then nothing – not even the offer of ships at well under full cost – will resurrect the corpse, unless another economic cycle is allowed to work. In this cycle, oversupply leads to price cuts and withdrawal of capacity, and turns into undersupply as demand recovers; prices then rise sharply; investment in new capacity then returns and, in the fullness of time, creates oversupply all over again.

As with all attempts to resist the laws of markets and economics, efforts to stockpile in the hope of avoiding these swings and roundabouts are doomed. The known existence of the stockpile restrains output, prices and recovery long – and painfully – after the natural moment of upturn. Since such hard economic laws determine events, it's no surprise that humanistic theories that impinge on those laws are always subject to alteration at short notice.

One Swedish shipyard, for instance, seemed to have achieved both productivity and profit by applying enlightened theories of man management. The yard concerned, Kockums, was quite right to treat its people intelligently and well; but when the economic storm blew down on the shipbuilders of Europe, the fabric of Kockums's prosperity was blown away, and so, equally inevitably, was the company's reputation as a worker of management miracles.

But, as the management theories come and go, each adds something of lasting value; and a few of the theories go on for ever; not because of the preternatural brilliance of their originators, but because they are rooted in both sides of the equation; the malleable material of human nature and the iron laws of economics.

*Make quality products, constantly strive to improve, take care of regular customers and maintain good relations with suppliers.*

Konosuke Matsushita is a man of profound simplicity, and the overlord of one of Japan's greatest electrical firms. No doubt, the simplicity is exaggerated – but this passage is an excellent illustration of Matsushita's personality:

> Considering that I am rather sickly by nature, I am extremely surprised at the fact that I have been able to continue my business for such a long time. I started with only two persons and, over sixty years, the number of my employees has gradually increased. Today my company has more than 100,000 employees . . . People say that I have become a great success in business . . . With the help of my wife and brother-in-law, I started a small electrical supply company simply in order to eat. Of course, there

were times when I considered how I might become successful in business. I tried to work hard, used common sense, and adhered to general maxims of practical business management in those days: 'Make quality products, constantly strive to improve, take care of regular customers, and maintain good relations with suppliers.' My business gradually prospered and expanded in both size and the number of employees.

You might suppose that this great Japanese businessman would continue by claiming that all his subsequent success had been founded on this simple formula. Wrong: he goes on to argue for 'a management philosophy' as the foundation of success. By this, Matsushita means an ethical system, a set of morally based principles and precepts that binds together all the members of a company in the interests of the organization they serve.

The idea comes more easily to a Japanese mind than a western one. But Matsushita is right – a company does need a unifying ethos, and the more deeply this reflects man's non-material needs, the greater the contribution the ethos will make to the company and to society. The heroes of the last pages of my *The Naked Manager* were the Quaker businessmen: men not only excellent at their primary business task, but also at building for the future and at pioneering the better treatment of people at work. Among the solid and great manufacturing firms of America's Midwest, the same pattern is often repeated: commercial success founded on and imbued by an ethical view of life and the value of work.

An essay like my present one, concerned mainly with ends, means and results, by implication ignores these broader, perhaps greater issues. It's wrong for managers to do so. They should, just as Matsushita says, have a philosophy; but that is essentially something that they (as Matsushita did) must work out for themselves. There is, however, one element that has an essential place in any management philosophy – and it's the element that the Japanese electrical supremo now tends gently to deprecate that early common-sense credo: 'Make quality products, constantly strive to improve, take care of regular customers, and maintain good relations with suppliers.'

Those few words have no great intellectual weight, and would never be written on tablets of stone. But maybe they should be. Their childish simplicity doesn't prevent them from being lastingly right. Many of the most important management truths share this same humdrum quality, but I don't hold that against them – although no less an authority than Robert Townsend, author of *Up The Organisation*, apparently does.

Writing a review of my first book, he described its Ten Truths of Management, which were printed on the back cover, as 'ho-hum'. Well, so (and here) they are:

1 Think before you act: it's not your money.
2 All good management is the expression of one great idea.
3 No executive devotes effort to proving himself wrong.
4 Cash in must exceed cash out.
5 Management capability is always less than the organization actually needs.
6 Either an executive can do his job or he cannot.
7 If sophisticated calculations are needed to justify an action, don't do it.
8 If you are doing something wrong, you will do it badly.
9 If you are attempting the impossible, you will fail.
10 The easiest way of making money is to stop losing it.

Nothing that happened in the 1970s has invalidated those ten ho-hum truths, any more than Matsushita's eighteen-word policy statement is less valid now than when he started in business sixty-one years ago. What's happened in the interim, above all, is to emphasize by example (much of it awful) the importance of mastering and sticking to what football coaches call 'the basics'. Once the corporate reflex has become to 'get the basics right' in a continuing process, the company's future and the success of its more complex plans should be assured.

But the key to mastering complexity, too, can be summed up in a favourite acronym: KISS. Standing for 'Keep It Simple, Stupid', it embodies (in the best KISS style) several much more profound observations: like that insistence of Moltke's on an army system mediocre officers can manage successfully, or the behavioural work showing how the chances of error are magnified with each additional level in the hierarchical structure.

It's another ho-hum truth, which the manager forgets at his peril, that even a hyper-intelligent man will master a simple system more readily than a complex system. Reducing the complicated to the simple is a key to success. *The simpler the task is made, the more easily it will be done*.

It follows that the fewer the tasks, the easier it is to simplify them. That's why concentration, on a few markets or a few products, or structuring a company so that its constituents can so concentrate, both simplifies and strengthens the firm. The marketing consultant Andrew Tessler has shown beyond question that UK exporters, in contrast to their far more successful German and French competitors, disperse and thus waste their effort by serving far more geographical markets. The same observation can be repeated anywhere in management: more means less – that is, MILO.

The translation is: Most Input for the Least Output. Every manager who has ever pruned a product line, removed a production unit, regrouped machines to eliminate unneeded ones, etc., etc., can produce anecdotes to confirm this truth. LIMO – Least Input for the Most Output – is the only sound policy and, as noted before, it's one that must include the time of managers, like all other inputs. Not only does this principle bar the sixteen-hour day, the eternal working weekend and other abuses (all of which are evidence of structural and operational defects); it also means not placing people in positions where their ability isn't used to the full.

To express the point positively, ability is more important than seniority, and talent is more important than age. That has immediate relevance to a subject unmentioned so far: women. I was once taken to task by a lady lecturer in management for giving 'a very chauvinist speech'. My sin was to use the pronoun 'he' for the manager – as in these pages. Adding 'or she' expresses my feelings accurately, but the extra verbiage doesn't add to the sense. Manager is a female as well as a male word, and any firm where a woman has no chance of reaching any line or staff position is suffering from a self-inflicted wound. Apart from anything else, it's ignoring *half* the available pool of talent – and making itself a less pleasant company for which to work.

Pleasant may be a strange adjective in the context of management, but it has a vital role. If a company isn't pleasant to work for, it probably isn't worth working for. One of the notable developments of our times, a process that has gathered force over the 1970s, is that companies have become more enjoyable places: in relatively trivial ways, like the introduction of flexible working hours; in broad social changes, like the spread of informality in manners and relationships; and in crucial managerial ways, like the devolution of real power to points closer to the real work of the business.

Under economic stress and strain, the company has continued to develop into a less stressful and strained form of organization. This social evolution has given managers a much better chance of performing well at their prime function – which is and must be economic, in both senses of the word: using resources economically in order to contribute to the economic well-being of society. The organization that wins and the manager who wins succeed by virtue of their economic contribution. And that is essentially a virtuous achievement, under any economic system known to man.

# 9 How to develop drive and overdrive

from *The Supermanagers*

*The Supermanagers* must have struck a multinational chord: it has been translated into many languages – and maybe this wide acceptance reflects its origins. I was on a Far East lecture tour: the first session, in Bangkok, had gone well enough, but I was dissatisfied. Had the managers (of many different nationalities) who gave up a day to attend the seminar gone away with anything personally useful?

The word 'personally' gave me the clue. On the flight from Thailand to Singapore I reworked the seminar material and tied the discussion to the personal, individual talents, achievements and ambitions of the manager. The new presentation was so much more effective with my other multinational audiences that the idea of the book followed naturally – and the first passage selected contains its essence: the belief that managers (and by extension managements) can improve their performance continuously and comprehensively.

The best way of proving the point was obviously to cite living proofs, which led to the plan of case histories followed by related themes. This inevitably meant that there was no grand flow of monolithic theory. But in any event, books that purvey such single-minded concepts are like grand attempts to reduce history to a single sweeping statement: impressive, sometimes, but always wildly disrespectful towards inconvenient truths.

Since respect for the truth is the foundation of truly excellent management, I prefer the approach in this book.

My brilliant American publisher, Truman Talley, made many

valuable contributions to *The Supermanagers*, including the request for an additional section on the new industries and the new management ideas that they had spawned and required. That set off a fascinating quest, still not finished, for the reliable managerial concepts in a high-technology world whose prime characteristic is an unreliability of managers and managements that utterly contradicts the amazing truthworthiness of their products. In fact, the new industries, in the end, obey the same economic laws as the old. But the action is enormously speeded up, like the chase scenes in silent comedies. As in those films, the crashes of corporate vehicles and their drivers are part of the scenario. It is one that staider industries are having to learn.

## The would-be millionaire

The businessman thought for a long time, staring out of the window at his suburban garden. He picked up his pen, put it down, picked it up again, and finally wrote this letter:

Dear Robert Heller,
With a strong urge to become a millionaire in the next five years, and £100,000 cash available, what would you suggest?

This book is the answer to that real-life letter – not the original reply, but the one that grew over years of investigating what really produces Supermanagements. My Would-be Millionaire, I realized, had several things going for him – not least, £100,000. But he'd also chosen a realistic target that could be put into words and figures. He had set a realistic time horizon for reaching his target. He was thinking in highly personal terms, as you must, if you want to get anywhere. And he knew that he needed help from other people to get what he wanted.

Above all, though, the Would-be Millionaire had one rare quality. He had ambition.

That's the first truth about Supermanagers. *Most people don't manage to the utmost of their ability because they don't want to.* You don't believe it? Then try this questionnaire based on a study in the *Harvard Business Review*.

> Do you have:
> A high level of drive and energy?
> Enough self-confidence to take carefully calculated, moderate risks?
> A clear idea of money as a way of keeping score, and as a means of generating more money still?
> The ability to get other people to work with and for you productively?
> High but realistic, achievable goals?
> Belief that you can control your own destiny?
> Readiness to learn from your own mistakes and failures?
> A long-term vision of the future of your business?
> Intensive competitive urge, with self-imposed standards?

If you have, in your opinion, half a dozen of the nine attributes, that's a higher score by far than that of the great majority of business executives who I've had answer the quiz. But unless you can score eight out of nine, you must be falling well short of your success potential. And unless you think you can get a perfect score, and want to, you're not truly ambitious.

That's the second truth about Supermanagement. *Every one of the qualities needed for executive success can be acquired, developed, or improved.*

You don't believe that, either? You think that some qualities are inborn, like 'a high level of drive and energy'? True, some people are born supercharged: the non-stop hustler, the fellows who can stay out drinking until three in the morning, start work at seven, wear out three secretaries before lunch, who can fire a failure as soon as look at him, and who force their projects to succeed by sheer energy. You're not like them, and neither am I. We don't have to be.

I prefer the pattern of a man named Maxwell Joseph. Sir Max was said hardly ever to work more than four hours a day or more than four days a week. Inside a decade, though, he parlayed a handful of obscure hotels into one of the largest chains in the world

– and that wasn't all, not by any means. His empire owned bars and breweries, liquor and L&M cigarettes, gambling and milk, and much, much more. Joseph had a high level of energy and drive, true. But the energy and drive were in the proper place – his head.

Nobody can succeed on his fabulous scale by just deciding to. But that method – just deciding to – is the way for anybody to achieve great improvements in any of the nine steps that lead to business success. There's no magic involved – except the magical results of *making* things happen instead of letting them happen. That's what the Supermanagers do, whether their native language is American, English, French, German, Japanese – or anything else.

## The men who made it

Energy and drive just as magnificent as Max's can thus be seen in the careers of Charles, Arnold, Royal, Ken, and Soichiro. They're five very different men from three different nations, but they have six shared characteristics – six highest common factors. And they also share a high, a very high, rating in the Supermanagement stakes.

The first, surnamed Forte, built up the largest European hotel and catering empire, with US interests that include the Travelodge motel chain. The second, Arnold Weinstock, created the General Electric Company's amazing growth record. The third, Royal D. Little, first the eccentric founder of the Textron conglomerate, later became the backer of innumerable management buy-outs. The fourth, Ken Olsen, is the computer engineer behind the phenomenal growth of Digital Equipment Corporation. The fifth, Soichiro Honda, is the motorbike and car tycoon whose story is maybe the most extraordinary fable of the Japanese miracle.

These men made happen what they wanted to happen by applying the following half-dozen highest common factors: tenacity; loyalty to long-lasting colleagues; tightness with money, coupled with tight controls; the money-making drive; the urge to simplify and to build on simple foundations; the ability to admit and learn from mistakes (Little even wrote a book entitled *How to Lose $100 Million and Other Useful Information*).

Once I was running through this list of qualities (which by no coincidence bears a close resemblance to the nine in the questionnaire). I mentioned things like tenacity, with which Honda overcame setback after setback, Lord Weinstock's reliance on right-hand men who came with him into GEC, Lord Forte's development of key and simple business ratios when he owned one milk bar, Olsen's uncarpeted offices in New England – and Little's lovely book. When I'd done, a businessman–politician stood up and questioned the truth of what I'd been saying.

Why, he said, nobody could have been more tenacious than himself. He'd stuck to it through thick and thin, and after ten years his company was at last in profit. As for loyalty, he still had the same nincompoops he'd had around from the very beginning. Tightness with money? He was the meanest man in the land. As for money, he never thought of anything else. Over the years, too, he'd simplified and improved constantly – because he wasn't afraid to admit his errors, of which he'd made plenty, and to correct them. So why wasn't he a Forte or a Weinstock or a Honda?

Two questions solved the puzzle. How big was his company? It did a million pounds' worth of turnover. What business was it in? Well, not one, actually, but five. They were unrelated, they were by definition small, and they gave away the game. Nobody who truly had the money-making drive would have stuck to such unrewarding divisions for a whole decade. Max, Royal, Arnold, Charles, Soichiro – any of them would either have found a way to make one of the businesses big and rich or moved on to lands of brighter promise.

The businessman–politician didn't know himself as he really was. His ambition actually lay elsewhere – in politics, of course. And that delusion – the cardinal one that explains why ambitious personal designs so often founder – was one error to which he couldn't confess and which he therefore couldn't correct.

Never make that same mistake. Instead, follow up the example of a Man Who Made It, a young entrepreneur named John Bray. He quit a family firm, despite his rapid rise and success in its employment. His reason? The family wouldn't give him a share in the business. The company he next joined, though also a family firm, did give him a stake. But far from being a red-hot success like his previous employer, this new one was ice cold. The business was dying, and Bray was forced to find another market. He started from the once and future foundation of any business – what it does well. Bray searched for a product to which the firm's existing technical skills could be applied, preferably in a large market, one where he could find all the sales volume he needed, even if he took only a tiny bite from the pie.

The chosen big market, in home decoration, was dominated by a very big company, but Bray wasn't intimidated by that. He knew that the larger the share one firm has of any market, the more vulnerable it is to mismanagement – to complacency, incompetence, and the depressing effects of large fixed assets and lumpy fixed thinking. Because he knew all this, and could clearly see the symptoms in this particular giant's market and marketing, Bray wasn't even distressed by the fact that sales in his chosen market were actually declining. He could (and did) still double the sales of his company, Coloroll, every year merely by raising his market share from minute to small. He planned to achieve that by finding a product advantage, something that would single out his product from the pack and that would have market appeal.

But Bray was also an expert at selling. He looked for the weaknesses in his huge competitor's distribution system so that he could both avoid them and turn his alternative approach into a strength. He introduced a stronger fashion element into the product. He recruited the best people he could find and used their own selfish drives to motivate them – so that they served his selfish ends as well.

Above all, Bray sold – and made everybody else sell. His initiatives were not immediately successful; new departures rarely are. Bray, however, was thoroughly tenacious. He changed the entire technology and raw-material base of the firm's original business, in paper bags, the one that was dying, and the new line of plastic bags also became a success. He invested up to the hilt in new machinery. No technical expert himself, he found the best technical adviser he could, and gave him full backing. And by those means he raised turnover from peanuts to £20 million, with profits up one hundredfold to £2 million, in only a few hectic years.

Then, he turned over the management to one of those highly motivated, selfish people he'd hired – which left Bray free for pastures new. What separates the men who make it from those who don't isn't just the highest common factors, important though they are, but the object to which they're applied and the will with which the aim is pursued. And, fortunately, getting clear – crystal clear – about the object helps wonderfully to create that all-conquering will.

## Be your own buy-out

If you can provide the self with its selfish motive, you can transform human performance for non-selfish ends and, with it, corporate performance. This principle is the non-financial essence of the 'leveraged buy-out' in which Royal D. Little specialized so successfully in his second career. When a group of managers 'buys out' the operation managed by themselves from its owner – usually some benighted conglomerate – they get all the advantages of 'leveraging', since the larger part of the 'buy-out' or purchase price is borrowed at fixed interest.

Levers are the oldest machines in the history of financial leger-demain. If you invest £100,000 of your own loot in a business and sell it a year later for £200,000, anybody can see that you've made a 100 per cent profit. But if you supply just £10,000 yourself, borrowing the rest even at 20 per cent interest, you make £82,000 profit on £10,000 investment – or 720 per cent. The arithmetic is very seductive, and it seduces even managers who by definition have brought no drive and no great success to a business (other-wise, why would it be for sale?).

One of the many buy-out mechanics who have swarmed on to the scene says that it's fascinating to find a sea change coming over managers with whom he discusses buy-outs. At first, they show the typical dumbstruck reaction of the typical dumb management in the typical dumb company to any bright new idea. But then he goes into that seductive arithmetic; they quickly discover that a 25 per cent equity stake divided among themselves can very easily multi-ply their capital (obtained by mortgaging their houses, wives, and anything else they can lay their hands on) by ten times for every doubling of profits.

Once that amazing thought has sunk in, along with the fact that they would be their own masters, they become changed men. They will go to endless pains, burning up the midnight oil and the calculator batteries to produce information and bring the deal to pass.

Just as mothers in all species fight ferociously only for their own young, so managers, in general, work most fiercely only for their own direct benefit. The best advice to the Would-be Millionaire is to put his £100,000 into a leveraged buy-out – that is, on the assumption that he doesn't have, or can't start, a business of his own. The best investment is almost always the one you have got to know most intimately by working in it. If your own business can't produce the desired pay-off (that aspiring Croesus wanted a tenfold gain in five years), then the chances of finding something else that will bear you fruit can't be good. But a buy-out must be the next best thing, for the following reasons:

1 You get an experienced team with a track record.
2 You can be reasonably sure that tolerable business systems exist.
3 You start with a substantial turnover, and an established position in the market – you don't face the inevitable horrors of building up from scratch.
4 You may very well be able to pick up the business cheap – the big company managers selling off the outfit won't be red-hot bargainers.
5 Making the management team put most of their money where their mouths are gives a much better incentive than buying into an operation that the entrepreneur started on a shoestring – and where his true stake is thus tiny.
6 Anyway, it's amazing what wonders of cost-cutting and profit-raising people can accomplish when they escape from big company overheads and have to run a business on their own – and with their own financial futures at stake.

Many entrepreneurs – none in more legendary style than the aforementioned Royal D. Little – have made fortunes out of demonstrating the apparently absurd proposition that the very same fuddy-duddy set of stumblebums who led the business nowhere can work wonders, *if* they are properly motivated by their perfectly proper selfish interests.

It's by no means entirely a matter of money. As noted above, the idea of being your own master is also powerfully attractive to those who work for other people. Indeed, the ideal situation for the hired hand is to feel that he is as much the master, as much in charge, as if he really did own the business lock, stock, and barrel.

Even the most illustrious of hired hands will tell you, though, that it's not quite the same thing – ownership does confer something other than property rights. But unless hired hands do feel they have an acceptable (to them) degree of control over their own destiny, unless they do feel that in some very real sense (real to them) the business is their own, their performance will remain stuck in the pre-buy-out syndrome. The fact of the matter is that all too many businesses are in that sad situation. The buy-out itself often rests on a *deus ex machina*, the Royal D. Little who appears from outer space to set the people free. The ambitious man or woman must learn to be his or her own Little – and it can be done.

## The would-be Robert Redfords

A hot-shot entrepreneur was asked by a friend to advise on the latter's money-losing business. The entrepreneur wanted to oblige, but didn't have much time to spend on the problem – especially for free. So he made a rush job of it. He went through the business at high speed, starting with goods inwards, following them all the way through to goods outwards. He could find no serious fault.

So he turned next to the office. A similar speedy search demonstrated that the financial and commercial systems, taking and making orders, were even better than the factory systems. So then he turned to the products; nothing wrong there, either. The next and last stop was the sales manager – and there the entrepreneur found his answer.

He called together the entire sales team and asked what their reaction would be if they were asked to study for the chance of a big part and a fat fee in a major Hollywood movie. Naturally they were all, as one man, ready to work every available hour in the evenings and on weekends. Given the opening he sought, the entrepreneur then suggested that the same effort and hours put into a really professional selling operation would pay dividends – as duly happened.

Up to then, under an undermotivated manager, these sales people, unmotivated themselves, hadn't harnessed their will, hadn't utilized the urge that would be stimulated by a chance to become a Robert Redford, and to earn a Robert Redford income. The will exists within most people. Without it you can achieve very little in management – and you certainly can't become a millionaire in five years.

## Work for only one SOB at a time

The Would-be Robert Redfords who became better salesmen, and the Bought-out Managers who became rich, largely by doing what was within their reach and capacity all along, should have kicked themselves for not having seen and seized their opportunities far earlier. It's true that the previous regime may have laid dead and deadening hands on the bought-out firm. But the managers didn't have to stay there. Their duty to themselves included the obligation to ensure that they were in the right job and employed in the right way – 'right' meaning what suits your wishes and abilities, and where both can be fully realized. Life is too short to be unhappy, uncommitted, or unsuccessful in your work, and there are always opportunities.

The likelihood is that, inside many great companies, businesses are underperforming because their managers are, and that the latter underperform because they are undermotivated. Money is the simplest way of committing them, though not the only one; nor is it necessarily effective on its own. It needs support from the way in which the whole organization operates. But unless the managers are motivated, the company has a large and growing problem, because the odds are that, having joined an organization, the person will stay there – very possibly underperforming all the way to the end of the line.

The tendency for the great majority of managers to stay put, despite the folklore of rapid and often violent changes of jobs, may be on the wane, judged by the latest statistics. Up to now, though, American managers have been no more likely to job-hop than those in West Germany, where youngsters still tend to join firms with the intention of resting (sometimes no doubt literally) there for life.

A good reason for staying put is that you love or like the job and the place so much that you simply don't want to leave, ever. A bad reason is fright, simple fear of the unknown. An unemotional reason is the calculation that in the key material respects, such as money or status, you will be unable to better yourself by change. The last sounds plausible, but is not likely to be true. Anybody who has ever had the misfortune to fire somebody else knows the feeling of blessed relief when, more often than not, the sacked person pops up in a visibly better job. If opportunities exist for failed managers, how many more must there be for those who are riding the crest of their own particular wave?

The difficulties are psychological. Change is traumatic, especially when it involves swapping a devil you've known for years for one you know not. Mostly, the only executives who take change in their stride are those who are forced to, like the executive inhabitants of multinationals, particularly those that are American-owned. Whether or not being shunted around the universe every three years is a good idea, it does instil into the executive the habit of moving – while the very mobility increases his outside value.

There is a school of thought, too, that holds that any period of service above three years is too long. Tex Thornton and Roy Ash, when riding high at the conglomerate Litton Industries, theorized that the first year is spent learning the job; in the second year the incumbent is at his peak; the third year sees the gradual onset of boredom, at the end of which it's time to move on.

The theory holds some truth (though Ash and Thornton at the time had held their jobs much longer than three years). The end of a three-year stint is a good time for taking stock. But the learning curve, the lovable process that improves performance with every repetition, continues after three years. There will come a point, too, where the position and the occupant are in perfect harmony. And that is the object of the personal quest – to find that point of near-maximum fulfilment – only *near*-maximum because human life isn't given to perfection.

At some point reasonably close to the summit, the ambitious executive is best advised to come to a stay, because three-quarters of the very top appointments are made from within. Even at the approach to the summit, though, two questions still have to be answered. Is the organization, or what I can make of it, able to satisfy my personal objectives? Have I got the personal abilities to exploit the opportunity? Often the only way to find the second answer is to take the job. That may prove a painfully hard route to a resounding 'No'. But in the end the time is likely to come in any manager's life when he has to discover just how good or bad he truly is, and that means taking one of the calculated risks that are inseparable from all management.

But don't take any risks with the company. Always assess a potential employer with as much care as if you were buying the company, which in a sense you are. The investment of part of a human life, especially your own, is no small down payment. The profile must cover: the company's market position, its current financial status, the consistency of its record, the future prospects for its sector, the return on investment.

In other words, you assess the upside potential and the downside risk as carefully as any buy-out backer looking at a possible candidate. It doesn't follow that a negative report on points like the above should put you off. Success in saving the day may do the executive far more personal good than joining a company in first-class fettle. That's because the corporate crisis provides both the compelling need to act and the urgent authority to do so – and many people in management do seem to require some abnormal outside stimulus, like a disaster, or the *deus ex machina* of the leveraged buy-out, to extract their best performance.

The chosen job should therefore be one where stimulus of one variety or another already exists, or where you can create it. But the most important pre-entry condition is the calibre of colleagues.

Just as this determines the potential of a buy-out, so it profoundly affects the desirability of letting yourself be bought in.

That's especially the case where the company is dominated by a powerful individual. One middle-aged executive who had plunged from a dull, large corporation into the excitements of a millionaire entrepreneur's court found some aspects of the change, including the financial ones, very attractive – but not the fact that he was now working, in his own words, for 'an SOB'. There's only one SOB you should ever work for – and that's yourself. And you shouldn't be one.

## The supermanager's sermon

The truly great leaders, in war or peace, are never bastards, anyway. They are intensely human and they treat other people in human and humane terms. Listen to these words from a boss whose smashing success turned him into a Supermanager. He arrived at a time when disaster after disaster, setback after setback, had demoralized the organization. Immediately on taking over he assembled his executives, many of them stuck deep in the mire of defeatism, and spoke to them as follows:

> You do not know me. I do not know you. But we have got to work together – therefore we must understand each other and we must have confidence in each other. I have been here only a few hours. But from what I have seen and heard since I arrived I am prepared to say, here and now, that I have confidence in you. We will then work together as a team. I believe that one of the first duties of [a boss] is to create what I call atmosphere. I do not like the general atmosphere I find here. It is an atmosphere of doubt, of looking back. All that must cease.

The Supermanager then made it absolutely clear that there was no alternative to success – it was win or nothing. 'I want to impress on everyone that the bad times are over. And it will be done. If anyone here thinks it can't be done, let him go at once – I don't want any doubters. It can be done and it will be done; beyond any possibility of doubt.' The Superboss rubbed home the lesson yet again. 'I understand there has been a great deal of "bellyaching". By bellyaching I mean inventing poor reasons for not doing what one has been told to do. All this is to stop at once. If anyone objects to doing what he has been told, then he can get out of it – and at once.'

After this stern stuff, the speaker lightened the tension by saying, 'I have little more to say just at present. And some of you may think it is quite enough and may wonder if I am mad. I assure you I am quite sane.' He stressed the 'atmosphere' that he wanted to permeate right down through the organization. Everybody 'must know what is wanted; when they see it coming to pass, there will be a surge of confidence throughout . . . I ask you to give me your confidence and to have faith that what I have said will come to pass.'

The short speech (compressed here) ended on an upbeat. Beating the arch-competitor 'will be quite easy. There is no doubt about it. He is definitely a nuisance. Therefore we will hit him a crack and finish with him.' The peremptory note gives away the game. This wasn't a civilian manager taking charge; it was General Montgomery laying down the law to his Eighth Army officers immediately on taking command in the fight against Hitler and the feared Field Marshal Rommel. Just two months later that demoralized and defeatist force won the decisive battle of El Alamein.

## Ten pillars of leadership

Analogies between the conduct of war and that of business should be handled with care. But Montgomery's speech of only a few hundred words to his officer/executives struck every note of effective management, every chord of turning group potential into successful achievement by the group and by the individuals who form the group. What was the Supermanager trying to establish? What principles was he following?

First, trust is a two-way process. The boss earns the trust of others ('We must have confidence in each other') in part by trusting them – and telling them so ('I am prepared to say, here and now, that I have confidence in you'). The corollary is that if you can't trust 'em, you don't keep 'em ('If anyone thinks it can't be done, let him go at once').

Second, the work of management can only be done together ('We will then work together as a team'). The more genuine this togetherness, the better the performance will be. But, third, the chances of effective collaboration, like everything else in the management of men and women, depend on the 'atmosphere', the climate, the culture; and that's one responsibility the boss can't evade ('one of the first duties . . . is to create what I call atmosphere'). He creates that atmosphere automatically, for good or ill, simply by being there, by being boss and by being what he is. With the very words 'I do not like the general atmosphere I find here', Montgomery had changed it – decisively and for the better.

Fourth, the objective of the enterprise must be sharply defined and determined. Montgomery's aim was to beat Rommel, and he had no compunction in telling these officers that it was do or die. Businesses should never be reduced to those stark alternatives – and neither should armies. But a world of difference lies between desperation and determination. Montgomery had no intention of dying, of failing: 'it will be done; beyond any possibility of doubt'.

Fifth, that aim must be communicated with total clarity, and (sixth and equally important) with the total confidence of the speaker. The self-confidence of the leader or leaders and the confidence of the organization go hand in hand. Both are created and enhanced by clarity of communication and objective (everybody 'must know what is wanted; when they see it coming to pass, there will be a surge of confidence').

The confidence will be false, seventh, unless it has material backup, unless the resources required are provided, and unless actions always support words. To prove that 'the bad times are over', Montgomery took pains to mention that 400 new tanks had just been off-loaded at Cairo. Exhortation has nothing to do with good management. Leadership is rather a matter of inspiration – of encouraging people to achieve what is possible, and insisting that they do so.

Eighth, total emphasis has to be placed on performance – on getting things done as and when they should be willingly and without excuses ('poor reasons for not doing what one has been told to do . . . If anyone objects to doing what he has been told, then he can get out of it – and at once').

The ninth essential is to temper discipline with humanity: the touch and the attitude that communicate caring. Montgomery forcefully established this point by telling the underbosses (a) that he wasn't mad and (b) that they were being moved at once to more comfortable, fly-free HQ near the sea, where they could work properly. Physical moves, incidentally, are one of the most effective ways of producing swift organizational change – provided, that is, that they are moves for the better and are used for their symbolic value, as well as for the rut-breaking that always stimulates moribund mentalities.

The tenth and final principle is aggression of the controlled and rational type – the urge to out-achieve the competition by applying the simplest possible strategy in the most effective possible way ('we will hit him a crack and finish with him'). In this respect, Montgomery made it crystal clear to his audience that nothing and nobody would make him move before he was good and ready. Beating Rommel would be 'quite easy' – but only when he had given his competitive, aggressive strategy the utmost chance of success by building up a massive superiority and by intensively training his forces to take full advantage of their greater strength.

Generals in war, of course, have advantages when it comes to being boss that are not shared by people managing in peacetime – or even by peacetime generals. Worldwide the trend has rightly been away from automatic, formal authority towards genuine co-operative, informal association. That increases the demands on the boss. But permissive, co-operative, non-authoritarian ways are not an end in themselves. They are means to an end, and the achievement of objectives is as important today as it was to those officers in the desert, listening in astonishment and hope to this fiery, crisp commander who was to change all their lives. The glove can be as velvet as you wish. But within it the iron fist of determined management must make use of the Montgomery method: trust, teamwork, atmosphere, objectives, clarity, confidence, backup, performance, humanity, and aggression – the Ten Pillars of Leadership.

# 10 How to manage the new industries

from *The Supermanagers*

## The writing on the pad

Supermanagement is always a combination of the old and the new. But it has been tilted towards the new by two developments: one, the rise of companies based exclusively on high, leading-edge technology, with information technology in the forefront; two, the soaring growth of service industries, whose stock in trade is ideas and information. Neither by nature fits the old hierarchical habits – illustrated by a couple of stories from the past.

A dominant tycoon figure, famed for his imperious ways, hired an executive for an important job. After the man had moved in, the boss sent a handwriting specimen to a famous graphologist. On getting the report from this genius, the tycoon marched into his new employee's office and fired him. The reason? 'You're emotionally unstable.'

Another boss, equally overbearing, hired a man from the civil service. On his first day, a meeting was held to discuss a project that was going grievously awry in the south. Turning towards the brand-new employee, he said, 'I suppose it would be grossly unfair to ask Hank, who's only just arrived, to go down there and live in a motel until this mess is sorted out?' Hank agreed that it would indeed be grossly unfair, and thought no more about it. The meeting continued. But as it ended, the tycoon, walking out with the company lawyer, said, 'I want that man fired' – and he was.

The sequels to both stories perfectly point the contrast between the old management and the new – and provide the explanation of the latter's triumph. The first tycoon was fired himself, by his boardroom colleagues. The reason? Because he wouldn't treat them as colleagues. The second tycoon led his company into a sensational collapse. The reason? Because if he hired good people, they wouldn't stay in an atmosphere where they were not colleagues but dominated underlings. The only people who would stay in that atmosphere were no good. No-good people in a service industry (this was finance) are walking disasters. And disasters are what they produce.

## If the cuckoo won't sing

The main difference between those who Supermanage and those who don't is that the former know that looking after, working with, and working on behalf of other people is the essence of the new collegiate style, or management by friends. The word 'friends' is used here as the movie director Mel Brooks did when he called his children 'those friends to whom we gave birth'. Most of any manager's colleagues are wished upon him by accidents of fate as bizarre as birth. But in any organization worth joining, the accident becomes a working friendship.

You can control the accidents to some extent by how you recruit. Pick badly, and you always have a disaster on your hands. Bad appointments result not only in bad performance but in doing bad things to people – and, if they have become in any sense your friends, bad is made even worse. But even if the appointment isn't a disaster in itself, an environment that doesn't allow and/or compel the appointee to give of his best will risk disaster.

The friendly, non-compulsive atmosphere is the ideal – but, in truth and alas, it's not the only environment that can achieve results. Management has its Gulag Archipelagos, and the pressure that is part of any successful management operation can be applied in an acceptable or unacceptable manner.

For example, at a business run by another pocket tycoon, just as megalomaniacal as the handwriting buff and the swift sacker, 'Board meetings were infrequent, papers were not circulated in advance. Non-executive directors had no chance to read often substantial documents until they were ushered into the boardroom as the meeting was due to begin . . . An attempt to take papers away afterwards produced an outcry,' as reported by a witness. This monster held undated letters of resignation from each of his executive directors, and neither they nor anyone else in the company had any pension entitlement. People who displeased the peerless leader left with nothing.

The boss's entry in *Who's Who* gave 'business' as the first of his very few interests, and he expected his managers to put in the same long hours that he worked himself. In some respects, their rewards were limited. Job titles varied at whim, and, said one senior executive, 'Promotion wasn't a thing he readily indulged in.' 'He wasn't difficult,' declared another manager. 'He was impossible.'

To retain people, the boss issued them with shares that could be traded only at par – say, a dollar. The prospects of having later to trade in at par shares worth several tens of thousands of dollars was obviously, whatever the discomforts of life in the company, a golden shackle to deter any potential leaver.

But the old man wouldn't leave himself, either. As his reign wore on into his seventies, the one-time Supermanager made one nomination after another as his successor, but, 'having appointed an heir apparent . . . repeatedly turned against his choice and sacked him or drove him out'. When the board finally appointed the successor, the ex-dictator was 'not on speaking terms with the choice, and publicly repudiated him'.

In the circumstances, it was amazing that the business, with total domination from the top and no management development, survived at all. But in the process, its record as a progressive growth company disappeared entirely. Over the 1970s, after allowing for inflation, its earnings per share fell by 10.5 per cent annually – Supermanagement had finally been turned sour by a man who had no friends.

Your own attitude along the gamut from Gulag to green fields can be tested by three statements. In which of them do you believe?

1  If the cuckoo won't sing, kill it.
2  If the cuckoo won't sing, make it sing.
3  If the cuckoo won't sing, let's wait until it does.

The statements comprise a form of haiku, a short Japanese poem that dates back to the sixteenth century. The first philosophy is hire and fire – the price of non-performance is dismissal. The second is the idea, basic to most western companies, that you need to coerce people to get decent work out of unwilling troops. The third, according to author Mitz Moda, writing in *Technology Review*, is the secret of Japanese success: you act on the assumption that the troops are willing and, given half a chance, will work excellently without recourse to fear or coercion.

Management in Japan doesn't kill its cuckoos or try to force them to sing, and so, freed from anxiety and happy in their work, they warble like crazy. Maybe so, maybe not – although there are some interesting confirmatory figures on killed salesmen, the implications of which have an obvious bearing on executives generally.

If you kill cuckoos for not singing, you will have high job turnover – not to be encouraged, if only because you must do all that interviewing all over again. Far worse: the study concerned, conducted in 1,029 US firms, showed no correlation whatsoever between sales performance and turnover of salesmen. The element and practice of dismissal, in other words, don't seem to have any effect, except to make the organization a nastier place in which to live. And in that environment, in this day and age, your cuckoos are much less likely to sing as well, say, as those of Soichiro Honda.

He and his partner, Takeo Fujisawa, were once addressed by a banker as follows: 'I think you have an outstanding business going for you. I presume, of course, that you will eventually hand over the company to your sons.' They replied as one man, 'We have no such thought whatsoever.' As Honda explained, with a rhetorical quote, 'If the company belonged to the . . . family, who would have the motivation to work for the company?'

The truly amazing Honda business career in motorbikes and cars really got under way only after a 1949 conversation between Honda and Fujisawa. Honda was then forty-two, and Fujisawa, four years younger, informed Honda, already known as a brilliant inventor, that 'I will work with you as a businessman. But when we part I am not going to end up with a loss. I'm not talking only about money. What I mean is that when we part, I hope I will have gained a sense of satisfaction and achievement.' A very Japanese wish, but a perfect expression of what business friendship means.

They never did part – retiring by mutual agreement on the same day twenty-two years later. You can get the flavour of their creation from a story about the initial build-up of Honda. It was based on a bike called 'Dream Type D'. The name arose when somebody, at a *sake* and sardine party to celebrate the prototype, remarked that it was 'like a dream'. At which point, Soichiro Honda yelled out, 'That's it! Dream!' The story comes from an excellent book entitled *Honda Motor: The Men, the Management, the Machines*, by Tetsuo Sakiya.

Don't run away with the idea, though, that Honda, or any other Japanese businessman, is some kind of superhuman as well as a Supermanager. Honda made plenty of mistakes, even in his own triumphant field of technology, where he scored stunning success after stunning success. Most seriously, he obstinately insisted, against all contrary opinion in the company, that air-cooled engines, not water-cooled, held the future for cars. The cuckoos couldn't sing, because he wouldn't let them. Finally, Fujisawa resolved the issue at dinner with his long-time partner. Here's Sakiya's fascinating account of the proceedings:

> They had not seen each other for quite some time and Fujisawa's mind was made up: 'If Mr Honda refuses a water-cooled engine, this would mean he is following a path different from mine. If the two of us cannot go in the same direction, our teamwork will not function.' At the dinner, Honda told Fujisawa, 'The same thing can be achieved with an air-cooled engine, but I guess that's difficult for a man like you to understand.' Fujisawa replied, 'You can do one of two things. You can continue to serve as the President of our company, or you can join the engineers at Honda Motor. I think you should choose now.'
>
> Honda looked unhappy to have to make such a decision, but replied, 'I'm sure I should continue to be the President.' 'Then,' said Fujisawa, 'you will permit your engineers to work on water-cooled engines, too,

won't you?' 'I will,' Honda agreed. Their conversation
had lasted no more than a few minutes, after which the
meeting turned into a party with both of them drinking
*sake* and singing old folk songs together. The next day
Honda went to the R. and D. centre and told the
engineers, 'OK, now you can work on water-cooled
engines.'

Although Honda was never seen to smile when anybody talked
about water-cooling thereafter, it's a marvellous Supermanagement story. If you, the boss, can't give in when you're wrong, you
can't be a fully effective leader, manager, partner – or friend – and
you certainly can't manage the new industries.

## The Mazda workers who sold

The principles applied in the case of Honda's water-cooled
engine, and exemplified in the cuckoo haiku, were familiar long ago
to western businessmen – whether they knew it or not. Collegiate
management is the essence of partnership; and that's how many of
today's great businesses began – with two or more people getting
together. When Hewlett met Packard the same alchemy took place
as when Rolls met Royce – and, as everybody knows who has ever
been in at such beginnings, everybody else in the business is a kind
of partner.

The growth and the excitement simply don't allow for the
limitations and demarcations of hierarchy. Usually, that comes
later, when the business has grown so far and fast that it needs a
corporate management structure. Sometimes, though, the business keeps that spirit of partnership when sales have soared into the
millions, the tens of millions – even the hundreds of millions and
beyond.

Increasingly, the preservation of partnership has become less a
way of life, more a necessity, for companies in high-tech industries
and the service businesses (some of which, like computer software,
are high-tech themselves). Again, there's nothing unfamiliar
about this aspect of service management. People in businesses like

publishing (which more often than not start as partnerships) rarely work in any other mode. In publishing magazines, which happens to be my own business, I can't achieve anything without my partners: the editor who turns the concept into a finished product, the publisher who handles the practical matters, the advertising manager who generates the revenue, and many others. It's not a question of treating these people as equals – they *are* equals.

In this kind of business, the time when people have to be given orders is the time when they have to move on. Of course, some Supermanagers do emerge in these conditions. They do so by virtue of having better ideas, greater skills, stronger personalities, but all these attributes can become worthless if they can't practise the arts and crafts of collegiate management. That is, in fact, one of the paradoxical secrets of Japanese success. Lifetime employment isn't a personnel policy, it's a cultural determinant, something that makes people behave in a particular way – as illustrated in a tale from Toyo Kogyo.

None of Japan's singing cuckoos has ever carolled more lustily than those employed at this company, which makes Mazda cars. It ran into one of the biggest brick walls in world industry when the 1973 quadrupling of oil prices hit the West amidships. The company had invested its future in the rotary engine. The rotary Mazda's appallingly high fuel consumption (8 m.p.g.) had a catastrophic impact on its sales. They crashed from 100,000 to a piddling 8,000 a year.

In a western company the necessary reaction would have been redundancies and lay-offs. Since, in a Japanese firm, these were unthinkable, the company turned to the co-operation of its employees. Factory workers by the thousand were shifted to the company's dealers to help in selling cars (the non-rotary ones). The workers and managers left behind at the plant met in small groups to find out how to improve productivity and tighten up quality control. Their efforts were a cardinal factor in nearly doubling productivity and converting a $44 million loss into $90 million profit.

Of course, other steps were taken. Working systems were improved, more automation was introduced, new models were developed and produced – including a rotary-engined sports car that picked up the flag dropped by the previous range. But the foundation of Mazda's miracle escape was that the cuckoos sang: management and work force were as one, equally willing to do anything to save the company – even to the extent of making door-to-door calls (the Japanese system) in the effort to sell cars. Many of the workers involved, when they returned to the factory one by one, did so with one piece of knowledge that most factory workers, even in successful firms, never have – they knew just what it takes to sell a car.

## The eagles who fly high

In the case of Mazda's singing cuckoos, it's hard to know who to admire more – the workers who went off and sold cars, or the managers who thought of sending them. Really, the two are inseparable. Good officers have good soldiers, and good soldiers make good officers better. Experts in recruitment are fond of listing the qualities to be sought in candidates: lists like (1) intellectual efficiency, (2) emotional maturity/stability, (3) human-relations skill, (4) insight into self and others, and (5) ability to organize/direct. But none of these qualities is any use without the help of others – indeed, a couple of the above factors specifically stress work with other people.

The process known as 'management development' (and, for that matter, management recruitment) must therefore keep those cuckoos in mind. One thing must follow if the object is to train managers who will neither kill birds that don't sing nor try to make them sing, but will rather patiently get them warbling for the love of it; that one necessity is that the managers themselves must be treated in the same cuckoo-loving way. What is true of workers is true of management: well and gently treated cuckoos – other things being equal – sing best. Which other things must be equal? You can see the answer to that from the answer to the following question.

What do you do with cuckoos who sing very well? The answer is, you turn them into eagles – high-fliers. (As a rough definition, to justify the description, they should have reached general management by thirty-two and have arrived at a very senior management level by forty-one.) According to a management professor, Charles Margerison, they should fly high in stages, of which the first is obvious from the definition of high-flying – and which also defines letting the cuckoo sing. You must give the cuckoo between the ages of twenty and thirty responsibility for a significant, personal part of the business.

That very first stage, like all its successors, must involve a position of leadership over others. As the eagle rises, stage by stage, he must get exposure to different aspects of the business in different functions. If the flier, at these stages, shows the necessary high need for achievement and the ability to work with and motivate others, you've got a candidate for the topmost eyrie.

'To work with and motivate others' – that's the essence of an effective relationship between colleagues, of a truly collegiate management. It has to rest, if you're serious about developing his powers of flight, on one unbreakable rule. If you ask somebody to do something for you, accept what they do. Otherwise, don't ask. The only result of second-guessing and interference, before the event, is to weaken the authority and the will of the person involved.

This doesn't rule out the right to criticize. No management can function properly without a severe critic on the premises, and no manager can be fully effective who isn't a good critic himself, especially (and most severely) of himself. The criticism, of course, must cut both ways: the subordinate must be as free to challenge his boss as the latter is to complain, goad, and grumble when work is not up to his standards.

It probably won't be up to standard if the subordinates are not fully involved in, and informed about, everything that impinges on their business. Apart from anything else, their opinions on the matter in hand should be valuable – otherwise they shouldn't be in the job. Moreover, you want everybody to be committed to achievement, not just for themselves, but for the organization. If you shut bits of the company away from these people, the commitment, similarly, will be less than total; and the action, since it isn't based on complete knowledge, will similarly be less than complete.

The only way to obtain the collective, collegiate style of management is to practise it. Every theory of management that has been promulgated in recent years, by no accident, revolves around the same central point of involvement: as enforced discipline has faded, so voluntary commitment to self-discipline has flourished. For instance, here is Max Taylor, a disciple of a consultant named Ralph Coverdale, writing in *Coverdale on Management* about taking over a new job (my italics):

1 Discover from your new staff how *they* tackle *their* own jobs. Get proposals from *them* on how working can be improved and what they would like to see done. Make sure that at least some of these are put into practice for the sake of morale, if for nothing else.
2 Discover the extent and the limits of *your* own authority.
3 Discover what is regarded as the essential purpose of *your* job.
4 Get clear success criteria. These should relate not only to the job's result, but to how *you* do it.

Whichever guru you turn to, every one will emphasize the you-and-them aspects of management, the inseparable dependence of colleagues on each other. There are plenty of companies in which these relationships are soured by hostility, insecurity, jealousy, and politics. Every atom of energy invested in these negative displays is energy lost to the real work of the organization. And in these hard times, organizations need all the management energy, and managers need all the friends, that they can get.

## The apple man who was IT

All the world's industry and commerce – with no exceptions worth making – is being profoundly affected in its products, processes, and possibilities by new technology, mostly (but by no means entirely) microelectronic. That means one thing for sure: all businesses will have changes in management methods and style imposed on them; changes many of which have just been discussed.

But the impact of change on one group of managements is and will be especially dramatic: the people who have the good fortune to be in the new industries, on whom everybody else depends technologically, and who include a whole new crop of Super-managers, often super-rich as well. The frequently eccentric, maverick behaviour of these new managements carries to its furthest point yet the nine-step formula for success, especially in the turbulent, explosive world of information technology. Theirs is a world of one-offs, not of archetypes – with one possible exception. If IT has produced a new breed of manager, then Steven Jobs is definitively *It*. Of all the gizmo-to-gold sagas of the Computer Age, Jobs has written the epic – whatever happens to his creation, Apple, in the tumultuous competition ahead. The Apple story isn't just that of Jobs, by any means. But he epitomized, at his peak, in a life-style that carried over from business to home and back again, the New Man, the Silicon Valley genus.

Seven years on, when Apple had become the quickest billion-dollar business in history, a journalist could still get a quote like the following on Jobs, from a friend: 'He still prefers to drive over to my place on his motorbike and sit around drinking wine, talking about what we'll do when we grow up.'

That was in 1983, when Jobs was twenty-eight, worth at least $150 million and facing the greatest challenge of his young, fabulously lucrative life: the onslaught of IBM, whose first anti-Apple product, the Personal Computer, has had such an electrifying effect on the market. In its bald facts, the story of Apple and Jobs reads like archetypal Hollywood hokum. Two men in their twenties start off in a garage in 1976 with $1,300 raised by selling a VW bus and a scientific calculator. Their first batch of fifty products is sold as kits for hobbyists to make their own computers. As demand increases, the two founders need more capacity and more management, for the jobs they held while moonlighting on their own business are no preparation for the big time – designing video games for Atari (Jobs) and working as an engineer for Hewlett-Packard (his partner, Stephen Wozniak).

As the fable continues, Jobs (jeans, sandals, long hair, and all) gets taken on at his third attempt by the PR king of Silicon Valley, Regis McKenna; McKenna introduces a venture capitalist, Don

Valentine; and Valentine introduces Mike Markkula, a marketing man whose credentials include experience with Intel and Fairchild Semiconductor and (possibly even more important) a small personal fortune, some of which he invests in the fledgling company, becoming equal partner and president. As one writer put it, the partners 'also did some market research and found that they had invented the personal computer'.

After that epochal discovery, the first Apple II is shipped in 1977; sales hit $774,000; four years on, sales have multiplied 432 times. The story is the stuff of which myths are made – and, in essence, the facts are quite correct. Apple did begin with what looked like (to quote another author) 'a couple of zany computer freaks building computers in a California garage to the blare of pop music'. But from an early date Jobs had the backing of two venture-capital firms (one of them Rockefeller-owned); of Art Rock, who sat on the Intel board; and of Henry Singleton, Chairman of the highly successful Teledyne conglomerate.

With that kind of backing, Jobs was able to capitalize on the critical invention, by another young genius, of VisiCalc, the financial software program available only on Apple II, which converted the latter from a domestic computer to a business machine – a development never envisaged in the original plans. True, with all this high professionalism going on, Jobs could still be highly eccentric. He resolved one stuck meeting by saying that if somebody didn't produce a decent name for the company in the next five minutes, it would be named after the apple he was eating.

The method may have been bizarre. But once McKenna had got brilliantly to work on the logo and the publicity, the name helped to position Apple perfectly as the friendly, lovable computer – an image that has been sedulously fostered by the technology and the marketing throughout a life story that owed far more to professional skills than to the revolution that's been styled 'Computer Lib' – and that needed far more of them as the revolution took its next turn.

## Mobilizing the mobile

The only parallel in history to the silicon chip is the internal-combustion engine. The explosion of entrepreneurs, of which Steve Jobs was the most conspicuous product, was prefigured by the rush of inventors as the Age of the Auto dawned. Just like that forerunner, the computer era is mutating fast as inventors run up against the hard rocks of business economics.

Thus Silicon Valley began with firms falling over each other in the pursuit of the better microcircuit. But as prices tumbled, and demand soared, the game became one in which only large companies could survive (and then not always with ease). The action has therefore moved on to products, led by personal computers – but here, too, the shake-out has started for exactly the same reasons that reduced Detroit from scads of competitors to only three. As the mass markets develop, the race goes to the business creators, not to the technological wizards.

But the difference is that the technology is developing so fast that new product fields (like video games or teleconferencing) are continually opening up. As the business opportunities proliferate, so do the career openings. The new manager has become highly mobile from an early age (Jobs, remember, was only twenty-one when he got going). It's not a question of how to keep them down on the ranch once they have seen Paree – it's how to keep them once they have seen the lure of a million bucks, or perhaps made it. Apple's 1980 public offering created 100 millionaires at one blow.

Plainly, one result has been to make the most successful electronic entrepreneurs into very special man-managers, able to handle their own kind. As Simon Caulkin wrote:

> Not surprisingly, the Valley's employment package is the most carefully thought out in the world. Extremely high pay ($36,000 for a fresh-minted Ph.D. at Intel) goes without saying. But other typical elements include preferential access to a company's own products (Apple); an eighteen-hour course, part of it taught by the chief executive, in 'company culture' (Intel); sabbaticals (Rolm); Friday afternoon swimming-pool parties

(Tandem); a variety of carnival gimmicks from free dentistry to company raffles (at AMD one winner picked up $240,000 last year); and high informality (general).

But more important ultimately than these, more important even than the 'golden handcuffs' (the stock options that create those millionaires), is the changed emphasis in management – or, to put it another way, the increased stress. First, high performance alone has value; a high level of mediocrity isn't good enough in an industry where the challenges come so thick and fast. Second, that performance is certain to be firmly based on technology, on what is still called, though engines have precious little to do with it, 'engineering'.

Like the automobile era before it, led by engineers such as the first Henry Ford and Charles Kettering, the silicon century has elevated the engineer into the driving seat. The financier has his function still, and a vital one, but it is probably exercised outside the company, following principles that have no echo in the time-honoured canyons of Wall Street. To quote Apple-backer Don Valentine of Sequoia Capital Fund, 'We're operating in areas of phenomenal ignorance. We're looking at businesses which two weeks ago didn't exist and about whose technology we haven't a clue.'

Valentine's previous career was in marketing, with Fairchild and National Semiconductor, which rubs in another point. The boundaries between disciplines have become fluid. The engineers who last the course to found lasting companies are those who build in the marketing, financial, and other skills required, either by self-development or by import – as Jobs did, first with Markkula and then with a new president, John Sculley, whose battle honours had been won mostly in marketing Pepsi (and whose fight for Apple's future ended in the ousting of Jobs – the man who recruited him).

So the game is played with high technology, but it is won ultimately by marketing. The dialogue between the engineers and the marketers had to be continuous in a way that the formal rigidities of the classic corporation notoriously discouraged. The informal, open structure of the West Coast company, which mimics and maybe derives from California culture, isn't just the natural way to run companies in the information industry – it's the only way.

All the trends in management have been moving inexorably in this direction. High technology merely accentuates the trend. That's why a successful Japanese high-tech company like Canon, different in every external respect, works in ways so strikingly similar to an Apple. The Japanese tradition of collective, expert professional management fits beautifully into the necessities of matching wholly new products to new and rapidly evolving markets.

The description makes it appear as if success is inevitable. The reverse is true. At the end of 1981 there were perhaps a hundred firms making personal computers. Very few had significant sales by 1987. This high rate of failure has been a fact of Silicon Valley for a long time. Venture capitalist Valentine has got well used to that fact, and doesn't mind: 'The trouble with the first-time entrepreneur is that he doesn't know what he doesn't know. After a failure, he *does* know what he doesn't know and can beat hell out of the people who have still to learn.' That's number six of the nine attributes of management. In the high-pressure world of high-tech business, all nine attributes are needed as nowhere else – and to the power of $n$.

## The stars that stumbled

The proof that management has changed can be found without any effort by pondering three of the most formidable names in new industry: Xerox, Hewlett-Packard, and Digital Equipment. All three have in common phenomenal growth records and the achievement of an imposing worldwide scale. In 1982, Xerox had $8.5 billion of sales – more than General Foods, PepsiCo, or 3M. Hewlett-Packard had $4 billion – more than Burroughs or Bendix, and DEC wasn't far behind.

Yet all three had something else in common: the need, after relatively short corporate lives, for a drastic rethink led by new men. At Xerox, clobbered by Japanese competition in large tracts of the copier market, the future clearly lies in office products, once headed by what *Fortune* magazine called 'one of the most unlikely people ever to work at Xerox'. For a start, the unlikely thirty-eight-year-old Donald Massaro was a multimillionaire, thanks to the price Xerox paid for his flexible-disk memory company.

Whether or not Massaro is 'a bull in the china shop' who is 'crazy, and . . . won't take no for an answer', one thing is certain. He didn't operate as Xerox used to when developing advanced products. As an insider told one of those involved, 'You'll know when you have a development programme for a real product. One day, you'll dig a bottomless pit out front. Come sun-up, the trailer trucks will start arriving with dollar bills and dumping them in. Your biggest problem will be traffic control.' The system seems to have worked well in copiers and duplicators: 'Buᵗ in developing office systems – which change constantly and have much shorter life cycles – the company drowned us in cash and the controls that come with cash. Xerox put all its eggs in one basket, which got so expensive we couldn't afford to take risks or move quickly.'

Massaro, typically for the new breed of entrepreneur, changed all that. He got independence for his division, rebuilt it entirely, settled a long-running and harmful dispute about whether to develop evolutionary products or go for something completely different, heavily intensified the sales effort – and turned an annual $50 million loss into a $5 million quarterly profit. With products like its latest electronic typewriters and its desktop workstation, Massaro's operation won the chance to cut a swath, not just through the market, but the whole method of operation and management in the Xerox Corporation. (Massaro, typically, broke away after a while to do his own thing again.)

Over at Hewlett-Packard, the new man, John Young, is a less conspicuous break with the past in personal terms. In his fifties, Young filled an age niche that was opened less by HP's failures than by the age of its brilliant founders, David Packard and William R. Hewlett, now both in their seventies. One measure of HP's need for a new management approach is that two of the most successful new firms in IT are partial breakaways; both Tandem and Apple had ex-HP founders.

Young's problem is not only to keep talent within the corporation, but to get out from under the competition in hot lines, like personal computers, where the conservatism of the two founders, the organizational overlaps within HP itself, and the lack of marketing orientation in the company had held back its progress. The paradox is that HP is the cynosure of high-tech companies, the one whose style has been most imitated up and down Silicon Valley. What Young is trying to do, as reported in *Business Week*, is preserve that HP style (the 'highly motivational' form of a small-division company made up of 'organizations that people can run like a small business') while making these small divisions move, and thus move the whole corporation, in vigorous step.

The only difference between the problem faced at HP and the upheaval at DEC is that the new man at the latter is the Old Man, founder Ken Olsen. Having previously handed over day-to-day operations, the fifty-seven-year-old Olsen had to move back to mastermind the recovery from an actual fall in net income, a previously unheard-of event at DEC. Like HP, the corporation had become a partial victim of its own success. Its scientific and engineering triumphs in minicomputers resulted in insufficient attention to the booming business market and (equally important) the different marketing approach needed to serve the latter.

The new products that DEC needed to become a convincing supplier in the office-systems market were also inhibited by an out-of-date, bureaucratic organization structure. The governing principle by which Olsen set out to beat the bureaucracy was to dismiss HQ staff and decentralize decision-making to market-based groups. Like Xerox and HP, DEC has the technology, for sure. But like them, it can hope to succeed only by harnessing that technology through radically revamped management – in DEC's case the fourth such shake-up since its foundation in 1957, and one that proved enormously successful. Whether a company is in Palo Alto, California, Rochester, New York, or Maynard, Massachusetts, the situation is the same – high new tech hinges on high new management, and nothing less will do.

## Knowing about knowledge

Was Steven Jobs truly typical of the new management? For a start, Silicon Valley is a California phenomenon, and the West Coast is a law unto itself. In the second place, the age of information technology wasn't born with Apple. It wasn't even born with Jobs in 1955. The new managers have been emerging in greater and greater numbers ever since the computer dawned; while Peter Drucker was writing presciently about the Knowledge Workers fifteen years ago.

You could meet the new managers in Boston in 1970, when Route 128 was the hottest spot in high-tech management. The characteristics of the breed were technical brilliance, verbal fluency, and a strong sense of the future. All those personal attributes translate readily into the pattern of the new management – technology, conceptualization, and vision are the watchwords.

In the first place, the tricks that can be played with technology are boundless, but the technology is tricky itself. As never before, the manager must manage technology. He needs the equipment to make rational choices, in the knowledge that the risks of error have become far greater, while the possibilities of error are also more substantial. You can't make such choices, against such a background, unless you can understand the technology.

That puts a premium on two types of people: the technologically expert person who can explain the consequences of the technology to the inexpert, and the manager, technologist or not, who can grasp the non-technological consequences of scientific advance. In other words, the new manager must be able to form and convey in ordinary language concepts based on the advance in technology. That's where Jobs, the Apple computer, and (still more) the newer Macintosh come in – bringing information technology down from the realms of the incomprehensible specialist into the reach of the competent layman.

Mac needs only a twenty-minute work-out before that layman can master its mysteries, or, rather, its non-mysteries. In this, the new computer represents the next logical advance in this particular technology – that of computing power made available for everyday purposes in small, convenient compass. The drawback of the computer has always been that it won't work in English, that a special breed of linguist was required to speak to the computer in a language it could understand.

The software packages like those that powered Apple's rise (especially VisiCalc) represented one huge step forward into intelligible computing. But the Mac leap into virtual self-management, so that anybody could interact directly with the machine, was the obvious next step. And the obvious truth of the new management is that the next step forward in any product must be taken now – while the first step is still in progress, maybe at its very first moment.

The principle isn't new. In the auto industry, with its four-year lead times, managers have long needed to finalize plans for the next model before launching its predecessor. That became a trap for Detroit, making its managements prisoners of what they were already doing, when the real task was to find out what had to be done – in and for the future. Information-technology managements can afford the luxury of conservatism even less. One after the other, the Seven Dwarfs in the famous old description of the industry (IBM and the Seven Dwarfs) missed the next step – sticking to the main-frame macro business where IBM was beating them hollow, and missing the micro move. It represented the future and one that, technologically speaking, the Dwarfs were well equipped to exploit.

The pace of advance in information technology is so fast that the innovator can bank on only a short time before his innovation is replicated. The same is true of every branch of microelectronics. Sony's Akio Morita has said that, when his company introduced the revolutionary Walkman portable cassette player, it did so in the certain knowledge that competition would appear within six months; thus Sony had to be ready to go with the second stage in a planned programme of updates and new features that would (and did) maintain its supremacy.

The need to think of the present in terms of the future, like the crucial importance of technology, and the basic essential of conceptualization, leaves no room for carelessness. The new breed of manager has to master his markets and his material resources, not just to win, but to have a chance of winning. Above all, he can't escape one single imperative – to THINK.

## The man who thought at IBM

By no coincidence, the theme that Thomas Watson Sr, the true founder of IBM, enjoined on his employees was enshrined in that one word – THINK. Objects bearing the word used to be ubiquitous at IBM. But the outward signs of common culture imposed by Watson have become much less conspicuous in the new age, whose new IBM men are epitomized by the man who took Watson's chair in the personal computer era, John Opel.

By comparison with Jobs of Apple, Opel was the man nobody knew, shy about where he lived, what car he drove (no motorbike here, presumably), what his personal life interests happened to be. But if Jobs is one variation, even one extreme, of the theme of the New Manager, Opel's version is just as legitimate: a self-confessed Corporation Man, one of the IBM-ers who still clung to white shirt, dark suit, and striped tie, the uniform that once, in the days of Tom Watson Sr, was obligatory.

Opel is no technologist, but a business graduate whose first job was selling for IBM in his own home town, Jefferson City, Iowa. There were eighteen more jobs to come. While one involved manufacturing and another a crucial spell in the private office of Tom Watson Jr, there was nothing on the record to indicate or apparently pave the way for his appointment to head up perhaps the most formidable technological powerhouse in the history of the world.

But that's the point. Information technology demands a new style of management – or, rather, a fresh and stronger emphasis on a tried and trusted principle, the Triple D: Divide, Decentralize, and Devolve. Rising up all those rungs on the ladder at IBM, Opel became convinced (just like many Supermanagers today) that centralization was a bad and frustrating form of management. As Opel expressed it to *Time* magazine, 'You have to have people free to act, or they become dependent. They don't have to be told, they have to be allowed.'

The role of the non-technological manager in the new world is thus to enable, to make possible, the release of technological energies. The more complex the range of technologies and possibilities, the more important the Triple D becomes. The Opel-type manager draws on all the strengths of the corporation that made him, and does so by the professionalism that knows its own strengths. 'No matter what I had in my jurisdiction,' Opel told *Time*, 'I typically felt I was more competent to deal with it than anybody else. And that wasn't conceit, it was just simple laws of nature.'

## Making a mammoth mighty

Another simple law or force of nature seemed to be IBM itself. No corporation has ever dominated so vital and profitable a business so comprehensively and for so long. Apart from its own might, the great corporation has spawned uncounted numbers of other companies in information technology as some of its fledglings have fled the nest – people like Gene Amdahl, whose large computers represented one of the few ways in which any main frame competitor has found chinks in IBM's armour.

The sheer strength of that armour-plating can be seen in one staggering statistic. IBM's *profits* in 1982 were roughly the same as the *sales* of the industry's second runner, DEC (a long-time chink exploiter) and four times the expected 1983 sales of Apple, which opened up an even more conspicuous chink by fostering the personal computer. The competition at that point had no more sapped IBM's market strength than the breakaways had weakened its collective executive ability. As those breakaways show, IBM cannot, in an individualistic western culture, and in so hotly competitive an industry, rely absolutely on the lifetime careerism that cements the Japanese company. But IBM does display very similar characteristics to the Japanese, all the same – and by no accident.

The lifetime career is the norm, and during that career IBM-ers are still expected to follow corporate norms of many kinds. True, the compulsory dress of dark suit, white shirt, and striped tie that

Opel favoured had been dropped, and so have other rules, such as teetotalism, favoured by the IBM progenitor, Thomas Watson Sr. While no angel in business ethics during his days with NCR (he was an expert at knocking out cash-register competition with underhand tactics), Watson laid down codes for his employees that added up to a whole corporate morality – and that still stands.

The current 32-page code of business ethics, however, is only one part of a monumental system of values that is the real source of IBM's massive resilience. There's nothing miraculous about this corporate culture any more than there is about Japanese success in world markets. People policies, marketing tenacity, and technological effectiveness are the tripod on which IBM has always rested. Often, the corporation, for all its wealth in financial and technological resources, has not been first into the newest technology or its latest application. It was actually and famously beaten by a mile into the computer age by Univac and into the PC age by Apple. But just like the Japanese, the IBM-ers, once they spot a threat or an opportunity, have so far reacted with a thoroughness and power that few competitors have been able to withstand.

The same reactive power drove IBM through its own worst mistakes, like the launch of the 360 computer series. Typically for IBM, the range didn't advance as far as technology would have allowed – but the step forward was far enough to land IBM in some very untypical messes in production and performance. They were cleared up, though at considerable expense, and no competitor was allowed to benefit from IBM's momentary but monumental lapse.

In moments of need, the corporation can call on those people policies and marketing muscles to pull it through. People are treated like the lifetime employees they will probably be, with high pay and good perquisites, and continual training, excellent communications, and powerful motivational methods, an employment package that has successfully excluded unions from almost all IBM plants. They also have the total job security of a corporation that has never laid off workers, but they don't have job permanence – IBM-ers have been moved at the corporation's will ever since the days of the elder Watson, and they usually start on the sales side, which is the bedrock of IBM.

That same tenacity that Watson applied in the cash-register wars has seen attack after attack repelled by methods fair and maybe less fair – for instance, the alleged announcement by IBM of new machines that never see the light of day, but whose phantom existence spikes the guns of some competitive threat. There's a London department store that boasts about its prices, 'never knowingly undersold'. IBM's famous THINK slogan should have as its companion 'never knowingly outsold' – and it was this sheer selling strength that enabled IBM to breeze past Univac in computers, to override the 360 troubles, and to thunder so successfully into a personal-computer market its management hadn't taken seriously – let alone as a serious threat.

But small computers and other changes in information technology that had by-passed IBM were responsible for the fall in its market share, from 60 per cent to 40 per cent, over the 1970s. In any less rapidly growing industry that would have spelled disaster. In real, inflation-corrected terms, in fact, IBM shareholders got no return on their investment for a decade – and that investment, remember, was in the world's most effective industrial giant. It did seem possible that IBM would go the way of nearly all corporate mammoths – stuck in its own bureaucratic mud: a nightmare that reared its head again as the profits got bogged down in the mid-1980s.

The IBM executive, after all, is the Corporation Man personified: the faceless lifetime employee who may do everything (even dressing) the company way, who doesn't (as the company insists) call on customers in the afternoon if he's had a Martini at lunch. Why has what would be a recipe for disaster in most companies not worked out that way? How was it that the 1970s turned out to be, not the prelude to IBM's comeuppance, but the preface to one of its dynamic patches? The answers tell a great deal, not just about IBM, but about the new management that the new technologies have called into being.

## The IBM-er who got personal

Before July 1980, hardly anybody outside IBM and the world of its watchers had heard of Philip Estridge. He came to rank ahead of Apple's Jobs in the explosive world of personal computers, yet his fame was confined by and large to readers of the magazines, which identified him as the divisional vice-president who led a Boca Raton group of a dozen people to the Personal Computer triumph.

The sentence in itself contains a clue to the success – entrusting the project to a task force, given a clear, single objective (within a year, get ready an Apple-eating model that would be 'user-friendly', in the industry phrase). Because of the short time-scale, the task force not only had to work Trojan 72-hour weeks but go outside IBM for virtually everything in the Personal Computer. The microprocessor (a sixteen-bit item with twice the power of the industry norm) came from Intel – a company in which IBM later bought a 12 per cent stake for $250 million. The software came from a Seattle company, Microsoft, which was one of the earliest into the PC project – and (taking a leaf off Apple's tree) the PC was designed so that anybody else could write software or design equipment that would work with the IBM machine (winning huge initial success at the cost of opening the door to massive sales of cheaper 'clones' in the mid-1980s).

Uncovenanted expansion of its uses as users invented new programs has been a major factor in Apple's astonishing popularity. One member of the huge Apple fan club has apparently programmed his computer to activate a small motor that rocks the crib when his baby has colic. Not the most commercial of uses, perhaps, but a vital ingredient in the marketing mix for the personal computer. By doing likewise, IBM soared to 35 per cent of the US market in 1983 and has given Apple (right down to 24 per cent) a very hard run for its money.

Nor was Estridge the only IBM executive to have been put in charge of small, discrete groups with specific tasks. The Boca Raton team that built the PC was one of seven independent business units set up by John Opel to operate within IBM – but to a large extent under their own steam.

The organizational method was one approach that was expected to prevent false starts like the 1970s launch of an IBM copier against Xerox – mismanaged technically and in marketing terms. With the 'office of the future' attracting competition from every powerful technology-based company East and West, IBM can't afford its new ventures to fare much less well than the PC team – and that exceeded IBM's most optimistic projections by far.

## Managers with four eyes

The new managers who can crack the big corporation code, you could say, have to be four-eyed. They need Independence, Identity, Iconoclasm, and Integrity – and the Personal Computer story at IBM strongly illustrated all four. The PC saga, though, isn't the only one inside this corporation. If it were, that particular IBM story could never have been written.

It's no paradox. Unless the culture of the corporation embraces the existence of task-oriented groups with the authority to shape their means to achieve their ends, the mechanism won't work. Many years before anybody dreamed of a personal computer, the great chemical company, Du Pont, tried setting up venture-based groups within a corporation whose culture was constructed entirely differently, built massively around the central fortress in Wilmington, Delaware. If Du Pont's groups achieved any wonders, they have been hidden from public sight. The truth at that time was that, although Du Pont prided itself on decentralization, every executive who mattered was in that one building, cheek by jowl with the top management which dominated the company.

IBM's centralization may have irritated and frustrated younger and newer managers like John Opel. But its structure was heavily influenced, not just by the huge disparity between markets like mainframe computers and typewriters, but by a geographical spread surpassed only by Coke. Because of the ardent nationalistic feelings aroused by computers, quite apart from practical considerations of control and closeness to markets, IBM has been forced to locate plants and research facilities overseas, to appoint and promote foreign nationals to run its overseas empire at a short arm's length from the US centre in Armonk, New York.

Just as the Japanese are now building plants abroad in an effort to blunt trade retaliation, so the IBM-ers for decades have adapted their policies to head off attacks on IBM – and very successfully. In most of its geographical markets, IBM won positions ranging from supremacy to near-monopoly. As evidence of its strategic success, it even got a strong market position (number two to Fujitsu, but struggling hard to regain its strength) in Japan – something few western manufacturers, in low or high technology, have contrived to achieve.

The political pressures have forced IBM in a direction the new management demands and that the corporation might well have followed, anyway – but maybe later, possibly even too late for its own good. These days, with talent in such terrific demand everywhere, companies need to hire it wherever they can find it, and whatever language it speaks. Also, local companies should be built around local markets, which they won't serve well unless they have those four-eyed managers.

*Independence*, the first of the qualities required, isn't just something you give a manager, though. It's something he has to earn. The stand-alone command of the resources required for a task is worthless if it's entrusted to the unfit. IBM units abroad don't get assigned new production tasks (significantly, 'missions' in IBM language) because of their managers' blue eyes, but as reward for their success in fulfilling earlier missions. Putting it round the other way, though, you won't get high-performing managers to perform at their peak unless they have not only independence, but the feeling of independence.

That implies *Identity* – not only a clear identification of the unit and the responsibilities of a clearly recognized boss, but also a clear aim, a practicable objective expressed in unambiguous terms, with a precise time-scale and budgetary framework. The big corporation HQ customarily not only interferes with sub-operations, thus undermining their essential independence, but surrounds them and their objectives with fuzziness.

For instance, new ventures are often budgeted on the same basis and in the same reporting framework as existing business. That's rubbish. In this way, the corporation loses clarity and blurs relationships between time and money (because the venture won't fit into the time-scale of the usual quarterly reporting periods); the mistake also distracts attention from what the spending and the work are meant to be achieving – a strong and viable new business for the future.

Of course, deviations of this kind cause heart attacks in some financial vice-presidents' offices. That's exactly where *Iconoclasm* comes in. The new management is totally uninterested in how the corporation customarily does things. It has the Independence, remember, to go after the Identified objective in whatever way is deemed necessary – even if that fractures the corporate norms. If the Boca Raton group had not broken with IBM's traditions, going outside the company across the board for the Personal Computer, the development could not have been completed within so short a time-scale; and IBM, late into the market already by years, might have been fatally delayed. It also might have had a product with more glitches; the PC had only a handful, none of them serious.

But how can a corporation retain its cohesion when executives are free to fly off in their own directions? That's where *Integrity*, the fourth I, comes in. Whatever the corporation does, and whatever is done in its name, must reinforce the corporate image and strengthen its hand. Down the years, that's always been one of IBM's great strengths. The company's name has become one of the most powerful brands in history, probably the most powerful of all – so strong that customers felt safer with an IBM product than with a perfectly good, maybe better, offering from a competitor.

Visually and commercially, the image must be kept whole – and there has to be a binding commitment. Old Tom Watson, with his hatred of losing a customer, set the theme, which evolved easily into the computer era – solving customers' problems. That was the magic ingredient that powered IBM past Univac at the dawn of the computer. The corporation's sales team and engineers brought the intimidating new machine into the ordinary lives of customer firms, making IBM one of the rare giants that have not slipped grievously when new technology (the computer replacing the punched-card machine in this case) breaks the market.

Apparently, the younger Watson was the catalyst in persuading his conservative father to plump for the newfangled contraptions. In doing so, he demonstrated the force of what should be the fifth I – *Intelligence*.

## The four-headed giant

Intelligence has many meanings, all of which are crucial to the new management. In any field where technology is moving fast, which means almost every field, the Supermanager needs to know what's happening and how to apply this knowledge – intelligently. What the information-technology companies have done instinctively the others have had to adopt with conscious intelligence – witness the case of 3M and Lewis Lehr.

The conglomerate Lehr heads has one of the outstanding records in US business – it's one of the stars chosen by Peters and Waterman as an exemplar of success. Based on coated materials (like Scotch tape), 3M has been an apparent model of innovative success. It boasts that a quarter of current sales comes from products that didn't exist five years ago. Great stuff – although it means, of course, that three-quarters of sales come from products that are *over* five years old, in many cases much older.

Lehr, in fact, came to feel strongly that 3M had spent too much of its time on just modifying products and had missed its chances – outstandingly so in the case of information technology, where 3M could and should have carved out strong positions in computers and telecommunications. For the 1980s that not only isn't good enough – it's potentially very dangerous. So in 1981 the 3M Goliath was restructured by Lehr. He set up four business sectors, each built around a coherent core of technologies selected from the eighty-five distinctive ones within 3M's competence.

The four sectors are graphics, life sciences, electronics, and industrial and consumer goods, with a research laboratory for each, and at the centre a 3M lab for basic research. Note that the principle of decentralization, a 3M article of faith since way back, hasn't been slung out of the window. The divisions retain their own labs, which are now held responsible for applied science in the product development and refinement cycle. In other words, the modifications and updatings of the products 3M already has, which are legion, are now clearly separate from the big issues of technology management: what technological leads to follow for the future; how to mesh together the resources 3M has and will develop; how to cross-fertilize technology between different parts of the business.

The corporation had a 'technology tsar' (a newly popular type of appointment in US industry), Dr Robert M. Adams. He explained to John Thackray that in the past 3M had grown by a process akin to spreading pancake batter. The big disadvantage of that, in the Age of Competition, is that each segment at the rim of the batter sees only a parochial and fragmented view of technology and the future. Adams claimed that, two years later, he was already getting faster technological responses to market needs, and more technology transfers.

3M's bosses know that it's going to need all the responses and transfers it can develop. 'We feel', says Adams, 'that technological productivity may be the last frontier for productivity enhancement.' Getting it, however, will be tough: 'Other types of productivity problems are easy by comparison.' Not getting it, however, will be tougher still. Those that stick with the batter process will simply get battered. Those that don't, win.

## Doing what comes naturally

There's a basic contradiction between the need of the big corporation to get dynamic, technology-based, entrepreneurial management and the fact that, simply, it is a big corporation. What's shown up in gross form by the failures of Exxon in diversifying out of its base business into information technology is the same syndrome that prevents giants, even in IT, from realizing their full technological and business potential. The centre gets in the way of its parts – so that a Hewlett-Packard, for example, doesn't respond to the desire of a Stephen Wozniak to build personal computers.

How many other potential Apples have been lost, not just to big corporations, but to the American economy, nobody knows. Nor is it clear that the appointment of technology tsars like 3M's Robert Adams will solve the problem in itself. That's another piece of corporate centralism, which can work, if it works at all, only at the periphery, where the individual businesses of which all corporations consist must battle against the competition and cope with the onrush of change.

The problem used to be much less severe before technology changed in nature. The gestation period (four years) and life-cycle (seven years in its first version alone) that were typical of an automobile and its engine (and still are) are luxuries of the past in many industries. Canon took only two and a half years from scratch to develop its personal copier. Japanese manufacturers can take as little as fourteen months to bring out a new machine tool. Fall behind the pace of innovation and you may never recover your position – not just in products but in a whole crucial technology.

As an earlier chapter has pointed out, RCA, which was the Big Daddy of the vacuum tube, is nowhere worth mentioning in modern semiconductors. Nor are any other tube-makers. As for the germanium-based semiconductors that killed off the tube, where are leading makers like Hughes and Transitron in the silicon devices that formed the next and current wave of change? They, too, have been left behind – and note that the gap couldn't be closed, even though managements must have known it was there. For example, nobody in electronics could have failed to spot the signal importance of developments in solid-state physics.

Yet a great technology-based company like General Electric stayed out of the semiconductor game – apparently, notes Harvard Business School professor Robert Hayes, because change was too hectic.

> When things did settle down a little in semiconductors, they found that those companies that had gone through all the thrashing around, pursuing false leads and so on, somehow had the technological base that enabled them to move ahead much more rapidly than the companies that didn't get involved. And the technological base could not be bought. So now General Electric finds itself fifteen years later buying a semiconductor house because it lacks semiconductor experience . . . The companies that wait for others to do all the work and then expect to

be in a position to be able to choose the right technology, much less be able to implement it once it's chosen, are fooling themselves.

For companies with more vulnerable market positions and less financial might than GE (which means nearly everybody), a completely different approach is needed – as exemplified by Gould Inc. and its brave (but ultimately failed) effort to transmute itself into a profitable high-tech company. According to David Simpson, Gould's British-born president,

> Not too many years ago we were building test instruments that were completely stand-alone, function-dedicated products. If you wanted a different job done, you designed a new machine. Today you find with oscilloscopes, and in other types of instruments, too, that you're really playing with the software to reconfigure the instrument's functions. Now, this software normally resides in read-only memories (ROMs). So then you come to the realization that you need ROM capabilities to exploit this trend. That's how we decided to develop a stranglehold on our own silicon technology.

The problem is that you may need simply too many stranglements – too many technologies may be relevant even with single product lines. Even companies as powerful and successful as the new Japanese high-tech stars have to come to terms with this reality. At Canon, for example, management knows full well that technology will power the future of the corporation, that it is the key to the future, as it was to the past. Optics and precision mechanics underpinned the growth of the 1950s. These two remained in the 1960s, to be joined by electronics, physics, and chemistry (the last needed for the copier business). In the 1970s, the classifications became broader: software, system technology, components, materials, communication. And in the 1980s . . . ?

The company's President, Ryuzaburo Kaku, has no doubt of the dimensions of the answer. He plans to develop 'at least ten very unique technologies – unique to Canon'. The technological drive covers not only products, but also processes. Canon's predilection for building its own machines leaps out from any of its factories, and its plans include major ambitions in equipment for manufacturing microcircuits. However, Kaku is well aware that the developing, acutely competitive world market is akin to feudal Japan, in which the boundaries were continually changing. His conclusion is that 'we must make our own power, but have a good diplomatic relationship' – which means that Canon will use its own technological successes as the bargaining counterweight in arranging exchanges of technology.

'Even today we have this kind of relationship,' he says, making it clear that, without partnership, 'we cannot survive'. Nor can that survival (which in Japanese terms means success) be achieved without a huge increase in planned spending on R. and D. Spending in the rest of the 1980s will at least double not only Canon's own existing level but also the going rate of competitors in office machinery and computers. Nor is there any lack of clarity about what the expenditure on R. and D. and on capital investment (another 10 per cent of sales) will produce.

The key word now is not products but systems – automation for the home, the factory, and the office, with Canon's stand-alone products serving as building blocks for these future systems. Kaku's thinking is that changes in technology provide the opportunity for outsiders to burst into markets – as Canon did in both calculators (only to suffer later in ruinous price-cutting wars) and typewriters, when electrics gave way to the electronic ones where Canon now competes. He is not interested in markets where there's 'no chance for us to win – when technology changes, that's the time when we can win'.

A case in current point is the camera side. The conventional equipment is the only mature product range in a portfolio that is otherwise on a series of growing curves. The business has been split into two: conventional and electronic imaging, where the obvious contender is Sony, which knew full well from the start that it couldn't bring its all-electronic, filmless camera to market without eliciting a strong response from Canon. The latter is working on technology that will enable six to seven hours' play on an ultracompact cassette, and when that becomes reality, Canon 'will enter very aggressively', with major impact, not just on photography, but on the whole video market.

The pattern is clear. The new managers have to manage their technology intensively, which means that it may not be theirs, but begged, borrowed, bought (preferably not stolen). 'Not Invented Here' has evidently gone out of the window when even the mighty IBM, with its twenty-nine laboratories and $3 billion of spending, and with far-out technologies across the whole spectrum of electronics, turns to outside suppliers for a personal computer. But the equally pernicious 'Invented Here But Not Used' has to be discarded, too – and there's no point in denying that technology transfer, within big corporations and between them, is among the most difficult arts of corporate management.

Or perhaps the truth is that corporate management makes it difficult. When Steven Jobs and his software supremo, John Couch, saw Smalltalk, a revolutionary program devised at PARC (the Xerox Palo Alto Research Center), it was love at first sight. The most striking feature was a hand-held control (the 'mouse') instead of just a keyboard. Jobs hired one of Smalltalk's top developers, and used the Xerox technology in the product revolution ushered in by Macintosh.

If you think about it, nothing is more natural than seeing what you want and using it; and nothing more unnatural than refusing to look, or seeing what you need and refusing to use it. Yet companies do that again and again, including some of the mightiest names of all. The tyre companies unanimously, and with catastrophic results, tried to avoid following Michelin down the obviously better route of the steel radial tyre. When NCR fell drastically behind the competition after the electronic cash register became technically possible, even after the supreme effort of corporate will at the Dayton head office had forced NCR back into the game, it still couldn't regain all its old supremacy in the market place.

What the new management boils down to is doing what comes naturally. In fairness, in the old days, the natural tendency to defend and build on the established technology in the firm probably made sense. A company like 3M could stick to the technologies of coating and bonding, a firm like Canon to optics, precision mechanics, and their derivatives. But the logical roads that lead to information technology, which come from many directions, are taking managements a long, long way from their bases. They will never complete the journey successfully unless they're prepared to decentralize decisions, to change anything and everything if necessary, and to be proud only of their results.

## The climb up Canon's Mount Fuji

The paradox is that all these themes of the new Super-manager are echoed and emphasized, not just among the hot-rod kids of Silicon Valley, but in the most tradition-dominated industrial society of them all – Japan. A typical example is Ryuzaburo Kaku, the President of Canon. The fact that he has spent most of his career in what seem to be head-office finance jobs looks like another western similarity; finance has long been a popular, common route to the top in the US and Britain.

But the resemblance is only skin-deep; corporate accountancy to the Japanese, and in Japanese, means more nearly 'controlling managers'. Kaku's career is that of a businessman and manager, although he did start in cost accountancy, counting sales slips on an abacus. Bored beyond distraction, it is said, Kaku got the idea of seeing just how quickly he could get through this tiresome task, and discovered that finding ways of increasing efficiency made the boring not only better, but fascinating.

That was the start of a central conviction that 'nothing is ever 100 per cent', that efficiency must be increased – not only for its own sake, but for the knock-on effects on morale, dedication, and corporate capability. The conviction led Kaku from early in his career to suggest a profit centre organization to recalcitrant superiors. They finally gave in, under the 1975 'embarrassment' of losing money and suspending the dividend; and the victory in this argument was presumably decisive in Kaku's elevation, on his predecessor's death, to his present job.

He makes no bones about his own performance in that role. Kaku is fifty-seven, short by western standards, a practised talker with touches of vivid humour, who smokes, blinks, and gestures as he expounds and expands on the Canon themes. He conveys a clear sense of the power he unquestionably wields: 'In Japanese companies the president has the utmost or dominant power.' There's no supervisory board of directors or individual shareholder breathing down his neck; he can even fix his own salary. As Kaku says, 'Unless you are a man with good self-control, you tend to be a tyrant-type boss.'

That Kaku is not. Objecting to the pure, naked capitalist with no corporate idealism, he says, 'In that sense, I'm not a capitalist, nor a tyrant.' In fact, the major change he made to correct the harsh fact that 'Canon was a company with very poor management' was to decentralize power – to give authority to the product group heads. Their groups now operate as self-contained companies, with their own balance sheets, own R. and D., own borrowings (from the core company), and own factories. The latter embody another Kaku reform. Before that, plants made a mix of unrelated products.

Throughout the company, the reform consisted fundamentally of pushing responsibility down the line, concentrating on strategic target-setting at the top, and leaving it to the lower levels to decide details of strategy and tactics, which feed back from the bottom for top approval. In other words, Canon operates the now standard American recipe for good organizational practice, but with far from standard success. Since 1975 sales have expanded by 385 per cent and net profits by 1,233 per cent, while the dividend is 158 per cent higher than it was before the 1975 suspension.

The main purpose was to add to Canon's existing strengths (high-precision products and excellent personnel relations) two more: higher productivity (easy for a Westerner to understand) and an expansion of Canon's management philosophy (not so easy). Kaku's 'premier company concept', though, is as real and important to him as the economic analysis of Canon's profit performance. That shows, going right back to 1950, how each major new product resulted in an upward burst in profits. 'Ever since I worked in Canon, I saw this point. But the voice of the low man on the totem pole cannot be heard by the man at the top.' After the 'tragedy' of 1975 had propelled Kaku to the top, however, he achieved a most remarkable demonstration of the strength of his ideas.

The quintupling of sales and thirteenfold rise in net profits since then surely prove Kaku's point. The major innovations since 1973 have totalled seven – as many as in the previous twenty-three years. Kaku has reached his target ('a climb to the top of Mount Fuji') of making Canon a 'premier' Japanese company in every respect – social, technological, and economic: 'This is what I have done in the past.'

For the future, he has started on a five-year second phase to achieve 'premier' status on the world scene, 'to get to the top of Mount Everest'. Since that means, as noted, raising the proportion of R. and D. spending to sales to some 10 per cent against 4 per cent in 1982, Kaku was ready to accept that for those five years profits would be 'more or less flat'. After this comes the third phase, for which he was 'dreaming that we can attain a similar growth rate' to the profits explosion of 1975–82.

Leaving aside (although you really shouldn't in Japan) the philosophical content and context of Kaku's extraordinary record, its elements are those that dominate the new management: setting a clear, strong overall corporate target; breaking that down into specific goals for specific businesses built around their markets; marshalling the resources of the firm (technological, design, financial, human, production) in support of the drive for the goals and the markets; animating the whole enterprise by a careful labour-relations policy designed to maximize the motivational power of the overall strategy.

It's one thing to have a recipe, though – quite another to cook the dish. The quiet power and total confidence radiated by Kaku ('there is no limit to Canon') almost conceals the fact that to fulfil 'the duty imposed on us', which 'is to live for ever as a going concern', he took a high-risk route up Mount Fuji. The continuing risks are certainly no lower, as Kaku perhaps acknowledges when he says, 'Maybe when you come back here in five years' time, Canon will be bankrupt. But I shan't be sitting here.' One of his little jokes.

## Mastering American management

The ascent of those mountains by the premier Japanese companies, both in the older industries and in the new technologies, has been so rapid that many Americans have attributed it to magic – or machination. But there's no secret, no magic, no mystery – only the repetition, in Asia, of a process that astonished the world a long time ago – in the United States.

Relentless innovation, ceaseless invasion of world markets, steeply rising productivity, domination of new industries, seemingly unbeatable market power, apparently infinite management superiority – all these were characteristic of America, or the attitude of others to America, until the Eisenhower era. The Japanese are emulating the American take-off, and over a much longer time-scale than it appears. The amazing growth of a company like Canon, from world nonentity to international sales of $2.5 billion, may seem a typical product of the gee-whiz 1970s. The true parallel is the expansion of an American firm of Polaroid's generation; Canon covers much the same time span as Polaroid, but with vastly greater latterday success.

The American company's sales got stuck at around $1.3 billion precisely because Polaroid did not, like Canon and other Japanese firms in older, maturing technologies, make a successful break into business machines, or find some other entry point into the new world of information technology. The Polaroid people, in the wake of Dr Edwin Land's departure, are trying to pick up where that Supermanager left off, finding computer-industry applications for their know-how. But they won't succeed in the new management unless they emulate the Japanese – and that means mastering not oriental mysteries but American management at its very best.

Japan's success stems from western-style objectives achieved predominantly by using and developing western methods. It may be more comforting for those who could have done likewise, but didn't, to blame their failure on irrelevancies like MITI, national culture, Japan Inc., bank money, protection, the cheap yen, dumping, etc., etc. The reality is far more uncomfortable. The best Japanese have just managed the new industries more efficiently – much more.

The tables have been turned only where companies have let them be turned. Take Xerox. That there should be one Japanese copier firm is remarkable enough, given the original patent-protected power of Xerox. That there are several is again evidence not just of competitive drive but of a competitive courage that is either lacking in the West or, if it does exist, often lacks the same intelligent strategic effort.

James Abegglen, of the Boston Consulting Group, a thirty-year veteran of the Japanese internecine wars, recalls warning the chief executive of Xerox that it was worth giving away the 914 copier in Japan, keeping the major profit, which comes from the consumables (paper, etc.), and keeping out the Japanese, who would otherwise go for the soft underbelly of the giant. The Xerox boss laughed; his successors are doing so on the other side of their faces. At Canon, Kaku now reckons to be ahead of Xerox in 'one-year placements' of copiers and says, ominously enough for the Rochester, New York, giant that 'we now have very unique technologies coming' – the age of the laser copier, for example, is about to dawn. Invented here or not invented here, Canon is determined to have the technology to meet its aims – 'as a final stage, to be number one'.

That is the starting point for the new management. Everybody can't be first, but those who don't try to win, and do all that is necessary for victory, will lose. In Japan, that urge runs right through the corporation, from top to bottom. 'Let's upgrade our ability to meet more challenging targets,' declares the challenging notice outside Canon's factory in Fukushima. Every identity card on every worker, from plant manager to guide, bears the initials ZD. It stands for 'zero defects'. Again, the temptation is to see this motivational zest as peculiarly Japanese, but it's the same rah-rah enthusiasm that used to offend European intellectuals as an expression of crude American materialism – and 'zero defects' is, of course, an American management technique, first introduced in California.

Wherever you go in a star Japanese company in information technology or any new industry, the same striking fact leaps out – America was there before. But while the best Americans still practise the technique to near-perfection, most Americans have forgotten what they're supposed to be doing, and the Japanese have improved on what they have learnt. Take quality. 'Quality improvement will bring about lower cost of production,' says one plant manager, echoing the pure doctrine of Frederick W. Deming, the American guru of statistical quality control. The Japanese have developed Deming's concept of his statistics to form production systems so rigorous that end-of-process defects are hardly worth enumerating.

Much the same is true even of management style. For all the hierarchy in Japanese companies, and for all the dominance of the president, the apparent behaviour of Japanese high-tech managers bears most resemblance to the democratic, horizontal, participatory style that is now the favoured managerial mode in the West. It's hardly surprising – for group loyalty and group working are, of course, the Japanese norm. Not only does the lifetime career mean that every manager, having worked from the bottom to the top, knows everything (and everyone) on the same gamut. But an executive in any capacity – whether he's a scientist or an accountant or a salesman or a personnel man – is expected to be thoroughly familiar with every aspect of the business that his fellow managers are doing, including their experiences out in the market place.

This doesn't mean that the Japanese manager has no personal ambition. True, the competition for power, status, and success inside the Japanese company is concealed both by the layers of deeply innate Japanese politeness (it's a language in which swearing is next to impossible) and by reticence before outsiders. But the competition is still there and, so it is said, fierce. It works, however, through the group and the company. The object is not only for the executive to succeed but for the company to win – and winning means being best, which in turn means largest.

That's no different from the King of the Market philosophy that has long animated western giants – although the best Japanese companies add another western ingredient, the concept of the product life-cycle. Firms like Canon didn't go into copiers, etc., for fun or to acquire 'second or third legs', but because the camera had plainly become a mature product. To stay on a growth track, let alone become a 'world premier' company, the firm had to have growth markets. The law of Japan's commercial jungle is survival.

True survival to a Japanese is success, and the mistake of all too many American giants was not to see (a) that products had reached the maturing stage of the life-cycle and (b) that only very important new markets, in which they could build a unique position, would fill the growth gap. Any American management professor could (and did) tell them so.

Any business historian could also have stressed the umbilical relationship between an end producer and his supplier – think only of the development of in-house supplies by companies such as AT & T or IBM. But the long-term relationships that quality and reliability imply haven't been taken to their logical conclusion – except in Japan. Where a western factory might have four vendors jockeying to supply an identical component, the Japanese have long-term relationships with single suppliers, regarded as part of the family. If that looks like one uniquely national feature, it isn't. The same principle has long been applied by efficient Westerners, who not only specify their requirements in exhaustive detail, but assist the supplier to meet the required standards – and, if need be, invest in that supplier.

IBM is doing just that by buying into Intel – while other investments (like that in Rolm, the private branch exchange, or PABX, company) are designed to strengthen IBM in areas of weakness. In modern conditions, even the strongest company can't be strong at all points – and Japanese companies have not only mastered the necessity of technology changes but, for the same reason, have incorporated the SWOT analysis as one of the bases for American-style corporate planning. That is indispensable in the new industries – not because these are more plannable, but because of their very uncertainties.

Analysing SWOT's (Strengths, Weaknesses, Opportunities and Threats) helps greatly to position the high-tech company as it pushes forward to meet its long-term objectives by following its medium-term, detailed course, allowing for contingencies as it proceeds. The basic procedures were pioneered by US companies like General Electric. But too many of GE's imitators thought the plan, rather than its objectives, was the name of the game. That often trapped them in ill-conceived acquisitions and outmoded technologies. The real object of planning is to achieve the optimum supply, allocation, and application of resources to meet high but realistic targets, which a Canon planner rightly sums up as 'to become rich by healthy growth'.

You won't get that, however, without a healthy relationship between all the people in the company. The adversary relationship between management and workforce that was allowed to grow up inside western companies isn't the natural order of things – it's most unnatural. The IBM approach is no different from that of the Japanese high-tech leaders. In the common labour policies of leading-edge innovators, the critical elements include (1) carefully controlled numbers, (2) good, progressive pay, (3) good jobs, (4) excellent training, (5) promotion by assessed merit, (6) continuous and effective motivation programmes, (7) constant communications, (8) highly accessible management, (9) social equality within the company, (10) growth and constant change in products and processes . . . and so on. Provide all that, and you don't need Japanese culture to get good labour relations and performance.

But none of this means that the Japanese are invincible or invulnerable. By definition, whatever they have done or are doing can be emulated, or has been pioneered, by companies in the US – companies that have many natural advantages over an Asian country with restricted land area and domestic markets. At Canon, for example, President Kaku became convinced that without investing in overseas production and in vastly higher R. and D., 'there is no future for Canon'. The same requirement applies to all industry in the IT era. Existing products, plants, and processes will not be enough without the plans and the planned spending to enhance and reinforce them.

Apart from anything else, the borders between industries are breaking down. Hence the new partnerships between not only IBM and Intel but also L. M. Ericsson (Swedish, telecommunications) and Honeywell (computers), AT & T and Olivetti (Italian, business machines) and Philips (Dutch, electronics). Just as departments within firms must learn to communicate rather than compete, so isolationism is impossible in tomorrow's industries – the manager needs to form partnerships, inside and outside the firm, as never before. The days have gone when one stand-alone product offered a golden key to an unlimited future. The new technologies offer future riches even greater than the phenomenal fortunes already created. But the evidence from Japan's successes, and from the equal triumphs of the best of the West, is that only excellence of all-round, common-sense, imaginative, competitive management will produce the necessary high-flying results.

# 11 *Damn* la différence

from *The Naked Market*

The evolution of business over the whole post-war period can be accurately described in one sentence: the world changed from a seller's market to a buyer's market. No matter what else had happened, this ineluctable trend swept along – and swept many formerly world-leading companies before it. Even in prosperous times, managements found themselves battling for market share against opponents who were more formidable than ever before. The Age of Competition had dawned – and *The Naked Market* proclaimed its coming.

The book began by pointing to a paradox:

> The years since 1973 have been a marvellous economic decade, believe it or not – even though the oil price explosion did end general rapid western economic expansion, perhaps for keeps. The marvel was that the same dismal decade saw the creation of more genuine new companies, more new self-made fortunes and more new revolutionary product successes than any such period in history. In the last quarter of the twentieth century world markets have been split wide open, old-line companies have been torn apart, and new-style entrepreneurs have poured through the openings.

I went on to strike a warning note:

> Partly, the opportunities have been created by the new technologies which have opened up new industrial

avenues, often whole vistas of change and wealth. But even in old markets, where neither microcircuits, nor genetic engineering, nor any other scientific marvel, has worked any wonders (or ever will), new market opportunities have multiplied. Managers who miss those chances will – as many already have – perish on the shore.

The ferocious competition created by differentiated, easy-to-enter and desire-driven markets means that a moment's marketing slumber can easily become the Big Sleep. The market has become naked in many ways; naked, because there's no protection against its forces (even if a government temporarily bails out the feeble, fate always gets them in the end): naked, because changes in management's own world (the job-hopping, the market research explosion, even downright theft) mean that few markets hold any secrets any more – no secrets, that is, that can be kept for long: naked, because most market places are now arenas for naked aggression.

I can't see any of the above losing its force this century. The excerpts here, however, look at an aspect of competition that has worried me from the days of *The Naked Manager*: diversification. Whichever route companies have taken – setting up new businesses from scratch or acquiring them – disasters and disappointments have been all too easy to achieve. The reasons, and the conclusions, have important consequences for management in general and for Wall Street and the City of London in particular.

As *The Naked Investor* pointed out (and a post-1987 sequel would stress *a fortiori*) the impetus behind mergers and acquisition booms is impurely financial – hinging on the excess equity values created in bull markets. That indicates where the ultimate weakness lies: in the lack of marketing logic and effective marketing management behind the acquisition, or the diversification. The grandfather of British marketers, Colonel Lyndall F. Urwick, could have told the dud diversifiers what was wrong – half a century ago.

Anyone can see that a multi-market company is inherently stronger than a single-market one; provided, that is, that the multiple markets are all strong. If the only result of diversification is to lose on the swings what you gain on the roundabouts, that provides stability, true. But the steady state isn't the object of business enterprise – especially in markets where competition cannot be beaten lying down.

Worse still, many companies, great and small, were forced in the late 1970s to recognize that their bold forays into new markets, by product or geography, had produced so much loss on the swings that the profitable roundabouts were revolving to less than no ultimate effect. The resulting wave of retrenchment might lead one to speak of a new spirit being abroad in world business – although in one of the cases of withdrawal, 'abroad' somewhat misses the point. The case is Gulf Oil's retreat from making petrochemicals in Europe. The invasion of the supposedly rich and growing Continent by the US chemical giants was one of the more striking examples of the famed American Challenge of the 1960s – so why was the new spirit abroad taking Gulf, as it were, back home?

A case from a quite different industry provides the answer. In mid-1981 Philip Morris bought a 22 per cent stake in Rothmans International (a $350 million puff) because it was dissatisfied with the results of its own diversification away from cigarettes. That bald announcement should have made any marketing professor swallow his Miller High Life beer down the wrong way – that brand being the key to a saga unsurpassed by any company diversifying into any business.

Using the marketing techniques it had refined with cigarette brands, led by Marlboro, Philip Morris expanded Miller's beer sales by 20 per cent to 30 per cent per annum, elevated it from seventh to second place in the industry, shook up the entire brewing industry from top to bottom by its success, and invented the whole low-calorie beer sector. Triumph could hardly have been more spectacular – so what was the trouble? The Philip Morris complaint was that, like Gulf's chemicals in Europe, the marketing game hadn't been worth the financial candle.

In the previous four years Miller's beer assets had yielded only two percentage points more than one-month Treasury bills. With 30 per cent of the group's total sales, Miller produced only 11 per cent of operating income. At that, it did better than the company's 1978 purchase, Seven Up, which cost $315 million and wasn't making a cent: though even that improves greatly on Gulf's £10 million losses on £300 million of European turnover. Small wonder that Gulf cancelled its £100 million expansion project in Rotterdam, and thus undermined the business of its existing plants in the one-time wonder Euromarket.

The Morris and Gulf cases differ in that Gulf made a basic strategic error (in hindsight), while the impact of Miller on the market must have gone more than according to plan. Seven Up in turn was given the full Miller treatment (sales force trebled, production capacity upped, prices raised, trademark and packaging revamped, massive new advertising). But all such endeavours, like Gulf's in Europe, raise the ante horrendously. Buying markets at the price of negative or inadequate returns in capital never makes any sense.

## What motivates mega-deals

Even mighty purchasers like US Steel, Du Pont and Occidental have ended up, after their billion-dollar oil buys, enmeshed in selling assets to reduce gigantic debts. But was economic motivation actually the force behind the mega-deals? Does that explain, say, the US mergers between Dart and Kraft, or Nabisco and Standard Brands? Dart and Kraft (which sounds like another pair of reindeer for Santa Claus) was formed by merger in the autumn of 1980. Kraft is familiar worldwide for those invincibly processed slices of cheese. But Dart presents a real puzzle for food marketing experts. Who they?

The answer is that they were, among other things, Tupperware and Duracell batteries. Now Tupperware is more likely to contain comestibles than anything else: but you can neither nibble, chew, nor digest a battery. Which only rubs in the point that, these days, a food company is most unlikely to confine itself to the gullet. After all, only £6.7 billion of Unilever's £14.1 billion sales was in human food in 1982 – although this figure still exceeded total sales for the second largest food firm, the virtually all-pure Nestlé.

Once upon a time food was food, and non-food was non-food, and never the twain did meet. But just as non-food companies, like the tobacco firms, had moved into foods (on the simple thesis that people have to eat), so food firms (like Borden, say) had moved into non-foods, because that delicious propensity to eat doesn't seem a good enough guarantee of the corporate future. To quote the *Financial Times*, 'In the mature food markets of the West the overall volume growth for food has become virtually static, which therefore encourages rationalization of processing facilities.'

Glossing over the fact that 'virtually static growth' seems to be a contradiction in terms, the amalgamations of Dart and Kraft, or Nabisco and Standard, can hardly rationalize anything at all, since the product overlaps are few or non-existent. So what did motivate the respective managements to merge? The probability is that running a $5.9 billion Nabisco–Standard combine as Nabisco Brands simply feels more comfortable than living lower down the big leagues: especially shortly after your old enemy, Kraft, has just jumped to the top by kraftily absorbing Dart.

The old line in prize-fighting is 'The bigger they are, the harder they fall.' In Big Food, apparently, the argument is, the bigger they are, the harder it is for them to fall. It's the same argument of stability all over again. In the case of Dart and Kraft, moreover, that's what seems to have been achieved in the decade to 1982. In earnings per share and total return to shareholders, the company was stuck exactly in the middle of *Fortune*'s annual ranking of the 500 largest US industries – and so was the merged Nabisco Brands. Of course, the supposed and expected benefits of the mergers had yet to flow: they never did – what man had put together was, astonishingly, put asunder. As the Dart–Kraft combine was split up, one of the most basic propositions in business was reaffirmed: that managing diversity is a business in itself – and one of the toughest tasks in management.

## The sum of the parts

Anybody who doesn't believe that should harken to these words. 'It is a very dangerous way to build a company – scary, too. It is logical that top management cannot sit in an office and build a company that way.' John H. Bryan Jr, Chairman and Chief Executive of Consolidated Foods, was speaking about his own company, which in 1974, to quote John Thackray in *Management Today*, 'was no less than 125 different businesses, and its $2,500 million-worth of sales all sprang from independent divisional fiefdoms which cared naught for headquarters direction from a scant staff of just 45'.

The divisional bosses were predominantly self-made men who had sold their businesses to Consolidated without relinquishing a shred of personal power. Bryan's family meat-processing business had the same character and origin, but he was subsequently forced to launch a mighty effort to reshape Consolidated into something more akin to Procter & Gamble, a unified corporation expert in making and marketing fast-moving packaged goods; finally renaming Consolidated after one of its major successes, Sara Lee.

This entailed getting rid of something like sixty businesses – in things like toy trains, curtain rods, men's shirts, women's clothing, and furniture. But disappearing unconsidered trifles like these is not the answer to the problems of diversified management. It can build successfully only round 'core' business: divisions that, paradoxically, are strong enough to stand on their own in markets which they dominate and which are worth dominating. Bryan simply didn't have enough of these – so he bought two, one of which, Hanes, is a fully-fashioned illustration of the point.

The business makes women's and men's hosiery and underwear, with $100 million in annual operating profits: half what Bryan paid for the entire company in 1977. The key products are L'eggs tights. Sold from store racks in egg-shaped containers, L'eggs propelled the company into the top position as a mass marketer of hosiery. The packaging, the promotion, and the merchandising (the stockings are sold like paperbacks, with Hanes filling racks at no cost or risk to the retailers) were brilliantly innovative, and rocketed Hanes right away from direct competition with the encroaching cheap private labels. In a trice L'eggs had half the market in supermarkets, drug stores, and discount stores – a market it proceeded to segment carefully into support tights, high-fashion items and heavier-knit winter wear.

Bryan is proud of efforts to achieve similar breakthroughs with Sara Lee (frozen croissants, now, as well as cakes) and the Capri Sun soft-drink-in-a-pouch idea imported from Germany; less proud of the flop of L'eggs-style cosmetics. But the efforts emphasize that paradoxical task of the diversified corporation: it can rise only on the undiversified success of significant units.

Their success, in turn, can be built only by: (1) Product innovation aimed at finding gaps in the market or opening up new market areas; (2) Finding gaps in the distribution system peculiar to their markets, and sending the innovative product into the gaps (Bryan's soft-drink business, for instance, undercuts the market leaders by shipping, not to retail outlets, but direct to retailers' warehouses). In other words, success depends overwhelmingly on skills and strategies that (unlike the principles of the national advertising that must support them) are intrinsic to the parts, not to the corporate whole.

For all Bryan's efforts, Consolidated's six main distinct activities, though now accounting for 93 per cent of sales, could hardly be much further apart without completely destroying any semblance of rationale for the company: frozen bakery products, processed meats, coffee (European mostly), soft drinks, hosiery and door-to-door vacuum cleaners. Bryan complained to Thackray that the same kind of criticism can be levelled at Procter & Gamble – which is in peanut butter, nappies, health-care products, coffee, etc. – or any other big packaged-goods company. So it can: that's why Wall Street has 'a clear view that companies like us have parts which are worth more than the whole corporation . . . which implies that we as managers of a big diversified company bring nothing to the sum of the parts'.

Of course, they do. But can they bring enough? Another of Thackray's interviewees in *Management Today* may well have the answer to the conundrum. 'A manager has got to know an industry intimately; to know and adjust to its mentality – it is amazing the variety of mentalities in different industries. You can't come in from the outside and hope to get that last 5 per cent.' The percentage to which the speaker, Richard M. Ringoen, refers is what results when you squeeze the last ounce of profit from the humdrum activities in which his company, Ball Corporation, earns its remarkable results.

Even Ringoen is 'just amazed at how well we do in some of the mundane businesses we're in. Because of this, we find the managers don't want to leave and go somewhere else in the company. They have their customers. They know the technology. What they want is to stick with it for ever.' The mundane businesses are in dreary, sometimes disaster areas like metal and glass containers, and zinc and plastic fabrication – in most of which Ball doesn't even have significant market shares: nothing like the fifth of the hosiery market won by L'eggs, for instance. It does get up to 15 per cent in glass jars for food: but in the two-piece beer and beverage can market, the figure is only 8–9 per cent. So how does Ball succeed?

First, its market-imbued managers concentrate on carefully selected niches: second, they are obsessed with achieving the lowest possible costs by the highest possible technology. In commodity markets like Ball's, as one analyst remarks, 'Manufacturers can't control prices. So they must control costs. The low-cost producer is the king of this business.' These two principles have carried Ball through recession and industrial shake-ups with far more success than competitors who have sought to diversify heavily away from packaging and containers: American Can into financial services, Continental into gas and oil, Owens–Illinois into hospital management. 'When you talk with most corporate managements, the conventional wisdom you hear is that a company should have a balanced portfolio of investments with countervailing cyclicalities,' says Thomas B. Clark, Director of Corporate Planning. But Ball 'found that it just wasn't true. The probability of being able to do this is minimal.'

In other words, Ball manages what is actually a fair degree of diversity by *not* acting like managers of diversity: another paradox, which Ringoen can explain. He treats all the business lines with an even strategic hand because 'I hate to see companies that allocate priorities and express preferences about their different lines of business and say, "This one is a cash cow, and that one a star."

Theoretically, we could squeeze all the cash out of the glass business and then plough it into high-technology defence areas – meanwhile telling the different management teams different things.' But 'you don't get the best results that way. It could be devastating for the motivation of young guys in glass. We want to treat them all alike, and expect each to do his best.'

What does Ball's centre do? It searches constantly for ways in which the individual businesses can better serve their markets and run themselves. In 1978, for instance, Ball bought a plastic injection moulding plant that was far more profitable than its own troubled business. Why? 'We got the founders, who were two brothers, to sit down and define their principles of operation: something they'd never done.' Among the principles they wrote down were a high level of automation, operating-room cleanliness, no secondary operations, and small productive units. That opened Ringoen's eyes to a principle of his own: make divisional bosses work out their own principles, and stick to them. In beverage containers, for instance, Ball's principles say it will make only 9- and 16-ounce cans, two sizes that together have 80 per cent of the US beverage can market. 'Every month, somewhere in the country somebody comes to our people with an idea for making a different size can – say a 7-ounce can for the wine market – but they know to tell him "no",' according to Ringoen. 'If the divisions manage within those self-imposed constraints they'll be left pretty much alone,' notes Clark.

Follow that kind of approach, and managing and marketing, even with businesses that vary far more widely than Ball's, become far easier and far more effective. The logic of diversification is ultimately the same as that of concentration. Bad businesses obey Gresham's Law and drive out good ones. The multi-form firm really needs to be managed like a product portfolio – in which no product is allowed ascendancy in the top managerial mind, but every product, as at Ball, gets the concentrated attention of the managements who actually have it in their ever-loving care.

# 12 Mergers make strange managers

from *The Naked Market*

You shouldn't always believe what companies say, even if the words have the effect of pillorying them. For instance, Robert Goizueta, promoted in a spectacular personal leap to revitalize Coca-Cola, promptly ran into heavy flak for bottling up Columbia Pictures with a $765 million bid. What, the Wall Street critics wanted to know, did peddling pop have in common with films like *Annie*, Columbia's $40 million musical?

The true answer is nothing at all – except that Old King Coke reckons to know a thing or three about marketing, especially promotion and merchandising, a field in which, by comparison, movie men are babes unborn. At least, that was one of the arguments adduced by Goizueta. But the analogy between promoting people into cinemas and into pop bottles doesn't bear much examination; films are essentially one-offs, and the universal, all but unbeatable, Coke franchise is based on continuity and repetition.

The salient fact, though, is that even Coke is not ultimately unbeatable. The reason why Goizueta, new broom and all, won his promotion was that Pepsi-Cola had been fizzing all too fast for the peace of the royally rich clique of Atlanta businessmen who are Coca-Cola's time-lords. Just like Jacques Bergerac, plucked from ITT by the legendary Charles Revson to run Revlon, the new Coke boss plainly saw that one quick route to financial targets (growing faster than inflation in Coke's case) is to buy that growth.

Funnily enough, Revlon did precisely that in one field, health care, which Goizueta examined and found wanting (maybe rightly, given Revlon's lacklustre later record). Why? Because it involved high technology – and that was one of Goizueta's diversification no-nos, along with high capital investment in plant and inability to grow rapidly without dramatic increase in market share. That last stipulation, obviously enough, would rule out Coke itself. After all those years of massive consumer bombardment, its chances of fast outgrowing the whole soft-drinks market are hardly high. It's a problem that eventually comes to all successful firms, even on far smaller stages: when you and the market have matured, what next? The movie market, of course, is even more aged in the wood than Coke's: the behaviour of audience statistics round the world has been as discouraging as the failure rate of feature films is sobering. Anyway, as Goizueta pointed out in his own defence, Columbia is only a tenth of Coca-Cola's size: which means that it can hardly make a mighty difference to the Atlanta giant's performance.

No: the drinks market was where Goizueta's cause had to be won or lost. The real reason for the Columbia buy was to provide a rich cash flow that would underpin the greatest shake-up the US soft-drinks empire had ever seen: distributor reorganization and executive revivalism went hand-in-hand with an unprecedented flow of new product launches, in which Diet Coke sprang out of nowhere to beat all-comers in its sector: including Coke's own Tab. The purpose of diversification must always be to add strength to the basic business, never to dilute the drink. As Goizueta's new ad slogan rightly said, 'Coke is it!' The basic business always is.

## The perils of purchase

Why Goizueta succeeded is made perfectly clear by why others failed. 'The bottom line in ten big mergers' ran the headline in a 1982 issue of *Fortune* magazine. Good or bad news for the whale-sized corporations which are still so avidly swallowing the smaller fry? Alas, for all the experience that should have been garnered in three decades of unexampled amalgamation, the thumbs still turn down – even though half the cases actually did have better 1981 earnings per share than they would hypothetically have made without their 1971 acquisition.

In four of the cases, the acquiring managements could say, hands on hearts, that the buy and its consequences were genuinely good. But even in two of the four, less encouraging notes are sounded. Drug firm Squibb, which in 1971 couldn't even 'spell out' the wondrous 'growth opportunities' that lay ahead of the Lanvin–Charles of the Ritz cosmetics business (a $206 million buy), admitted, 'We made some mistakes because we didn't understand the business.' Another drug firm, American Cyanamid, also went into cosmetics, with Shulton (for $106 million), and confessed that 'synergy in research took too long to come'. Funnily enough, relative failures said much the same – as in: 'We made our share of mistakes; we took too long to move down the learning curve.'

That was Heublein, the brewers, talking about Kentucky Fried Chicken ($237 million). Then, take a drug-maker treading the same route as Squibb and Cyanamid into cosmetics, etc. – Schering. It found that its 'international people didn't adapt well to consumer products. That synergism took longer than we thought.' Its $644 million purchase of Plough knocked 19 per cent off hypothetical 1981 earnings. Plough was the most expensive of the ten buys – both absolutely and as a percentage of the purchaser's book value (815 per cent no less). But expense, absolute or relative, has no visible correlation with success or failure. Nor does closeness of fit with the acquirer's own business.

Thus drugs and toiletries don't sound impossibly far apart – but only look at Schering. The answer, which is no surprise, lies in management, in the speed and the skill the acquirer applies, or makes sure is applied, in its new market. Even so, the task of managing unfamiliar markets brings no bonanzas. Relating net profits in 1981 dollars to the purchase price in good old 1971 bucks gives yield figures for the four successes ranging from 7 per cent to 13 per cent.

Merely think of what those 1971 purchase prices were really worth in buying power ten years later, and the old lesson is doubled or redoubled. A purchasing company is buying one of the toughest management tasks, as four of the ten proved in the hardest possible way. Three of the businesses they bought in 1971 had been sold, with one more allegedly up for grabs. If you can't manage 'em, sell 'em, is a sensible policy; but it is, of course, an admission of failure. The failures, note, were not failures of the acquired companies, but of the acquiring managements.

That diagnosis is made clear by studying the many large, merged failures formed out of competitors. Post-mortem analysis usually reveals that the union was never properly consummated for years after the parties formally became one. The problem wasn't that of managing diversity (the problem that lays low most major companies that try to buy their way into new markets); rather, the problem is one of managing *tout court* – of imposing the common direction, common controls, and common sense any operation needs.

That explains why multi-millionaire financiers often batten even richer from ventures of baffling diversity without ever leaving their luxurious pads for some lugubrious office. They know what they own, they know what they want, and they know what to do if they don't get it: they shoot the pianist. The businesses stay firmly rooted in their own markets, and the authoritarian drive motivates their managers.

Take the career of Sir Maxwell Joseph. His passing removed a man who, on the record, must have been one of the great originals in marketing. Yet he wasn't a shopkeeper, like the late Sir Jack Cohen of Tesco; he wasn't a caterer, like Lord Forte, and he wasn't a hotelier, milkman, or brewer, either. All the same, he ended up with an extraordinarily varied and rich marketing portfolio – beer, wine and spirits, food, restaurants, cigarettes, milk, retailing, industrial catering, hotels worldwide, etc., all brought (or bought) together amazingly fast.

If there was nothing else to it, Joseph could be discussed as just another conglomerating financier. The hallmark of that breed, however, is often that very inability to exploit the accumulated enterprises which laid *Fortune*'s unlucky acquirers low. But under the Joseph aegis the Eden Vale arm of Express Dairy, for one example, chalked up some notable new products. While few of the Joseph enterprises are famed far and wide for marketing excellence, their worst days and mistakes mostly predated the Master: the Watney's Red beer fiasco, for example, was all Watney's own.

By and large, Grand Metropolitan operations easily survive

critical scrutiny – including that of customers who are over-whelmingly located in the large-scale markets. But how could a man brought up in the wheel-and-deal, fat-cat world of property develop so competent a touch with the consuming masses? One answer is that Joseph, even when confined to a handful of modest West End hotels (as he was so remarkably late as 1969), thought in straight marketing terms. Very early on, for instance, he appointed people to market his hotel rooms, then a rare activity in Britain.

When he broke out of the medium time, too, Joseph bought big: while his deals could generally be justified in property terms, Joseph in fact went for significant consumer franchises, especially serving the richer South of England, and all in the high-cash-flow businesses needed to extract him from the high debt incurred by such costly purchases. Above all, Joseph demonstrated the truth that any marketing business consists of two things: the fixed assets, and the consumer franchise (which is also an asset). Of necessity, Joseph's approach (not to mention his own personality, which included a taste for conspicuously short working weeks) meant decentralized management of businesses that kept their separate market identity – and that is why they worked.

## Conran's happy marriage

That same essential quality – knowing what you want and how to make others get it – explains how Sir Terence Conran overcame the problem of the enormous contrast in style, though not in sector, embodied in the Habitat–Mothercare merger. Happily it wasn't a contrast of personalities, since Mothercare's Selim Zilkha, very wisely, bowed out of the shop door at once. The world of difference lay in the development and nature of the two organizations: one a large, £169.7 million retail chain, set up and built up in deliberate imitation of the Marks & Spencer model; the other a much smaller, specialist business, whose retail outlets seem to have developed from the merchandise.

Where Terence Conran had created his Habitat market as a brilliant taste-maker, Zilkha concentrated on cornering parts of the business already being done by other stores. Where Zilkha could initially draw on the family fortune to finance his early hard climb, Conran fought his way through his own vicissitudes with pluck and a great willingness to learn: it's typical that he agreed to a behind-the-boardroom-door TV programme on Habitat when its fortunes were being heavily battered.

Since those traumatic days Conran has seasoned his expansionism with heavy doses of prudence. Where Mothercare went for the US market in a big way, and earned big losses for its pains, Habitat proceeded step by step, keeping its downside American risks as low as possible – and perhaps (who knows?) sacrificing some upside potential as a result. The Conran strategy has been well judged for the purposes of a group that has evolved into a significant retailer specifically by shunning the mass market. Yet an overwhelming proportion of the merged companies' sales are a long way down from Habitat's original NW1 segment.

There was no immediate evidence from the past that the smaller company's management had either the down-market or the up-management skills that were required. But Conran and Co., by prudently applying what lessons of their past were relevant, and learning some new tricks fast, succeeded in rapidly establishing the combined viability of their disparate chain. Where Mothercare had doubled its turnover since 1978, while net profits had risen by only a fifth, Conran's management elevated the business's performance on all measures with what looked like surprising ease.

Pre-tax profits up by 90 per cent on a turnover rise of just over half gave early, convincing evidence that the new Mothercare was working. The principles were simple: change through consultation, not dictate; refitting all shops with a new colour scheme; uplifting the quality and image of the products. The Conran team drew on its experience both in the Habitat retail operation and as designer for other retailers to do the simple and obvious well and smoothly.

The simple and the obvious are highlighted by a banal, but true, observation from Conran – 'If people are offered well-designed, well-made products at a sensible price, they will like and buy them'; and by another commonplace from John Stephenson, the director who masterminded the Mothercare operation – 'I've been asked when Mothercare will be finished. That's a stupid question: it has to be a continuing process of evaluation and change.' In that process, obvious or not, the £110 million price paid for Mothercare began to seem perfectly reasonable – because of perfectly reasonable management.

In the beginning and the end, the purchase of another business, diversified or complementary, is just another commercial venture, no different from a new factory or new product, in that its justification depends on the planning, the cost, the execution and the results – in that inevitable order. Ignore the market-place realities, allow a gap to emerge and grow between that real-life potential and the actual costs, and you get a disaster – which you richly deserve.

# 13 The discontinuous present

from *The Naked Market*

Do today's corporate essentials represent a break in continuity? Has management in general, and marketing in particular, been changed radically by the brave new markets? According to an article in *Fortune*, the answer is a resounding Yea. It quotes one academic to the effect that 'all of a sudden, industrial products are like Hula Hoops'. Without a doubt, the pace of markets has hotted up to relative frenzy; product life-cycles have shortened by as much as a third; product innovations follow hard on each other's heels; no price structure is safe.

All very true: but more important by far than events is how management reacts to them. In the reactions described by the magazine, the starting point is that everywhere the customer is king. One man at Hewlett-Packard told *Fortune* that 'we'd never heard of' focus groups. But once they had, getting a bunch of computer purchasers to talk proved invaluable – surprise, surprise. Over at Texas Instruments, the example cited is the $660 million collapse in home computers, blamed on inadequate observance of the marketing injunction, Know Your Competitor. When it launched a price war, TI just didn't know that Commodore's costs were decisively lower.

Lesson Three is Know the Man Next Door. You can no longer afford to let design, manufacturing, and marketing operate as separate, sometimes warring factions, especially when it comes to innovation. In a move led by IBM, companies are thus even putting design and manufacture under combined command. Speed is the fourth necessity: speed in development, speed into the market place. You can get it more easily by simply stopping engineers making the big changes they love *after* the initial process of market identification and product design is complete.

Fifth, and obviously vital at a time of fast change, cannibalize, even supersede your own miracle before some other swine does. If necessary, join the other swine – form joint ventures (as AT & T did with Olivetti, say) rather than go it alone, however rich you are in money and technology.

Through all these five points there runs a note of impending, if not onrushing doom, an 'or else' based on the hard facts of rapid corporate disaster in the naked markets. In the light of actual events, nobody could accuse *Fortune* of scaremongering. Indeed, beware of being Mattelled or Warnered is a warning that should be engraved deep on the hearts of the new entrepreneurial companies. Few firms have ever expanded so explosively as Mattel, whose electronic games doubled to $556 million in a single year; and Warner's Atari division multiplied its sales ten times in five years to an incredible $2 billion. Yet both crashed into horrendous losses – and the warning is that the calamities were not beyond control.

Indeed, control is the key word. Rapid growth of highly profitable business (Mattel had $67 million of electronic earnings in 1982–3) customarily covers up a multitude of sins. Though Mattel won its rapid success by leapfrogging Atari, it then failed to upgrade its game player; missed out on video-game cartridges; and came to market with a $150 computer, $50 dearer than the competition. Exit computer. Exit Mattel, back to toys, out of electronics altogether.

Where the toy company failed was in not building up management to control and match the explosive electronic growth. At Atari, lack of control showed most conspicuously as disorganization: a dozen separate uncoordinated divisions, according to *Time* magazine, with forty-nine scattered buildings, five finance departments, terrible overlaps, no pay structure, too many products, and too many people (now cut from 9,800 to 3,500). Apple showed much the same syndrome – its Macintosh white hope, for one example, was produced independently from and without any reference to the Lisa computer, which used identical technology.

Explosive-growth companies need to be reminded that they are mortal, and that the management basics they blithely ignore in boom time will be desperately needed when market conditions change – as change they will. What makes the Atari and Mattel horror stories so striking is the speed and severity of change, as the bottom dropped out of games and home-computer markets and prices: Mattel's Intellivision in 1984 was fetching a sixth of its 1982 price, while the Sinclair computer, under the Timex name, was selling at the same time at pocket-calculator levels. Small wonder that Timex, itself the victim of poor control, had to follow Texas Instruments, Mattel, and others out of the US computer market. The pace of change in markets is so fast today that even growth companies have little time to repair their basic deficiencies – after, that is, those errors have found them out.

## Mark the market

Nor is it only the growth companies. In an industry mature to the point of grey hairs, BAT lost enormous face for a group of such size (£11.5 billion in sales) and sophistication by losing £53 million on its UK cigarette trade, ignominiously halved by a semi-pullout in early 1984. This isn't, after all, a trade where management knew naught. True, the lush learning curve up which BAT's tobacco profits had risen didn't apply to the UK, thanks to the time-dishonoured carve-up that kept Imperial Tobacco out of overseas markets, and BAT exclusively in them. Over the post-war years, this separation from home built up into strong frustration among BAT managers who, flushed with success abroad, were sure they could burn Imps badly in Britain.

Their subsequent five-year failure to catch fire has three possible causes. Either the BATmen were not so white hot at marketing as they thought, or they simply made a hash (which happens to the hottest of marketers at least once in their lives), or anybody would have burnt out against the dark background of a 25 per cent fall in smoking. It's churlish, though inevitable, to say that market research should have given some warning of the latter collapse. But all factors, the unavoidable and the voluntary alike, played a part; not only was it impossible to out-market Imps, but BAT's chosen strategy, excessive promotion in support of none-too-brilliant brands, was unwise.

The BAT brands had no strong selling proposition, unique or otherwise. Spending couldn't make up the deficiency – given that full frontal assault hardly ever succeeds without a three-to-one advantage in resources. BAT couldn't outspend and undercut Imps indefinitely. The lesson is that today a giant barging into a new market is subject to much the same limitations as a relative midget.

The unavoidable nature of these limitations – the fact that nobody can buck the market – emerges clearly from the ten-year growth listing *Management Today* published in March 1984. The rampant retailers stuck out a mile. Habitat–Mothercare, MFI, Burton, Superdrug and Comet were respectively third, fifth, sixth, seventh and ninth: a concentration that emphasizes not just that, these days, the shop is mightier than the workshop, but that the market is mightier than anybody.

The retail predominance alone was none too surprising in a Britain whose manufacturers had mostly long since given up, if not the ghost, at least any hope of growth on the strict conditions met so triumphantly by the ace retailers: a ten-year rise in earnings per share, after correction for inflation. On this all too real criterion, BAT suffered a decline exceeding 5 per cent annually, during a decade when Comet rocketed away by nearly 22 per cent per annum.

True, the famous five shot up from bases that, back in 1973–4, were knee high, either because so was the company's stature, or because it was performing drearily in the Sagging Seventies: like Burton. However, the retail stardom also has a highest common factor. Each in its own way, the wonder-chains won by identifying new market trends and smartly adapting strategies and products to match. Michael Hollingbery, who built up Comet from a single inherited shop in Hull, is explicit on the subject.

Observing (simply enough) that the death of retail price maintenance meant the birth of cut-price retailing, and that the pervasive car made possible purveying out of town, he moved swiftly because (as he told *Management Today*), 'I was frightened that if we didn't do it, Tesco would.' (The fact that Tesco didn't may partly explain why it ranked seventy-nine places below Comet, with a negative figure for growth in earnings per share.) Differentiate, specialize, segment – and do it all with speed and conviction: that formula for retail riches has an oddly familiar ring.

It's precisely the policy the pundits have been trying to force down the throats of manufacturing industry – along with the warning (also voiced by Hollingbery) to 'give the customer what he wants, or go broke'. What explains the dearth of successful British firms supplying the things that the gee-whiz retailers sell? In case after case, the thing-makers allowed their strategies to be shaped by what they made, rather than by what could be marketed profitably.

That is nothing but the oldest of business basics. Hark back, too, to that list of the new management necessities as established by *Fortune*. Any old marketing hand should experience a sense, not of brave new management, but of *déjà vu*. Isn't this what marketing has always been about? Keeping close to the customer, watching the competition like an especially famished hawk, bringing the functions together on co-ordinated product development, getting products through development at maximum speed, beating competition to the punch: these are among the oldest rules of the game. They have also, true, been honoured more in the breach than in the observance. But there is something new under the sun: the fact that, because of the newly ferocious pace, rule-breakers may expect (like TI in computers, BAT in British smokes, Atari and Mattel) to get broken – and that right soon.

## Triumph in turbulence

'Turbulence' is the word used by Bill Ramsay, Director of Development of General Foods in the UK, to describe these conditions in world markets. He pointed out, in a paper on brand marketing, that the world economy had gone from growth through crisis to flatness; that brand marketing had passed from proliferation through rationalization to polarization; that consumer requirements had moved from choice to price/value to identity; that the source of profit, market expansion in the 1960s, became margin improvement in the next decade: now it is winning the battle for market share. This all means that management has had to switch its attention from diversification through resource allocation to competitive strategy – which is where this chapter began, with the huge competitive pressure being felt by US companies and its consequences for management.

Ramsay's conclusions on what these consequences are for brand marketing were emphatic:

1 Recognize that the brand is in a state of flux and transition. The conditions of the 1960s have disappeared for ever. Anticipate the changes to come.
2 Build a strategic view of your brand adjusted to the new realities. Learn and relearn the key leverages that affect the market you are in. Look for segmentation opportunities. Think how you would enter your market if you were a new competitor.
3 Analyse your consumers. They are no longer conformist and uncomplicated. The role of women is changing. They are smarter, less predictable.
4 The manufacturer and the trade are strategically inter-dependent. Each needs the other. The manufacturer needs a detailed trade marketing plan, the trade needs a brand marketing plan.
5 Invest heavily in advertising when you have a new brand, a new item or a genuinely improved product (or service).
6 Use research and development to improve or at least maintain your competitive quality.
7 Accept innovation as a necessity for your category and organize accordingly. New products need to be tech-nologically driven as well as market driven.

Once again the wisdom is ancient, but the urgency is new – and powerful. Ramsay quoted from a *Harvard Business Review* article a passage that should be engraved on the marketing mind. 'The key to long-term success – even survival – is what it has always been: to invest, to innovate, to create value. Such determination, such striving to excel requires leaders.' So there *is* strong continuity: the difference is that the lessons of what has always been true have to be observed in a setting so strongly discontinuous that what is old can look frighteningly new.

# 14 *Opportunities in changing times*

from *The Supermarketers*

*The Supermarketers* builds on the foundations of *The Naked Market* to explore what has become a preoccupation of mine, and for management at large in the closing years of the century: how to turn words into deeds. More even than its predecessors this book dwelt on the successes of Japanese management, of which the greatest (since it underpins all the others) is the ability to understand and exploit western markets and methods more ably than the West itself.

Writing in the West, though, as a committed friend of the US and a committed supporter of a united Europe, my concern must be with western striving to return the compliment and reverse the slide. The task is far from easy, but it can be done – not, however, by clinging to the modes of the past.

After *The Supermarketers* was written, IBM's struggle to maintain its profitability provided a piquant illustration of this vital point. Discovering that, for all its emphasis on being led by the customer and driven by the market, it had lost touch with both, IBM dispensed with tens of thousands of marketing support staff and sought to return to 'the way it was'. The book's message, however, is that 'the way it was', in such fast-changing times, is most unlikely to be the way it should be.

The times are not only moving rapidly, carrying reputations away before them: they are kaleidoscopic, and the changing patterns of challenge and response impose new imperatives on marketing management – which simply has to mean all management. The higher commands of companies will claim that they are indeed wholly imbued with the marketing philosophy, wholly committed to the innovation and quality issues round which that philosophy must revolve. But the words are too often lip service: this particular book was intended to make managers put their money and their attentions where their mouths are – in the market place.

To repeat, this isn't because marketing has become more important. It's because the pressure of competition has completed the fusion of what was a function with the entire life of the corporation. British companies used to be urged to 'export or die'. That may have been wrong-headed. But there's no doubt of the imperative now: it's 'market or die'. For the great majority of significant companies the markets concerned are those of the entire world. That's a crucial concept in which, yet again, the Japanese are leading the West – and the Westerners have no choice but to follow.

## The inertia of Texas Instruments

Failure may have few friends, but it has plenty of remedies – so many and so well known that nobody attempting a turnaround from disaster lacks examples and precepts. But how do you tackle what is usually a far more difficult problem? How do you cope with success?

The problem is twofold. Not only does a smash marketing hit, like a personal triumph, often go to the head, but the winning company, bumptious or not, will sooner or later face the real and agonizing questions of how to build on and sustain its success. Thomas V. Bonoma, writing in the *Harvard Business Review*, came up with a telling phrase to describe one aspect of this potential crisis: 'marketing inertia' – the title of an article that takes a swipe at some US names famous for getting stuck with ideas of their own marketing brilliance, even though the ideas were founded on enormous market success.

Thus Texas Instruments passionately believes that 'low prices lead to market-share dominance'. Sounds OK. But TI followed this philosophy when marketing its cheaper calculators at discount prices through department stores and other mass outlets. It thus neatly poleaxed its standing with the office-equipment specialists, who had been selling Texas Instruments' more expensive, higher-margin machines. In 1981, after similar pursuit of the cheap and dominant, TI had to withdraw in disarray from the watch market. A couple of years later, exactly the same fate overtook its home computers. Low-priced, mass-volume consumption goods just aren't its bag.

Then there is Coors, a beer that became famous for the quality ('product superiority') to which the family management attributed its success. Bonoma points out that 'quality is determined more by customers' preferences than by family formulas' – and, in the case of Coors, customers preferred a beer that they could actually buy. Poor distribution made the quality quite academic. At Coors, as at TI, marketing actions were attuned not to the market, but to preconceived notions of how it would or should behave. Two younger Coors family managers had to break with the past to set the brewery on a new course of profitable growth.

At that, Coors was lucky to have a pair of insiders who could recognize and conquer the corporate inertia; and the two were lucky, in a sense, that the facts of market share and profitability made an overwhelming case for change. If a company is held to be wholly successful by most of its own management as well as everybody on the outside, and by the family shareholders, the victory of inertia might seem inevitable. Surely nobody will see the need to jolt the business into reforming its inert ways? The favoured jolting technique in a family-dominated firm is to appoint a chief executive who is not a family member. And, in a rare reaction to incipient inertia, that is exactly what happened at one of the very few retail businesses that's as famous outside its country as inside: the mighty and once-marvellous Marks & Spencer.

## Good is never good enough

'Anatomy of Britain's most efficiently managed company': so ran the subtitle of a book by a Hong Kong manager named Dr K. K. Tse. Ask any informed Brit which company that is, and the answer, nine times out of ten, would be Marks & Spencer. Whether the judgement is correct, of course, is a matter of opinion, and a prickly one at that. *Efficient* is a difficult word to define; 'efficiently managed' almost suggests that there's some discrete activity, like abstract painting, that exists in its own wondrous right.

Efficient management without efficient results sounds contradictory. But the book musters an array of reasonably objective financial counts, on all of which M & S leads, and often dwarfs, its retail competitors. The genius of its business, though, is that it actually has little head-on competition. The M & S principles have profoundly influenced retail businesses all over the world: build dominant shares of consumer markets on limited ranges of products (in its case, clothing and food), all carrying the chain's own brand, all produced to the chain's specification and under its tight control, and majoring on high 'VFM' – the value for money being achieved by combining superior quality with moderate prices.

Its closest rival on financial measures is the British supermarket chain J. Sainsbury, but the M & S food-and-drink business overlaps only part of Sainsbury's spread – and the higher margin portion, at that. The real similarity between the two is their brilliant (and certainly efficient) use of the house brand. Against Marks's one-third of all British bras, Sainsbury boasts one-seventh of Britain's wine sales – maybe the more remarkable statistic of the two, given that competitive bottles are distributed more widely than uplift.

Speaking of uplift, Sainsbury does outscore M & S heavily on one financial count that Dr Tse doesn't use: growth. From 1973 to 1983, the St Michael's brigade raised sales by 338 per cent and profits by 209 per cent; the Sainsbury figures were 518 per cent and 637 per cent. Moreover, the 1981 supremacy of M & S on other scores is no longer complete – Sainsbury easily outdid the champ in 1985 for return on shareholders' equity (18.9 per cent versus 13.9 per cent, pre-tax).

You could (and should) argue that growth isn't relevant to the 'most efficiently managed' title, as Sainsbury was expanding from a regional to a national base, which M & S had long occupied; and this very process of rapid expansion has helped to generate the supermarket chain's rise in profitability. All the same, that doesn't dodge the fact that, while Marks's margins have remained commendably stable (never higher than 12 per cent or lower than 10.2 per cent since 1977), the productivity of its capital has slumped. A fall from 36.1 per cent (1974–5), or 31.4 per cent (1978–9), to the recent 22.2 per cent isn't what is generally meant by efficient management.

Thus, when the chief executive torch at Marks & Spencer passed to a non-family manager, a case for fundamental change could certainly have been argued. But M & S's new leader, Lord Rayner, was no newly made broom. After his long years in the country's most admired retail chain, he was as thoroughly indoctrinated in the group's culture as any of the ruling Sieff family. That corporate culture, in turn, is among the most powerful ever created, as you'd expect with so many forceful men concentrating on so narrow a front for so long.

But was the front, for all the product diversification of recent years, including the crucial post-war food expansion, still too narrow? A business whose shops are obviously good, by subjective and objective standards, is desperately hard to criticize. But if you adjust the group's rise in earnings per share for inflation (as *Management Today* does annually), the result turns out to be negative over the decade to 1982: a 2.4 per cent annual *decline*.

True, that was better than 127 other companies in Britain's top 200, and by 1985 the decade's figure was up to a positive 8 per cent, against 21 per cent for Sainsbury. These figures don't dispel the nagging feeling that so intensively managed and superbly integrated an operation should have generated greater rewards. The reasons why it hasn't are obvious. Britain's sluggish economy has inevitably cramped the style of a group that was confined largely to those stagnant shores, that has near-saturation shares of mature markets, and within which that all-powerful culture was dead set on organic growth, not acquisition. When these characteristics were described to an American financier wanting to know if Marks might like to take a billion-dollar retail bauble off his hands, he listened in silence, then said: 'I seem to have picked on exactly the wrong company.' At that time, he sure had.

Maybe the missing phase in the great chain's development would have made it the *right* company. After all, Sears Roebuck in the United States would be a mere smidgen of its $39 billion size (seven times that of M & S) had it stuck to mail order. The evidence is that Marks has long been pressing against the natural and national barriers to the expansion of its magnificent patented method: the vertically integrated, limited-catalogue variety store, stocking own-brand merchandise and steadily expanding the lines and sidelines. The way out is either to export the method (which Marks began, only to find the overseas sledding slow and sometimes painful), or to follow Sears in adding other consumer-based operations.

In the great Marks and Sieff eras, the company did not bring its usual scrupulous intensity to exploiting the base asset: its unique experience of the consumer. This could be because M & S has, in a sense, created its own consumers. The genius of its founders was to change people's buying habits and thus turn a store into a national brand. But serving mature markets in mature ways with a mature corporate culture is unlikely to produce rich growth.

There couldn't be a more conspicuous example of the fact that managing efficiently carries a hidden price: that of creating a hard act for yourself to follow. Markets (like bras, in a manner of speaking) get saturated. New areas are less rewarding, at least initially, than are old. And the harder the cost lemon is squeezed, the less juice is left. Whoever said that nothing succeeds like success didn't know what he was talking about. Success is only the beginning; building on it is the tough, and vital, part.

## Whatever happened to Baby Hoover?

In some cases neglect of a business is so extreme, so puzzling, and the results so drastic as to raise that doom-laden question, Whatever happened to . . . ? For example, Whatever happened to Baby Hoover? This British company, child of an American parent, grew so strong that it became the brightest jewel in the parental crown. In 1960 few companies seemed better poised for rich and lasting success: multinational, Europe-oriented, leader in unsaturated consumer markets with weak domestic opposition, proud possessor of a great household name, famous for productive efficiency, blessed with access to American know-how and market developments through its US ownership. How could it fail?

Yet success didn't come. The closing of Perivale, once the focal point of the whole British appliance industry, was only symbolic of a long and sad two-stage decline. From 1971 to 1981, on cumulative sales figures of $2.5 billion, Hoover earned a total net profit of $80 million – a pitiful 3.5 per cent. That followed a desperately dreary decade in the 1960s (1969 sales were only $4.5 million up on those of 1959). In the early 1970s Hoover did smartly pull up its socks and its sales, but the rot set in again. In 1980 turnover was only 27 per cent up on 1975, while the accompanying five-year plunge in profits had reached the vanishing point. By contrast Black and Decker had tripled its British profits and sales between 1973 and 1979.

Even if you argue that Black and Decker's markets for electrically powered appliances were better ones, who deserves the credit for that? It was an Englishman, Robert Appleby, who built this UK subsidiary of an American parent into an intensively managed model of how to conduct and develop a fast mover in consumer durables. Another Englishman, Sir Charles Colston, had created Hoover's enormously strong position in Britain and Europe in an earlier era. But whereas Appleby was rewarded with honours and the number-two spot at the parent organization, Colston was awarded the boot – kicked out by Herbert Hoover Jr himself.

That wouldn't have mattered if, after an affronted US management putsched Herbie himself in 1967, the UK operation had sustained development either on B & D lines (as a crack, independent subsidiary) or on those of British Ford (as part of a US-controlled, trans-European, locally and strongly co-ordinated organization). Perhaps the critical moment was the 1965 success in breaking the back of a challenger who sold awful cut-price washing machines door-to-door, but who proved, before his crash, that he was more in touch with Hoover's market than was Hoover itself. As far stronger challengers arrived from places like Italy, it's small wonder that the Princes of Perivale found themselves being bashed in turn by the Borgias of the appliance industry. Machiavelli could have told them what to do. If you hold mastery in the market place, you never, never let go.

That truth was one that Hoover's parent back in the States had cause to rue, as it succumbed in 1985 to takeover by Chicago Pacific. By that time, western Europe was producing only $13 million of Hoover's total operating profit, on $270 million of sales. The United States, with only $30 million more in revenues, generated $30 million more profit. The price tag on the Hoover deal wasn't low, at $530 million, but how much more would the company have fetched if the European business had emulated the efficiency and inexorable rise of Sweden's Electrolux? Had it done so, would Hoover have lost its independence at all?

The *Financial Times* noted at takeover time that Hoover's European picture was brightening up:

> Within the past three years, virtually every product
> manufactured by Hoover has been changed or radically
> redesigned, to take account of improving technology and
> make more profitable use of Hoover's market shares . . .
> Its new Turbo vacuum cleaner, for example, has a
> completely redesigned engine as well as other novel
> features such as an incorporated air freshener.

Better late than never, maybe. But Hoover's fault was the same as that which turned the future of Westland, the helicopter company, over to United Technologies and its Sikorsky managers, after a political fracas that cost two British cabinet ministers their jobs and brought Prime Minister Margaret Thatcher into some peril. Westland, like Hoover, had been mismarketed for two or three decades. And in the main theatre of that failure there's a vital lesson. In the 1960s and 1970s, it paid to innovate; in the 1980s, it kills not to.

Even if Westland had been better at production (it was poor, and not much better with its financial controls, either), it would have been brought low by its failure over all that time to come up with profitably competitive models of its own design. Licences from Sikorsky were Westland's mainstay – and also its main weakness. Effectively the company was shut out of the world's best markets, led by the United States. Every company needs its USP: the unique selling proposition that's yours and yours alone, that nobody else can better, and that you can sell in all markets.

That's the reality that lies behind innovation. Not only must a business possess that unique product or service (which is the starting point for most businesses), but the edge has to be constantly sharpened. If you don't achieve that sharpness, you'll be Hoovered: after establishing an apparently invulnerable market position, the company failed to keep pace with the significant changes and improvements in its markets. If you don't even develop your own successful line, you'll be Westlanded.

## Questions of innovation

How can a company avoid the fate of either a Hoover or a Westland? There is no single answer, but a dozen highly suggestive ones were given by 400 top businesses and 600 of their executives. This is how their answers ranked, in order of importance, the actions that a company can take in the essential effort to obtain innovative success:

1 Increase or improve market research efforts or capacity.
2 Get top management commitment and support or leadership.
3 Increase rewards or establish a reward system for innovative groups and individuals.
4 Encourage risk-taking and avoid penalizing mistakes.
5 Improve or establish a positive, more entrepreneurial climate for innovation.
6 Increase creative, entrepreneurial, far-sighted thinking and behaviour.
7 Establish separate or small organizational units responsible for innovative activities.
8 Establish clear priorities, goals, objectives.
9 Delegate authority and responsibility – decentralize.
10 Develop differentiation in products or services.

11 Use innovative strategies and formulate an innovation plan.
12 Persist in innovation efforts.

One important point: don't imagine that innovation is only about products or even services. The survey, absolutely rightly, defines it as 'any new product, service, process or organizational activity through which a company expects to solve a problem, satisfy a need, or achieve a goal'. The barbershop chain, cited by Peter Drucker, that used time-and-motion study to reduce haircut time, while opening in several locations at once, was innovating just as much as the publisher of free magazines who got recipients to register if they wanted to keep getting the publications – and both were just as innovative as the man who gave Sony the Walkman.

Why? Because the barber chain could afford to use local TV advertising, offering a short maximum wait – or you got a free haircut. Predictably lucrative results ensued. The publisher could not only prove the demand for his giveaway but could deliver far more information to advertisers about their audience. Every business needs continual review, formalized in regular meetings, of the key activities that generate costs or income to see if there are new ways in which either or both can be improved: in other words, innovation.

It's *never* trouble-free, though. Doing new things is the most exciting and often the most rewarding part of business, but it's also the most exhausting and nerve-racking. Also, the innovator has to face a number of man-made obstacles. If these are in your path, do your utmost to remove them:

1 Red tape; cumbersome 'decision and review' structure or process
2 Lack of funds for innovation
3 Preoccupation with current operations at the expense of future opportunities
4 Failure to engage in innovative thinking; insistence on tradition

5 Lack of top management support, commitment, or innovativeness

6 Organizational structure that discourages innovation.

Plans to surmount these obstacles may run into more barriers. The following list ranks the barriers in their most common order of occurrence. Note that these are all very closely akin to the sales objections you receive from people who don't want to buy, but prefer not to say so. The arguments are shot through with illogic and emotion. They can be overcome – but you need good sales skills and persistence to achieve your end.

1 Cannot afford; inadequate return on investment
2 Tendency to protect an existing investment or livelihood
3 Fear of failure or risk-taking
4 The 'not-invented-here' syndrome
5 'Let's postpone it, give it some more thought'
6 Opposes custom, habit, fashion, taste
7 'That product won't work' or 'It didn't work last time'
8 We are basically followers, not leaders.

Suppose you sell yourself and your innovation over all the barriers – your troubles still aren't over. The novelty may fail (the majority actually do). Westland came out with civil helicopter projects of its own, but totally failed to win the sales the company desperately needed to offset its dependence on orders from the good old Ministry of Defence. The following are the hard questions you have to answer in the hardest-nosed manner possible before plunging into the unknown – for that describes the future of any innovation in a product or service. Again, the questions are ranked in order of importance:

1 Has our analysis of market and customer needs been full enough, thorough enough, and accurate enough?
2 Has the competition been fully, thoroughly, and accurately assessed?
3 Is the offering sufficiently different – that is, not too much of a 'me-too'?

4 Are we straying too far from our real areas of corporate and marketing expertise?

5 Are we allocating the proper amount of time to development and marketing: not too little, not too much, but just right?

6 Is top management sufficiently involved and committed?

All these questions are important, but the first, judging by the responses to the survey, is crucial. Over 60 per cent of those replying gave insufficient or faulty market or customer analysis as the prime reason for failure. Certainly, one new venture in publishing was shown by post mortem to have failed this test. Because of fears about security, the research concentrated entirely on the size of the market, paying no attention to the buying patterns of the customers. Because of this basic defect, the product's ability to take market share from the competition was greatly exaggerated.

The stupidity is that independent market research, given time, could have solved the problems. But the companies responding to the survey (conducted by Arthur Young and reported in *Advanced Management Report* by the firm's Cesar L. Pereira and William K. Foster) often had a low opinion of their research abilities. Only half of them thought themselves 'relatively strong' at research. Given that companies generally overstate their strengths, that is a dismal picture. It's one, however, that's not only easy to improve but that will pay richly in both mistakes avoided and masterstrokes made – and not just in innovation.

## The double whopper at VW

Every success carries within it the seeds of its own potential destruction. Successful managements ignore this truism precisely because they are successful. It explains how one great company let sales of its most important product in its most valuable foreign market halve in a single year. The company was Volkswagen; the beleaguered market was the United States; and the product was the Rabbit. The year was 1982, and one reason for the collapse, of course, was the general US recession, courtesy of

President Reagan. But the Rabbit run-down also raises two fascinating questions:

1 Had VW kept the Rabbit running too long because it thought of it as another Beetle?
2 Had VW's decision to assemble its cars in the United States, and to promulgate that fact assiduously, backfired – because, to quote an analyst, 'people were willing to pay more for a foreign car, [but] . . . it became hard to convince consumers that there was something unique about a car made in Pennsylvania'?

On the first point, VW got in the deepest possible trouble with the Beetle itself. It had lived on far, far too long, with the entire company's fortunes pinned to its snub nose, because the management couldn't bring itself to admit its beloved Beetle was obsolete – or to agree on how to replace it. In today's world market, you can't afford to run a Rabbit (launched in 1974) indefinitely, certainly not at a time when Ford had launched its three lower-priced ranges in 1977, 1980, and 1982.

As for that 'made in America' label, the advertising stress was making the best of a bad job. VW felt that US assembly was essential to counteract the strength of the Deutschmark. But once the boot was on the dollar's foot, the Rabbit, despite price cuts, cost notably more than its Mazda or Toyota rivals. As in its calamitous purchase of Triumph-Adler's business machines (offloaded on Olivetti in 1986), VW simply got its strategy wrong, but this time in its base business and key markets.

The company had come back from the edge of the grave famously before. After record-breaking losses, new management pushed through a total revamp of production facilities and model range in a single amazing year, as Rabbits ousted Beetles. But some journeys back are too long ever to be made. Note three vital statistics: 500,000, the American sales of VWs (mostly Beetles) in 1971; 150,000, the sales in 1984; and 560,000, the US sales figure for Toyota in 1984. Clearly nothing short of a new Beetle, probably not even the excellent new Rabbit, could restore VW to the palmy American days of eleven years earlier. In marketing you can get away with one whopping error, but seldom with two – especially if it's the *same* error.

## Starring, European-style

Gigantic companies like VW seldom face the ultimate sanctions of total collapse or private takeover. This is not simply because they are so gigantic and their debts so huge that banks and governments won't let them go under, but also because of the regenerative powers of any company that has retained a real hold over large volume markets. What VW lost for keeps in America, it won back in Europe thanks to the launch in 1985 of the new Golf, an obvious winner from its first appearance. By early 1986 the West German company had over $16 billion in sales and was on course for a $600 million profit in 1988, a performance strong enough to win an honourable mention in *Management Today*'s roster of Western Europe's best companies.

The key to that assessment (and to the turnaround itself) was VW's 12.8 per cent of the European market. That pushed sales value just above those of the European paradigm, ranked head and shoulders above all competitors in esteem: Daimler-Benz. The very fact that the latter is a long-running saga, a prime case, says the magazine, of 'taking a long-term view of the market, rigorously building up its presence and steadily increasing its economies of scale', explains the accolades. But the most striking aspect of Europe in the mid-1980s was less stamina than resurgence, of which VW is only one conspicuous exemplar.

In the same motor industry, Italy's Fiat staged an equally impressive comeback, based on a massive revamp of the model line. The same style of rejuvenation also explained the nomination of Peugeot, whose troubles had been created not only by model obsolescence but by the troubled takeovers of Citroën and Chrysler's European interests. The auto renaissance, though, was outshone by the dazzling performance of Olivetti under Carlo de Benedetti, lauded by *Time* magazine in 1985 as 'an inspiring example of a fresh entrepreneurial spirit that is beginning to rustle through western Europe'.

That quotation marks an emphatic change of mood in American attitudes towards the Old World economies. Until quite recently US reports had concluded that Europe, plagued by conservatism and heavy unemployment, had run out of manufacturing and commercial vitality. The running in international reputation had been made by Japanese and, to a lesser extent, US companies, as their leaders pushed steadily into new markets, Europe among them. These powerful competitors rebuked European complacency with their efficiency and productivity in the Japanese case, and their entrepreneurial high technology in the American one. The dollar's fall and the oil-price collapse have prompted some of the swing in mood back in Europe's favour, but the evidence of European corporate resurgence has also been compelling.

There's a common thread binding the fifty-odd stars listed by *Management Today*, whether they are comebacks like VW, golden oldies like Daimler-Benz or Siemens, new companies sprung from the imagination of a post-war entrepreneur like the late Heinz Nixdorf, or reassembled, rejuvenated old-line groups like Moët-Hennessy ('the ultimate yuppie company', according to one admirer). All have sought to build or rebuild market share by reliance on products, new or old, that offer the purchaser a strong perceived advantage over the competition's entry. Most important, though, is the combination of this basic strategy with another quality: high ambition.

De Benedetti, for example, aims to make Olivetti 'the IBM of Europe' (a position IBM thinks it already occupies). That may sound grandiose, but Olivetti's current European position is founded on a relatively small base in the Italian home market, and the small-base syndrome can be a source of strength. It explains why several European stars have been forced to pick targets that sound overambitious to anybody except a Japanese. Like the latter, the ambitious European has created his own definition of impossibility. Thus a German maker, Heidelberger Druckmaschinen, makes 'more printing machines in Japan than all the Japanese companies combined'; the Swedish firm Tetra Pak supplies 'nearly all the milk and juice cartons *everywhere* in Western Europe'; the Danish compressor-to-hydraulics company Danfoss exports 90 per cent of its production to 105 countries.

Even for companies based in larger and richer markets than Italy, Sweden, or Denmark, the achievements are often out of proportion to reasonable expectation. West Germany's Robert Bosch, praised for a 'bull's-eye strategy, excellently executed', has three-quarters of the rapidly growing and lush market in fuel injection. It pioneered this market so successfully that its Chairman could boast to *Fortune* that, among European car makers, 'the only alternative to Bosch is Bosch'. It's much the same approach, applied business worlds apart, as that of Louis Vuitton, the fine luggage makers, whose management has at all costs 'maintained the exclusivity and quality of the products'.

In the 1980s the quality of ambition is as vital as that of the product or service being marketed; in neither case does the Supermarketer settle for second best. From the narrow Swedish base, Hans Werthen of Electrolux (whose own choices of top European company start with Siemens and Bosch) expanded the company into Europe's largest white-goods producer by excellent engineering-based management and judicious takeover. One recent foray, the US purchase of White Consolidated, not only went a long way towards making up for a deficient presence in the richest market but gave Electrolux world leadership – reinforced by buying Italy's Zanussi.

From the equally narrow base of West Germany's data-processing industry in 1968, Nixdorf built one of IBM's few forceful and profitable competitors. By 1984, Nixdorf had multi-plied revenues thirty-one times and stockholder's equity by forty-nine, thanks to gearing its business not to computer hardware but to computer solutions, giving IBM a ferocious race in selling computers and terminals to European banks. The Nixdorf emph-asis on close co-operation with the customer, rapidly assimilating new market trends and new ideas, with swift translation into innovative products, backed by superior service, is the classic niche recipe. But like Electrolux before buying White, Nixdorf has a western weak spot: a mere 1 per cent of US minicomputer sales.

In general, the Europeans' record in the American market compares badly not only with the Japanese penetration but with their own ambitions. Another weakness is that post-1950s start-ups that have achieved world status in the 1980s are thin on the

European ground. Yet the best Europeans have added to continuity (the traditional strong point) an unexpected resilience in adversity and a readiness to embrace new ambitions that have produced some evidently lasting achievements, often out of unpromising circumstances. In doing so, they have demonstrated the extraordinary diversity of late twentieth-century markets and the even greater range of marketing strategies with which ingenious Supermarketers can create winning positions from vaulting ambitions – even when they start from ground as soggy as Europe's in the wake of the gone, but not forgotten, oil-price shocks.

## The industry of Big Mac

There'll be plenty more opportunities, but they won't be in traditional industry. Indeed, what is industry? This sounds like a silly question, until you consider a fact like this: the fifth or so largest employer in the United States isn't in cars, or oil, or steel, or computers. It's in hamburgers – none other than Big Mac itself.

If industry means converting raw materials into consumable products, McDonald's is as industrious, so to speak, as General Motors. True, the product isn't durable, and the materials consist entirely of food. But food manufacturers count as an industry – so why is a fast-food processor a mere service? Anyway, why are services 'mere'? For that matter, how many of the people employed in industry, such as marketers, are much more remote from actually making things than a short-order cook?

The definitions matter for both the economy and the business of management. What's traditionally defined as *industry* notoriously employs far fewer people than it once did – especially at the blunt end. At the sharp end, where the product meets the customer, industry employs more and more, directly and indirectly. The analogy is with agriculture. Numbers actually working on the land have become minute, but great hordes are now occupied in transforming farm produce and delivering the results, often in fantastical guises, to waiting mouths. Really, the staffs of Carnation, General Mills, Kellogg, Heinz, and McDonald's are all part of the agricultural industry.

Agriculture's dwindling away as an employer of labour is an optical illusion. The action has simply moved downstream. True, in some cases (like steel), the action has moved away from a whole industry, for reasons that won't be reversed. In others, though, like cars, the action has moved from blunt-end companies to sharp, market-oriented ones; the extraordinary results of BMW and Mercedes, growing rich yet again while rivals groaned, rest on superbly efficient service of defined market segments. Similarly, Sweden's L. M. Ericsson won an absurdly high world-market share in public telephone exchanges, which was a just reward for starting at the sharp end and setting out deliberately to provide customers with their hearts' desire in electronic switching.

That is the sharp clue to nearly all Supermarketing success in the 1980s: the sharp end. Acute knowledge of acutely defined markets not only separates the sheep from the goats, it divides the high returns from the low.

## Winning the American way

The Supermarketers of the 1980s don't think of themselves as operating in broad industries. They flourish in specific product sectors – sometimes many more than one. But the number doesn't make any difference to the principle: whatever they are, the best companies specialize. They possess, in their segment, sector, or niche, the offerings that are most wanted; and they serve its public devotedly to sustain the high market shares and high yields from which continued leadership can be financed.

Consider this list of corporations: American Home Products, Dow Jones, Mitchell Energy, SmithKline Beckman, Kellogg, Deluxe Check Printers, Worthington Industries, Maytag, Merck, Nalco Chemical, IBM, Dover, and Coca-Cola. Ostensibly they share nothing, but they are bound by a common statistical excellence. In April 1984, *Fortune* found that these thirteen companies, and they alone among the magazine's list of 500, had averaged at least a 20 per cent return on year-end shareholders' equity over the decade to 1983, without ever dipping below 15 per cent. Look again at the list, though, and a non-statistical similarity emerges. By and large, these are older-line, conservative companies. Each has a strong and generally leading position in a desirable market. But the strength and the leadership spring from solid virtues applied over a sustained period.

That follows axiomatically from the acid test. No company can earn such high returns over a decade without being built for the long haul. But there's more to it than that. Only the energy business, Mitchell, financed its performance with heavy debt (and later fell out of bed in consequence). The others succeeded in large measure in self-financing their market leadership. Again, that outcome is axiomatic. The higher the return on current capital, the less the need to obtain additional capital from outside. The axiom is not that straightforward, however. Other things being equal, high leverage is supposed to lever upwards the return on shareholders' equity. So why were these companies the supreme exponents on that vital score?

Clearly other things aren't equal. Is there a connection between the kind of marketing management that farms its territory most assiduously for long-term yield and the mentality that dislikes deep entry into hock? Maybe so. The fact is that customers, like these companies, are fundamentally conservative. They flock to the genuinely new, whether it's a videocassette recorder or a new munchie or an anti-ulcer drug. But once flocked, they tend to stay with the supplier who, year in and year out, gives them what they want, as they want it, when they want it.

Even better, they are willing to pay more for the privilege. *Fortune* cites two highly relevant examples to show that, when market leaders risk losing business by raising prices, 'a strong brand name or a rock-solid reputation for service will usually carry the day'. Thus Kellogg didn't rescind all of its earlier price rises, necessitated by mounting cereal costs, when those costs fell. Return on equity soared joyously from 20 to 26 per cent. At Dow Jones, continual increases in the cost of paper, excused by rising costs, were readily absorbed by readers who found the *Wall Street Journal* irreplaceable at any price.

Mind you, it greatly helps if the product has an absolute or virtual monopoly, such as the *Journal*'s. The objective of the long-term Supermarketer is to achieve, if not an actual monopoly, the benefits of absolute market ownership. Even in a commodity business like cheque printing, the determined company can achieve incredible market shares, like Deluxe's better than 50 per cent, a figure that is claimed to rise slightly each year. The key was a Japanese standard of error-free service (99 per cent perfect, with over 95 per cent of orders delivered inside two days) based on Japanese-style adoption of the best technology – without which Deluxe would have run out of the supplies required to meet the demand.

That's another characteristic of the champions. They concentrate on the supply side as much as on the demand. Maytag's boss, Daniel J. Krumm, started expanding plant capacity for its appliances by three-quarters in the recessionary conditions of 1974. The $60 million he put at risk paid off triumphantly with capacity that Krumm expected to last out the 1980s – and to deliver high quality at efficient costs. High investment of that nature can pay off even when demand disappears. Dover's Norris division tripled its capacity for the sucker rods used in oil drilling. When their prices crumbled, Norris might have looked a sucker indeed, but, so Chairman Thomas C. Sutton told *Fortune*: 'When the circus comes to town, you rent every room in the hotel, at the best prices you can get . . . Norris totally capitalized on the market place. We earned an awful lot of money for the shareholders.'

The common themes of reliable supply (in both quantity and quality), deep understanding of markets, low costs (combined with premium prices), and conservative finance are no coincidence. A similar exercise in Britain by *Management Today* came up with eight companies that had achieved, alone among the nation's 250 largest, more than 17.6 per cent return on invested capital over a decade and had never fallen below 13.2 per cent. Their core businesses were defence electronics, out-of-town shopping, discount supermarkets, health care, pest control, and building products. Two of them, the Beecham drugs and foods to toothpaste and cosmetics business, and the brilliant BTR conglomerate, were multimarket. But they were no exceptions to the rule.

Like the single-market firms, they are marked by the absence of flashiness and the presence of solid common sense. All eight, like the American thirteen, had built their profitability primarily by exploiting the potential of well-understood markets. As in the United States, so in Britain: high achievement can be realized in low-growth markets and hot technologies alike. Actually, the core business that year after year provides good and growing profits in response to careful and continuous nurture has one supreme advantage over the runaway growth market – for example, the personal computer in its heyday. Products like SmithKline's Tagamet drug or Beecham's synthetic penicillins generate vast profits but are desperately hard acts to follow. A boom market always creates the what-to-do-for-an-encore syndrome, superbly solved by IBM when it belatedly grabbed the PC opportunity; but what comes after that?

Ambition does more than provide the kind of desire that makes former Chairman Frank Cary rate IBM's chances of repeating the past ten years' profitability performance as 100 per cent, or that underlies Sir Owen Green's belief at BTR that, having grown from $220 million of sales to $5.6 billion in a decade, 'we can continue for as long as we choose to continue'. Translated into numbers, into targets, ambition provides the mechanical driving force of these far-from-mechanistic businesses. For the British bunch, however, ambition has produced one visible difference from the Americans, taken as a whole: in the sunset circumstances of the 1970s, any British manager worth the name had to look outside the domestic market – and all six of the non-retailers in the *Management Today* article consequently have heavy international presence.

Evidently, a business like BPB, the building-products firm, with 94 per cent of the British plasterboard market, hasn't much left to harvest at home (note, again, the monopoly achievement). For such a company, North America is a powerful magnet. The attraction isn't so great in reverse. But most of the American thirteen already have global operations, and in an increasingly global world, would-be US Supermarketers will have to widen their vision even as they retain their narrow concentration on high service at low costs – and with rich reward to the investors.

It sounds paradoxical that, thanks to their superb cash generation, these companies have tended to provide that abundant reward more in higher dividends and less in exceptional stock-market performance. Those who find that disappointing should reflect on one final lesson of the Fine Thirteen and the Excellent Eight. Isn't that how capitalism (and Supermarketing) are supposed to work?

## Blue bloods, and shotguns and pickups

Selling rat poison? Or prune juice? Marshmallows, antacids? Then go west, or east, young marketer, to Grand Rapids, Miami, Salt Lake City, or Atlanta – those being, according to an article in *Fortune* magazine, the respective prime US markets for these products. It doesn't say whether Grand Rapids is also the rat capital of America, which is a logical assumption. And there's no apparent reason why Atlanta stomachs should reach (or retch) for the Pepto-Bismol more than those in Savannah – which holds the gastronomic (or gastric) lead in monosodium glutamate and meat tenderizers (again for no apparent cause).

Illogical or not, that's the way things are. And it provides the way out of many a marketing dilemma. According to Thomas Moore's article, S. C. Johnson and Son, facing a static 40 per cent market share for its Raid insecticides, went for the throats of the cockroaches in Houston and New York and of the fleas in Tampa and Birmingham, all in due season. The result? Bigger market shares in sixteen out of eighteen regions; a 5 per cent rise in national market guzzle; and food for thought for any company (which means almost every company) that is divided into sales or marketing regions.

If these divisions are purely organizational, rather than tactical or strategic, the company is certainly missing major market opportunities. Targeted promotion always makes more sense – if, that is, you can locate the target. Thanks to new technological wonders like computers and laser scanners, as *Fortune* points out, the targets can be picked up, and picked off, with an ease unknown to previous generations. An operation named Prizm divides neighbourhoods into forty-odd groups under such redolent names as 'Blue-Blood Estates' and 'Shotguns and Pickups' (the latter vehicles, incidentally, being a bull market in the Southwest). Advertising agency

Ogilvy and Mather has the same message; it operates its marketing smarts on eight profiles of different US 'nations'.

Using this concept state by state, the brewing giant Anheuser-Busch frothed up its national market share from 22.6 per cent to 36.7 per cent in only a few years. Note that the key doesn't lie in regional advertising, but in altering the whole marketing platform to suit specific conditions and tastes, season by season, product by product. That's how the whole marketing game has changed: place by place, season by season, product by product. And that's how the Supermarketers play the game: witness the progress of PepsiCo.

## What pepped up Pepsi's marketing

In the naked market today's hero company is quite likely to be tomorrow's – if not next minute's – bum. Take Coca-Cola and Procter & Gamble, respectively fourth and eighth in *Fortune*'s January 1986 list of America's most admired corporations. In February of the same year, *Business Week* included them in another, less honourable roll: that of 'marketing powerhouses' that had 'tumbled' – P & G with old toothpaste and new disposable nappies and orange juice, Coca-Cola with the 'ill-fated' introduction of New Coke.

The roll of dubious honour is completed by Philip Morris, whose double stumble takes in beer (once a claim to marketing fame second only to Marlboro) and Seven Up. The stumbling powerhouse had put the latter up for sale, after years of losses that had mocked Philip Morris's marketing prowess, to the magazine's new hero: PepsiCo. Without question, the Pepsi people could parade impressive credentials ranging from the embarrassment of Coke to the Personal Pan Pizza. But so could P & G, Coca-Cola, and Philip Morris, in their long moments of undisputed glory. What grounds were there for supposing that Pepsi had some magic ingredient, more potent than its cola formula, that would avoid the dreaded development of feet of marketing clay?

The attributes that, at least for this season, work so effectively include:

1 Shooting from the hip, ranking speed of response over deliberation. To quote chief executive officer D. Wayne Calloway, it's 'ready, fire, aim'.

2 Strong belief in decentralization and insistence on its practice (in contrast to the top-down decision-making said to stamp the P & G management style, all the way down to detailed questions of advertising and package design).

3 Heavy pressure on the managers, in return for their autonomy, to move fast and perform competitive wonders. *Business Week* quotes a consultant to this effect: 'These are people who like to win. Virtually everybody is overworked.'

4 Readiness to take investment risks. The 100 per cent Nutra-Sweet formula for Diet Pepsi was launched without testing, 'on the basis of a gut feeling that the time was right' – and sales subsequently rose by a quarter in just over a year.

5 Quick competitive reflexes. The magazine quotes the three new flavours of Slice with which Pepsi greeted the first two flavours of the Coke product designed to muscle into the soda-plus-real-juice market created by Pepsi.

6 Massive investment in advertising based on the use of celebrities: $460 million in a single year, a figure that grew by more than the increase in revenues, to promote products via personalities ranging from Michael Jackson to Marvelous Marvin Hagler.

7 Emphasis on a rapid flow of speedily produced new products. At the time of the article, Frito-Lay was testing some half-dozen new snacks to follow the success of the $150 million O'Grady's thick-cut potato chips. Their two years from lab to test market, though, had been shortened to six months for two newer products.

8 Continual close attention to markets: 'looking, listening and learning'. According to Calloway, 'You hear a lot of conversations around Pepsi about what's going on with the consumer, what's going on at the supermarket, what the competition is doing. You'll seldom hear about internal things, like a controller's report.'

One point leaps out from those eight: nothing in the Pepsi marketing magic is either novel or magical, and most marketing and management experts would come up with largely similar prescriptions for any company that wishes to hold its ground, let alone forge ahead, in the current decade and the next. Action before words; delegation of real authority to managers in the market; insistence on high performance from the devolved units; risk-taking investment; swift response to competition; heavy investment in telling promotion; innovative power; eyes and ears on the ground of markets; and total customer orientation. Throughout this book, the virtue of these virtues has been constantly stressed.

Indeed, any one of the three stumbling powerhouses could point to striking examples of some, if not all, of the eight virtuous qualities. Never in the whole history of marketing has any company made an investment in innovation that involved more risk than the launch of New Coke. Because it was rushed, and based more on gut feeling than convincing research, Coke was totally unprepared for the backlash that forced it to reintroduce its original formula as Classic Coke. While that bifurcation gave Coke more combined shelf space in the supermarkets, it left Pepsi as indisputably the biggest brand in soft drinks – and by early 1986 began to look like what might be called a mitigated disaster.

In other words, Pepsi's marketing looks like magic because some of it has worked like magic. By the nature of modern markets, there will be more setbacks like its Grandma's packaged cookies, which failed to become a national brand. As the marketing powerhouses square off against each other over vast tracts of consumer territory, from fast food to tortilla chips, soft drinks to cookies, each tract subdivided into increasingly complex segments, the result is the same for everybody: you win a few, you lose a few.

As *Business Week* pointed out, 'Major technological breakthroughs are rare, markets change fast, and competitors can easily rip off each other's ideas.' Such conditions guarantee flux. The pepped-up corporation can best ensure that its wins outweigh its losses by noting that the Pepsi Eight are in danger of becoming marketing clichés. Any idol company that degenerates into cliché management is measuring itself for a set of clay feet.

## The classic case of IBM

The combative pressures of the 1980s leave nobody unscathed, not even an IBM lording it over Apple. Like the former champion underdog, the latecomer champion has had to grapple with classic marketing problems in personal computers. IBM's amazing decision early in 1985 to drop the PC Jr was as powerful evidence of unresolved dilemmas as Apple's one-week production shutdown at the same time. The events are intimately connected, since it was IBM's revamped Jr, marketed with utmost belligerence, that helped build Apple's mountain of surplus.

IBM's classic conundrum started with cannibalization. With the original PC a runaway success in the higher price bracket, the temptation to head into down-market territory was irresistible. The difficulty of doing so without hurting PC Sr sales, though, was obvious and formidable. No doubt this explains why Jr appeared with cheap features like a rubber keyboard; the strategem kept the new baby away from Little Daddy, all right, but also kept away the customers – in droves.

When a chastened IBM bit the bullet, it took, in *Fortune*'s words, 'brilliant moves . . . to strengthen its product line, including its one weak link, the PC Jr'. But that fortification, along with aggressive pricing, cannibalized like crazy. In the retail market, Jr overtook Sr, but at a heavy toll on profits. With the down-market Jr and up-market AT model both having dire difficulties, Philip Estridge, the father of the PC, moved swiftly from much-praised divisional hero to unsung corporate staffer.

Even if IBM had decided on a policy of *reculer pour mieux sauter* – coming back later in force with a better differentiated, deadly weapon – the morals would have been the same. First, no strategy, especially not this one, makes economic sense in modern markets if the trade-off for the economic benefit is a sacrifice in product attributes.

Second, don't expect lightning to strike in the same place. The rapid and unpredicted triumph of the PC must have encouraged IBM to think that its almighty brand would repeat the runaway success lower down. When Jr flopped, the price cut and promotion blitz then thrown at customers tarnished the brand image while destroying the economics of the venture. That mistake in turn must have helped the IBM clones to halve its market share.

All the above, of course, is hindsight: nobody could logically have foreseen the PC surge, or the Jr flop, or the retreat. Yet it would be utterly wrong to conclude that there were defects in the original idea of setting up Estridge away from the organization and shibboleths of IBM's centre. That was brilliantly right. But the perfect set-up for a crash launch of a wholly new product in a wholly new market may be disastrous when consolidation takes command. You simply need a different kind of hero, and of heroics. To put it another way, the Supermarketer had better be prepared for change at all times; for all times, and everybody's markets are now subject to change – often with precious little notice.

## Omnipresence of change

That omnipresence of change is a cliché of the 1980s. Yet the full significance of what has already happened in the naked world market, let alone what is going to happen in the period to the 1990s and beyond, has only started to sink in. The first certainty is that there are no certainties – and anybody who doubts that need look only at the forecasts that predicted oil shortage and price escalation forever.

What actually happened, the crumbling away in the oil market, is a powerful and maybe ominous demonstration that the basic law of all markets will never be suspended: what goes up must come down. If what's rising is a price, sooner or later the higher cost will choke off demand, encourage substitution, and create a mounting surplus. With equal certainty, that glut will press harder and harder on prices until – presto! – it's no longer Yamani or your life.

But the law doesn't apply only to prices. Lovely, soaring profits eventually have the ugly effect of attracting competition, so that even a superb computer company like Digital Equipment finds its market share receding inexorably, to the point where it can no longer take recession in its stride. Instead, it suffers severe decline in profits. If that sounds painful, look at the slaughter that affected weaker firms, as IBM's PC took its inevitable lion's share of a market where far too many kittens had been making their small fortunes.

Even big Apple, having hired its first-ever marketing supremo, had to solve some vile problems as it fought back against IBM, striving to sell the make-or-break Macintosh marvels without undermining too soon its vital business with the great Apple II. When a market breaks, as have both Apple's and Sheikh Yamani's, those engaged have to remember one thing above all: the process is ineluctable. Once the basic economies of the market place have asserted themselves in this way, they can't be overturned.

Hence the truth that you can fix all of the markets some of the time, but none of the markets all of the time. The textbook answer to these dilemmas is that the company should establish so clear a marketing superiority that it is invulnerable – offering the highest perceived value at the highest price. The paradigm of this approach is Caterpillar Tractor. Yet it made losses for the first time in its history because of recession coupled with inability to match the fleetness of foot of Komatsu, its once far tinier Japanese competitor.

The tragedy is that the superior marketer may build so superior a market share and saturate the market so efficiently that the company has nowhere to hide when recession strikes. The only course is to recognize that, one day, marketing's law of gravity will affect every business, and that the force bringing the law into play, as likely as not, will be international competition. The global transportation revolution is basic here, but so is the new technology that allows, for example, unskilled Asians to assemble and export high-tech products.

To make matters worse, currency movements make it impossible to predict exactly where the most cutting competition will emerge. In early 1982 the joker in the pack was the United States, whose currency had fallen so heavily against the Deutschmark that exporting suddenly became fun for American corporations – and much more profitable. That challenge passed, but in 1985–6 the dollar was down again – and the yen so far up as to threaten Japanese prosperity. With its inefficient domestic economy and total need for imported raw materials, Japan has no option but to develop still more highly competitive export industries.

Since most western economies will also be trying to export more (if only to eliminate their energy deficits), you can bank on tough competition for as far as the eye dares to see. So how does the poor marketer manage? Actually, much as he or she was forced to manage from 1973 on.

1 Seeking higher added value first, rather than higher volume, by optimizing prices and reducing costs.
2 Going for specialized world markets rather than domestic commodity ones.
3 Taking all microeconomic opportunities you can find.
4 Developing as the main management strength the ability to compete – the crucial factor in today's markets.

Even for the best-placed companies, with the enormous boon of a rich market virtually to themselves, sooner or later somebody is likely to try muscling in. The Supermarketer of the 1980s and 1990s must become brilliant at repelling boarders and must learn to seize opportunities, but without being an opportunist. For this is a situation where it's essential to . . .

*Take a long-term view*. Don't jump in and out of markets and businesses, but aim to build a business that's good not just for this management generation but for the next, and the next. Having made up your mind on a market, show the utmost tenacity in sticking to it through thick and thin. By and large, in this effort to build long-term businesses . . .

*Grow internally*. Many growth companies starting in the stock market make acquisitions. But the Supermarketers know that buys designed to get you into a new business area never work without a great deal of sweat supplied by the buyer, and reckon that it's cheaper to build on your existing strengths – as Sears Roebuck, in its greatest days, did by adding stores to mail order. But in old and new businesses alike . . .

*Go for the largest attainable and profitable market share*. Be less interested in short-term profits than in pushing up your share of viable markets in the belief that long-term profits come from market strength. This means, of course, knowing enough about the market to have an accurate picture of what your share actually is. But that's no problem if you understand the necessity to . . .

*Spare no effort in getting all the information you can about the businesses and markets in which you're interested.* The amount that can be learned about competitors, without industrial espionage, is amazing. It's also amazing how many firms are ill-informed about themselves, let alone other firms. That makes it far more difficult, among other things, to be sufficiently alert to . . .

*Follow the leader.* Being first isn't always best. When other people do the pioneering, you can learn their lessons at their expense, strike while the iron is hot, and have a target to aim at: the pioneering Number One. Which means, of course, that you must have confidence in your ability to . . .

*Develop new products and services.* That has to be the prime aim of competition – with no nonsense about development being the task of engineers or some other separate group. Everybody in the business must be deeply involved – with the people at the sharp end, where the customers are, calling the tune. Don't rest until the offering meets all market needs. Which, of course, means *never* resting; and, even more important, you can then afford to . . .

*Compete on everything except price.* In export markets (essential because exporting builds volume and lowers unit costs), heavy price cutting is often enforced. At home, where things should be under better control, do all in your legal power to maintain prices – if possible, premium ones. Only a fool, goes the doctrine, charges less than the customer is ready to pay. If prices crumble, that robs you of the profit benefits you should get if you . . .

*Concentrate on strengths.* Search exhaustively for some asset you have that the competition hasn't, and that you can exploit to gain the upper hand. It might be high-volume, low-cost manufacture. It might be the best sales back-up in the business. It might be top quality. Or some combination of the above. Your strengths should provide the USP – the Unique Sales Proposition – yours and yours alone, which convinces the customers to buy from you and you alone. That's the strongest way to . . .

*Build a customer franchise.* The paying customers will come back again and again if they trust and like what you provide. The classic case in big business is IBM. Other American firms have had no trouble making products that are better than IBM's. But customers ignored them, by and large, because the IBM name was reassuring – and rightly so. With a strong customer franchise you can safely proceed to . . .

*Minimize risk*. Obviously, you can't avoid risk – that's life. But the business ideas that make Supermarketers rich are ones that are certain to succeed, provided they execute the plans well. One risk you'll never avoid is that you might do something badly. Leave that as little as possible to chance. Thoroughness and painstaking deliberation are essential, as is conservative finance; but, paradoxically, care and caution must be allied to quick reaction, speed of foot, and daring. Once you decide to move, and once everything is ready, move very fast. One of the key principles of competition, in fact, is that of continual reaction to changes in the market place, to whatever the opposition (closely monitored, of course) is up to, wherever it competes.

This guide to competitive success, by no coincidence, fits exactly the methods by which the Japanese companies have achieved what have truly been wonders of marketing. To produce premium products at lower cost than anybody else is a fabulous achievement in itself. But to use such abilities to crack strange market after strange market, in which you don't speak the language, and in which neither the buying habits nor the practices in any way resemble your own – that has to rank as the supreme demonstration of Supermarketing in our time.

The lesson for management is that strategy must at one and the same time be grand and limited. Whatever its resources and scale, the company of the 1980s and 1990s has no option but to specialize in intelligently selected markets in which it can hope to capitalize on its special skills. Yet the number of major business sectors in which any company, however great, can afford to miss out in the conditions of the 1980s is limited as well. Too many missed businesses, and a company is somebody else's potential purchase.

For all that the sovereign importance of establishing a stranglehold on the prime market or markets is inescapable. Do that, as the Supermarketing companies do, and at best the company will live happily and profitably ever after. At worst, the purchaser, hated or welcomed, will be forced to pay through the nose.

Note, too, that in an era when victory has been expected to go to the big battalions, market after market has been scooped by the relatively small. From now to the end of the century, the old, across-the-board markets that made corporations mighty will no longer hold sway. The emperor is as naked as everybody else in marketing when the specialities are so infinite. This has made Supermarketing a game anybody can play, with one supreme proviso: he or she must play it superbly.

# 15 Battle of the bestsellers

from *The New Naked Manager*

When I came to update *The Naked Manager*, the task originally seemed easy: just a straightforward run over the old, and largely unchanged territory. But the subject matter started to impose its own imperatives, and the book ended up as largely new in its material, though not in its basic philosophy. Of the many matters that had to be noted, one was in my own territory: the business book, where *In Search of Excellence* had shattered, smashed and superseded all sales records.

Not only that, but what was tantamount to a whole new genre of business autobiographies had also outsold any predecessors by millions – notably *Iacocca*. At Truman Talley's suggestion, I investigated the phenomenon, and found it a fascinating area. The bestsellers, autobiographical or not, were based largely on anecdote. So, in fact, is the vast bulk of management literature, even the academic and pseudo-academic. The strength of the ideas, fortunately, doesn't depend on that of the anecdotes: because time and again the anecdotal reporting and/or analysis proves to be in error – which at the least (*Excellence* being an excellent example) lays the authors wide open to criticism.

What the autobiographies do is to uncover one of the main causes of false reports: falsified accounts by managers. The problem was highlighted in *The Naked Manager* and my subsequent books. It isn't necessarily that managers lie: rather, that they don't tell the truth – although they may honestly believe in what they are saying. Add to that the instinctive (but often wrong) equation of brilliant financial results with brilliant management, and you easily end up with wrong-headed evaluation of heroes – companies and entrepreneurs alike.

Beyond that, however, fashions in management literature are like those in every other field. Of themselves, they reveal the important underlying trends of the times. Thus all the big bestselling books mentioned are American: and the most crucial trend here, in my view, is the effort – essential, belated and somewhat baffled – of the American manager to reassert the global business hegemony that his predecessors had frittered away.

The wondrous boom in management of the post-1973 era quite inevitably meant a wonderful something else: a boom in management literature. Managers desperately needed more knowledge to cover their nakedness, and books are where knowledge resides. Robert Townsend's *Up The Organisation* and Lawrence Peter's *The Peter Principle* proved to be the iconoclastic forerunners of a stream of non-academic tomes that became a spate – and then turned off in a new and unexpected direction. Even *In Search of Excellence* (the book that brought new riches to consultancy) did so in the time-honoured manner, writing about the great and the good.

Time (and honour) have changed, however. Now the great, the good and the not-so-good write about themselves. True, Townsend used his turnaround triumph at Avis as a peg on which to hang his enthusiastic ideas about permissive, Theory $\Upsilon$ management. But it was still definitely a management book. In 1984, though, the runaway, unprecedented bestseller success of Lee Iacocca's life and good times changed the name of the game. Iacocca's book is a full-blooded autobiography, more in the vein of John De Lorean's literary work – the self-justifying effort of a failure with a great deal to justify.

In one way or another, though, all the tycoon texts are as interested in justifying or glorifying the self as in offering precepts for management. Since this vainglorious element is so obvious, what explains the public's hunger for reading the works?

One answer is simply that the tycoons (or their publishers) mostly had the wit to employ professional writers, and even to name them. Once upon a time, businessmen confined their literary ambitions to inter-office memos and annual reports, and that's how most of them write. But beyond the literary professionalism, and far more important, lies the same quest for certainty in an uncertain world that explained the equally unprecedented multimillion sales of *In Search of Excellence*, or the high-rise sales of books promising to reveal the secrets of Japanese business success. The management readers want reassurance; they want to hear that, if they only imitate this marvellous man, or adopt that magical recipe, they can rise above the toughest challenges, as Iacocca did so superbly at Chrysler.

Not that more than a portion of Iacocca's amazing sales were confined to managers. But any budding boardroom authors inspired by its success should beware. Few other executives have lived through such tumult. None have become preternaturally famous through appearing (in 97 per cent of US households, 63 times each) in their own commercials ('If you can find a better car – buy it'). Few can tell a story that has so many elements of a *Dallas*-type television blockbuster. The Ford years alone brim with blood and thunder: the ageing 'despot' (Iacocca's word for Henry II) maintaining his cramping grip on a lavish and indulgent court at the price of destroying the ambitious, brilliant, thrusting Crown Prince . . .

Similarly, Mark McCormack has enough fame as the entrepreneur/agent who made Arnold Palmer into a multinational, megabuck corporation to give any book a flying start. But celebrity isn't the sole explanation: the sales of his *What They Don't Teach You at Harvard Business School*, of *Iacocca*, and of *Managing*, the testament of ITT's Harold Geneen, are also symptoms of a general upsurge of interest in the business of business. The issue is whether the books do anything for management other than line the already richly coated pockets of their prime authors; whether the readers obtain anything for the expenditure of a few bucks other than a warm feeling in the heart.

To be fair, that question can be asked of any management book, including this one. The *Iacocca* phenomenon is only a mite more remarkable than that of *In Search of Excellence* – or that of *The One-Minute Manager* and its 60-second progeny. That first slim (or minute) volume basically consisted of a crisp lesson as old as management itself, if not older: 'Don't hire a dog and bark yourself.' Apart from that incontrovertible advice on delegation, and a simplistic three-stage guide to retaining control and motivation while delegating, *The One-Minute Manager* has little to offer except brevity. That's no criticism of the book, though, for the limited range of its lore isn't at all exceptional.

The eight basic attributes, the highest common factors, which the two consultant authors found in their search for *Excellence* among America's leading corporations can also be summed up in one page and read aloud in one minute. That's a vital mark of the business-book bonanza: the essential message, even if the volume, like *What They Don't Teach*, runs to 249 pages, can be expressed in very short compass. Thus, McCormack's argument is that what Harvard doesn't 'teach you is what they *can't* teach you, which is how to read people and how to use that knowledge to get what you want'. His 'seven-step plan' to supply this academic deficiency occupies just two and a half pages and twenty-four key words ('listen aggressively; observe aggressively; talk less; take a second look at first impressions; take time to use what you've learned; be discreet; be detached').

Good, sound advice it is too. There are other equally pithy summaries *en route* to the epilogue, like how to deal with employees: (1) Pay them what they are worth, (2) Make them feel that they are important, yet (3) Make them think for themselves, and (4) Separate office life from social life. Again, the words are worth their weight in silver, if not in gold: but they are hardly enough to fill a book. So what does?

The answer in McCormack's case is a wealth of anecdote, much of it inconsequential, and a welter of advice, mostly disconnected. The anecdotes are about sports more than management, for McCormack appreciates better than anybody (he should) the value of dropping a good heroic name; viz. 'I bring up Arnold Palmer's name in business conversations all the time.' But McCormack isn't as original or non-academic as he would have you believe. Some of the lessons he offers are in fact taught at Harvard (like the 80–20 rule, which lays down that 20 per cent of your customers provide 80 per cent of your sales, etc.) and the art of positioning (which tells you where to place and price your offerings in the market place).

What Lee Iacocca learned in the hard school of Detroit, too, wouldn't surprise any Harvard professor. In the 16 pages (out of 341) which he devotes to 'The Key to Management', the Chrysler hero advises on quarterly review of subordinates' performance (his favourite nostrum), on decision-making, on motivation, on delegation, on the importance of having a strong ego (but never a large one) and on the vital role of team spirit. The note the Chrysler saviour strikes here is similar to Mark McCormack's, and for similar reasons: both men are great salesmen. Iacocca's management methods – including the review device – derive from managing the salesman and sharing his prejudices: thus Iacocca waxes quite lyrical about the inherent conflict between 'the guys in sales and marketing' and 'the bean-counters'.

The latter are the accountants, a breed of whom Iacocca is wary, even though, as he stresses, the terrifying problems at Chrysler included the fact that nobody was counting the beans properly. Without getting crisp, clear financial information about just how and where Chrysler was losing so many hundreds of millions, Iacocca and his team couldn't begin to stem the loss of corporate blood. But Iacocca wasn't really concerned to discuss the finer, or even the coarser points of management. He was far more concerned to demonstrate that the Ford Motor board were deeply culpable for agreeing to the demand of Henry Ford (that 'evil man') for the head of so splendid a president.

You certainly can't argue with at least three of the great man's achievements – anyway, not as he tells them. As the head of the Ford Division ('the happiest period of my life'), he found 'a market in search of a car' and launched the Mustang, which netted over $1 billion in its first two years. That was after killing the Cardinal, a potentially disastrous plan to build a European-designed compact in the US.

Later triumphs recorded by their author included the billion-dollar project, another crucial decision, to launch the small Fiesta in Europe. Add the revamp of the Lincoln division with the Mark models (one Mark equalling ten Falcons in profit terms) and you have a terrific track record. Which raises two questions. One, obviously, is why Henry Ford fired the champ. The other is why, with so much Iacocca goodness going for it, Ford failed under him to emerge as a great, deeply admired, powerhouse super-challenger to General Motors and the world – especially Japan.

Iacocca's thesis is that the two answers are linked. Bad decisions by Henry (like his veto of a terrific deal to buy Honda power trains for a US-made small car) offset the Iacocca brainwaves, while the hero's good management was vitiated by Henry's bad habits, like firing his brightest and best – including Iacocca's top auto man, Hal Sperlich (the hero weakly complied with this execution), and above all Iacocca himself. Yet consider this passage:

> The day after I was fired, Henry sent off a letter to every Ford dealer in the country, trying to reassure them all that they wouldn't be neglected: 'The Company has a strong and experienced management team. Our North American Automotive Operations are headed by talented executives who are well known to you and who are fully attuned to your needs and the needs of the retail market.' Of course [writes Iacocca], if that were really true, there would have been no need for the letter.

But if that were *not* really true, if Ford *didn't* have a strong and experienced management team, whose fault was that? Iacocca had been President for eight years, after all. Then, consider the Pinto disaster. After 'a number of accidents where the car burst into flames after a rear-end collision', Ford was charged with 'reckless homicide. Ford was acquitted, but the damage to the company was incalculable . . . We resisted making any change, and that hurt us badly.'

Iacocca himself asks 'Whose fault was it?' and concedes that 'One obvious answer is that it was the fault of Ford's management – including me.' But surely, again, it was more Iacocca's fault than anybody's, on the basic management principle that the buck stops here – at the desk of the million-a-year man in operational charge. Presumably it was mere coincidence that 'we voluntarily recalled almost a million and a half Pintos . . . in June 1978, the month before I was fired'. But Iacocca conveys a strong impression of taking 90 per cent of the credit for all Ford's feats and little or none for its flops.

What that proves is that super-managers aren't superhuman. They feel such common-or-garden human urges as the need to present themselves in the best possible light, their enemies in the worst. Given the chance to write history, they rewrite it to suit (literally) their book. In that they are no different from ex-Presidents of the United States. Just like the White House heroes, too, the tycoons can now, thanks to the bestseller industry, reap huge financial rewards – even if, as in Iacocca's case, the need for still more personal millions isn't especially apparent.

It's a fair guess that the money motive, even if powerful, comes well behind the passionate drive to justify the self. This essential element of self-justification is as strong, if not stronger, in a book that doesn't even call itself after its hero – *Managing*. To read this work, you would imagine that its author, Harold S. Geneen, was one of America's most successful managers. And so he was, up to a point: that point being when he stepped down from the chairmanship of the company, ITT, of which he was the second founder.

In management, the evil that powerful men do lives after them – and (like Iacocca with Ford) Geneen would have to shoulder some responsibility for ITT's unhappy recent history, its sell-offs, slump in earnings and vulnerability to predators, even if he hadn't hung on, Godfather-like, as a powerful and interventionist presence on the board. None of that is recounted in his book, though. The innocent manager would suppose that ITT was still regarded with deepest respect, even awe, at the time of writing. The less innocent manager, though, will guess from Geneen's own account, which does not spare self-praise, how the seeds of defeat were sown in the master's victories, and why they were bound to yield a bitter harvest. He tells, for instance, of 350 buys, mergers and absorptions, many hasty, most acquired at asking price. Just how do you manage a consequently enormous spread of 250 profit centres? Many, moreover, were bound, on the law of averages alone, to be duds – and expensive ones, at that.

In answer, Geneen's overall principle is 'You read a book from the beginning to the end. You run a business the opposite way. You start with the end, and then you do everything you have to do to reach the bottom line.' The bottom-most line was ITT's target growth in earnings per share: 10 per cent per annum compound. To achieve the bottom line (as he did, remarkably enough), Geneen set up an elaborate, exacting system of budgets, monthly reports and interventionist visits at will by his staff experts anywhere in the company. Geneen calls this invigilation 'open communications'; no doubt some of the invigilated gave it less pleasant names.

But the centrepiece of the system was the General Managers Meeting. All 250 managing directors met Geneen and his cohorts (a strike force of 40-odd executives) once a month, either in Brussels or in New York, for sessions lasting at least 12 hours daily over several days. In all, says Geneen, ITT management spent 35 weeks of every year on planning, budgeting, and the notoriously inquisitorial meetings. Allowing for vacations, 'That left a scant 13 weeks of "other time" to run the company.' Some men cracked under the stress of the inquisitions. But setting that aside, their still worse defect, shared with the whole apparatus, was just what the quote implies: most of the time, Geneen was running the system, not the company.

It was a system, too, that could be worked only by one brilliant, driven and driving man: Harold S. Geneen. Moreover, it was a system uniquely equipped to seize tight control of an uncontrolled empire and provide a framework into which acquisitions could be speedily slotted and where they could be duly disciplined in turn. But Geneen, with his concentration on short-term results and distrust of planning ('There will be no more long-range planning' is the entire text of one early memo), seems to miss a vital point – that every business has two bottom lines: the financial one, of which he was the supreme maestro, and the organic one, which determines its future.

The organic bottom line would have included such objectives as intensifying ITT's technological power in its base telecommunications markets, instead of allowing it to slip behind, perhaps fatefully. The ITT giant was in too many businesses to manage them centrally, but its central system was much too strong for them to be managed independently. So long as Geneen was there, his own dynamic performance partially hid this reality. With him removed, painful reality came bursting through – but not for Geneen.

He writes witheringly about the man who 'becomes unwilling to accept information which is contrary to some preconceived notion or image of himself held in his mind . . . (who) believes that he is smarter than everyone else, that everyone else is there to serve him'. Outsiders at the time of his personal domination of ITT were led to think this scathing description of the 'supreme egotist in corporate life' to be an excellent one of Geneen himself: it's an image that his book does little to dispel.

Inability to see themselves as others see them, even such spectacular blindness as Geneen's, isn't confined to managers. Self-deception is a common managerial vice – and blindness to personal defects, even worse, easily goes with the avoidance or ignorance of unpleasant truths about the business. Maybe the supermanager memoirs should all be accompanied by an antidote, a commentary supplied by a candid friend, or even an honest enemy, so the reader at least learns that the great man's character and conduct have a side other than the one he chooses to display.

There are also, of course, alternative views of the events he describes. Robert Townsend's version of events at Avis has been questioned by his co-workers, for example. In a famous passage in *Up The Organisation*, Townsend describes how White Plains was chosen as the head office site by imagining where 'a man from Mars' would land as his chosen centre for a multinational car rental business. The revisionists say that the decisive factor came, not from outer space, but from the fact that most of the decision-makers lived nearby. Similarly, one old Avis hand complained that, sure, Townsend (as he reports) had no secretary – but he used everybody else's, and they hated it.

Be that as it may, does it matter? The 'man from Mars' technique – trying to shake free of all acquired attitudes and received ideas before making a decision – is no worse for being based (if it is) on a misleading anecdote. Actually, the idea is very sound – and all the sounder if you gather, from the revised version, how difficult it is to be honestly Martian, truly aloof from preconceptions and predispositions. The issue of secretaries, what they are used for, whether they are truly needed, is one that's rarely faced, but should be. The story helps focus the mind, like all parables. And if you find that it may be a fib, that might help you to examine your own conscience for fibs, possibly harmful ones, of your own.

Does it matter any more if the account misleads about actual and important events? If Lee Iacocca wasn't, say, as he has always claimed, 'the father of the Mustang'? In the authorized, or Iacocca version, the project sprang from his brain and was carried to sensational fruition by his energy. According to Ford's designer, not so: Iacocca was presented with a completed model on taking over his beloved Ford Division, and then ran with the ball. The truth matters in one sense, because truth always matters. But in terms of the managerial value of *Iacocca*, as of *Up The Organisation*, that worth lies in the inspirational example – and the description of the market analysis that targeted the Mustang's sector is unquestionably valuable, whoever first dreamt up the car.

All the same, the battle of the bestsellers has taken the managerial book far away from the scholarly, deeply researched, thoughtful works of a pioneering writer such as Peter Drucker: far away, too, from a book like *My Years with General Motors*, in which the between-wars super-manager Alfred P. Sloan Jr wrote not about himself but about the history of the great corporation of which he was the architect. It took Sloan 467 pages to tell a story that is still an indispensable management text. No doubt, gilded lilies and misreported events occur in Sloan's narrative, but it's difficult to believe, when reading that careful, dispassionate, fact-filled prose, that the lapses from grace are many.

For that reason, Sloan's *magnum opus* will probably still be around when today's mega-sellers and their hectic, 'as-told-to' journalistic prose are long forgotten. That, too, may not matter. As Sloan wrote of the corporation: 'No company ever stops changing. Change will come for better or worse . . . The task of management is not to apply a formula but to decide issues on a case-by-case basis.'

What's true of the corporation is true of management in general. Behind the hype and the hoop-la, the bestsellers gain their currency (in both senses of the word) from a direct relevance to real and deep concerns of changing times, even if the relevance isn't too obvious. There *is* a strong backlash against the B-school academicism enshrined at Harvard, for instance. There *is* a powerful reaction against the awful internal and external abuses of corporations like Henry Ford II's Ford or the pre-Iacocca Chrysler.

There is, too, a general wave of acute awareness that the American corporation has been long overdue for renaissance, for just the kind of managerial renewal that the sage Sloan foresaw. Whatever the motives and misdeeds of the hero authors, and however many millions their books coin, reading about the experience of other managers is the best (and cheapest) method around of giving naked managers a few more clothes. It helps greatly if they don't fall for the super-manager myths, to be sure. It helps even more if they learn from their reading not to create myths of their own.

# 16 If you can't be careful, be good

from *The Common Millionaire*

The last two chapters in this anthology should be read together. While a philosophy of management and human affairs does, I profoundly hope, run implicitly through all my writing, the closing chapters of two books – *The Common Millionaire* and *The New Naked Manager* – express these beliefs explicitly. The connection between the books is clear: successful business management creates great personal wealth, and in both the getting and the spending fundamental questions about society and the individual's duties towards society are inevitably raised.

Raised, yes; answered, no. What exclusively concerned thinkers like Rousseau and Marx has passed into the history of political thought, not into its present. The dearth and death of political philosophy, the subject that absorbed the Greeks and occupied some of the greatest minds from the Middle Ages to the twentieth century, is an extraordinary development. Capitalist or communist, the world has settled for what it has: new orders are not wanted.

Widening affluence (in only the developed world, alas) has produced this social acceptance and stability – and I revel, as anybody must, in the amazing success of the post-war economies in giving ordinary people options, opportunities and even opulence that they had never before envisaged, let alone enjoyed. But that generalization of wealth has made the exceptions – what John Kenneth Galbraith called the contrast between private affluence and public squalor – only more glaring and unacceptable. These are issues that the millionaires and the great

corporate magnates (often one and the same) would be unwise to
ignore.

I go into these socio-political issues more deeply in a new
book, *The Age of the Common Millionaire*: the Crash of '87 has lent
greater force to its ideas by baring the fragile foundations of
western prosperity. I do not expect the house to come tumbling
down: after seeing meltdown after meltdown averted (if only
just), I remain optimistic about the future of economic man, just
as I am about human nature itself.

The two are indivisible, of course, and I have wanted, with all
my books, to work towards a blend of humanism, humanity and
human reason (man's unique quality) with business economics.
These two chapters sum up my conviction that the blend is not
only feasible, but also the best long-term guarantee of profit and
prosperity – without which all other human goods are infinitely
more difficult to achieve.

> *A recipe to regain high moral standing which has never*
> *been known to fail in the most desperate cases of ill-gotten*
> *gains . . . and which starts with the recognition that all*
> *great gains, by virtue of their greatness alone, are to a true*
> *extent gotten ill.*

There are no golden rules for achieving the seven-digit nirvana; but
there are golden rules, guiding principles, for use on the way up,
while on top, and, if the best comes to the worst, on the way down.
Like every set of rules compiled since the Ten Commandments,
every item isn't relevant on every occasion or to every worshipper:
the man or woman who covets his neighbour's ox (or Boeing 727)
may have no use whatsoever for adultery.

But the charm of rules is that they can be broken, every single
one of them, and the breaker can still win. Making money, after all,
is a competitive sport; and success in competition doesn't depend
on your observation of precept, it depends on whether you outscore the competition.

It may help to achieve this result by sandbagging the poor
fellow, putting anti-pep dope in his tea, taking pep dope yourself,

lining his track shoes with lead, tripping him, and so forth. But cheating isn't necessary, even if many millions have been made by cheats. The rich in fact divide into three categories: those who would trample over their grandmothers on any pretext, because that is their horrible nature; those who, faced with the choice of losing money or grandma, would kiss the old lady a tender goodbye; those who would honour their grandmother in any circumstances, no matter what the cost.

The general view of economic history is that most millionaires fit into the middle category. They behave decently, or no more indecently than the mass of mortals, unless pushed, when no holds are barred. A small but significant number are natural grandma-tramplers; and a tiny minority are upright, benevolent and honourable at all times.

Virtue in this sense has nothing to do with good works: all the Rockefeller benefactions can no more wash away the memory of the old boy's sins than the perfume of Araby could cleanse the hands of Lady Macbeth. Many godly religious sects have been handsomely financed by royal flushes of fortune – notably in Texas – but the common assumption is that these benefactions are more often expiations for past offences committed in the service of Mammon, than expressions of great goodness.

It's the same with noble motives: they do not invariably express noble natures. John Spedan Lewis, a second generation genius who transformed his family department store inheritance, handed over control of his business to all the employees under a unique partnership scheme. True, the Lewis family was inordinately rich by this time – but Lewis also gave the staff his Longstock Park mansion, complete with contents, plus a handsome riverside estate for their partnerly recreation.

Those bald facts might imply that Lewis was a saint among men, let alone millionaires. In truth, however, for all his partnership ideals, Lewis was a highly autocratic, high-handed ruler who, after surrendering control, tended to regret the surrender. Admonitions to his successors would appear embarrassingly in the partnership magazine, despatched from his self-styled 'burrow in Longstock Park' – and in Lewis's version of partnership it has always been clear that, to paraphrase Orwell, some partners are very much more equal than others. Generosity with material goods is not the same as a generous attitude to power.

Much the same tale can be told of another great social reformer, who was indifferent to personal wealth: Gottlieb Duttweiler, the brave Swiss who spotted that big companies were ganging up on the customer by charging unnecessarily high prices; Dutti undercut the over-chargers by selling first from vans, then from his chain of Migros outlets. Migros was a co-operative, owned by its grateful customers in Switzerland, or so it was supposed by those who had not studied the Migros constitution. The set-up left Dutti and his family a controlling interest, special rights and effective power for as long as they cared to exercise it – which in Dutti's case was until death did him part.

There is the case of the greatest banker ever to bounce a cheque, A. P. Giannini, who steadfastly refused to make his family superrich from his building of the Bank of America; and there is that of the Tatas in India, whose former wealth is vested in charitable foundations, but who still rule the East's biggest private industrial empire with iron rods.

The cynical view (and cynics have a saving habit of being right) is that capital accumulation in the private sector plays the same role as tax in the public sector – it provides the means by which the mighty and their minions exercise their power. Indeed, the millionaire's millions, no less than the Revenue's riches, represent a tax levied involuntarily from the citizenry.

The citizen contemplating a war in Vietnam knows that the finance came from him and his fellows; contemplating the Bar Harbor estate of the Rockefellers, the sizeable choice acreages of Europe owned by the Rothschilds, or the whopping incomes of the Japanese industrialists, the citizen never thinks that this money came from exactly the same source as the tax dollar: from a percentage of the earnings of the masses. (Not to dwell on the fact that sometimes the private dollars and the tax dollars are one and the same, transferred to the private sector from the public by the beneficence or corruption of the politicians.)

In public life, it was long ago recognized that politicians have to be kept under constant scrutiny and ultimate control if they are not to abuse their power. That process works imperfectly; but the devices for controlling malefactors of great wealth, in Teddy Roosevelt's phrase, are less powerful to start with, are less numerous than the political restraints and work no more effectively.

This fact should intensify the pressure on the financially potent to exercise restraint on themselves – although nobody can expect them to behave in those ways considered normal by people who think themselves normal.

The rich begin by being exceptional, original, unusual, eccentric in varying degrees and styles. Their differences start them on their way, and the rush of power to their purses accentuates their differentiated traits. But to all the rich one law applies: if they have to count the money, pound by pound, dollar by dollar, something is wrong, somewhere – a clerk in the counting house is running away with the loot, or an investment is haemorrhaging, or Midas himself has mislaid his touch. And the sensation that something, somewhere is awry must never be ignored – like a pain in the abdomen, it's nature's warning, not to be ignored.

The messages of nature are a millionaire's most valuable communications. Few fortunes could have been created without a successful hunch, a display of divine intuition. Hunch is not luck, however lucky a hunch may seem. Instead, the computer in the skull has run through a whole series of complicated routines, operational research sums, market-research equations, multiple regression analyses, discounted cash-flow calculations, opportunity costings, decision trees complete with probability factors. All these mathematical marvels have flashed through the brain's maze of electro-chemical circuits with speed so dazzling that the computer's owner himself is unaware of the brilliant series of algebraic assessments that lead him to express a hunch or 'gut feeling'.

To ignore this highly sophisticated machine is a folly – akin to that of the owners of a computer, programmed to play the stock market, who refused to believe the thing when it resolutely refused to buy a single stock. 'Computer,' said they to it, 'there must be something you want to buy.' It thought again, and still said no. 'Computer,' they sadly observed, 'you must have made a mistake somewhere. We're going to have to override you.' The market promptly went into a flat spin, vindicating the computer and mortifying its masters.

The lesson, which applies to millionaires and non-millionaires alike, is to heed your computer: it will even obligingly provide extra warnings, not flashing lights, but physical symptoms (a tightening sensation in the stomach, tingling of the scalp, pulsations in the stomach, commotions in the bowels). These messages from inner space mean that your computer has evaluated whatever asininity you propose to undertake and found it bad.

The warnings seldom come from the conscience. Only the moral have moral qualms – the immoral or amoral, like the denizens of Richard Nixon's White House, believe self-righteously that their ends (self-evidently right) justify their means. There's no argument on this point: the virtuous course (like not stabbing some unsuspecting partner between the clavicles) is always clear, and virtue should always be pursued, even if it costs money. After all, few sensations are more pleasant or enduring than the odour of true sanctity: it's worth every penny.

As a bonus, bear in mind that although virtue is not its own reward, the wages of sin are sometimes death. Grave misdemeanours (as Bernie Cornfeld, *et al.*, must have reflected) frequently have grave consequences. For every Rockefeller I who escapes scot-free with his moral crimes, there is a Krupp III who reaps the harvest of his ancestor's misdeeds. Admittedly, finding a fault-free tycoon appears to be only slightly easier than hunting through a haystack for that recalcitrant needle.

Two separate inquiries into the iniquities of wealth (*The Rich and the Super-Rich* and *America, Inc*) each came up with only one candidate for goodness and pelf combined: the same man, T. R. Danforth of Ralston Purina. All that this paucity of saintly candidates implies is that, in making money, as in most areas of achievement, idols have not feet but entire lower limbs of clay.

Goodness is a private matter. What is known about Danforth is not the whole picture; maybe the entirety would reinforce the good image, maybe not. The good that men do lives after them; the evil is oft interred with their bones. If evil, or quasi-evil, does litter your path, however, the same rule applies as to any other vice: don't carry it to excess. If you must cheat somebody, for instance, don't try to cheat the same man or men again; next time round, they may be ready.

It pays, in any event, to be careful who you pick to cheat, out-bargain or battle with. Remember the natural law that money flows upwards from the weak to the strong, from the many to the few, from the poor to the rich. It is flying in the face of nature to tangle with a richer tycoon. (A contest with a corporation, as we have seen time and time again, is a different matter. The odds are on David's side because, in all probability, he is both richer and craftier than the paid servants of Goliath). The plain millionaire who seeks advantage from dealing with a fancy multi-millionaire needs a large insurance policy.

Not only does the richer man have more resources: the chances are that he arrived at his higher status by deploying greater wiliness and garnering greater bargaining skills along his path. Anyway, he has an inherent advantage. By definition, the sum at stake is more important to the smaller man, which makes him more eager to consummate the deal. In that over-eagerness, he is apt to overpay. Far better to stay on the top side.

Keeping the top slice is also highly advisable. Common Millionaires derive their wealth from equity interests. Dilution of that equity – that is, reducing the proportion of profits or assets to which it is entitled – is justified only if compensated for by a nourishing increase in capital worth. But the most tempting form of dilution is rarely justified: and that's the ancient game of sending bad money after good. If a venture blasts off rapidly and then requires further infusion of capital, the sound course is to raise the money from some friendly neighbourhood banker. The return on equity must fall sharply if the millionaire dips into his own resources. Cutting others in on the game is always to be encouraged so long as that first or top slice grows thicker and fatter as a result.

If you are predominantly interested in the money rather than the business, moreover, it makes no sense to maintain any stake higher than respectability demands. You can reduce a controlling interest to 20 per cent before anybody smells either a rat or a sinking ship. A high stock rating should always be cashed in by a cash addict, for the simple reason that what goes up must come down, and always does.

Recognition of that law of financial gravity demands the virtue of humility, which is the essential element in goodness – and one that goes against the driving urge. So the driven man should propel himself to as lofty a height as possible while the propulsion works: he can then more easily withstand a terrible fall. The megalomaniac John H. Patterson of National Cash Register was a loony who insisted on his minions chewing each mouthful thirty-two times, who closed down his Dayton plants entirely to teach the city fathers a lesson, and who absented himself for two years in Europe – all without destroying the cash-generating power of a mighty business. His successors, with not a smidgen of a mania between them, did more harm by the mistakes in computery and product development that wiped out NCR's profits in 1972: the moral there is that mad inspiration beats dull honesty every time.

For Patterson was also a notable breaker of laws. It's easier for the rich and powerful to offend against statute, not only because the legal authorities are more reluctant to proceed against plutocrats than pickpockets, but also because the rich, and the rich company, can afford rich lawyers, and because the laws the wealthy break are often so complex that it takes squads of lawyers several years to work their way through the maze (a tangle made more impenetrable still by the tendency of the rich and their legal eagles to complicate the simplest transactions).

After Calouste Gulbenkian's 5 per cent deal with his partners in Iraq's oilfields had been rewritten, one of the lawyers remarked that these contracts could never be the subject of litigation, because nobody would ever be able to understand them. The labyrinth in which financial minotaurs like Bernie Cornfeld lie in wait for their prey similarly appeals to the labyrinthine mind, and is the final defence of the ungodly. But some brave Theseus will wend his way through in the end; and it is a matter of historical fact that, by and large, the criminal millionaire (or for that matter the millionaire criminal) although he may die in luxury, and honours, often does suffer some blow or fate that punishes his sins like a Capone imprisoned for tax evasion and dying of syphilis, or a Buggsy Siegel bullet-holed by his pals.

This Calvinist-sounding truth has morals as well as morality on its side. He who already has millions no longer has any excuse for immorality, even the usual badness. He can afford to be good, which doesn't mean donating wealth to charity, still less to tax-dodging charitable foundations. It means following strict standards of decency – and that demands the hardest self-sacrifice of all, which is for the human leopard to change his spots.

One tycoon, caught in a mess of deceitful accounting by his bright young men, was bewailing his bad luck to a business associate – such a mess had entangled him before, he moaned, referring to a well-known incident a few years back in which he had been widely castigated as a crook. His version of the old story utterly convinced his hearer: as the tycoon reasonably argued, he was over sixty and very rich – why on earth would he have engaged in any personal skulduggery?

The true answer was simple: he did, just because he didn't need to. The honest crook, so to speak, lies and cheats because he must, and at the time (let alone in hindsight) can't tell the difference between fact and fiction. In this case, not only had the tycoon in the first place been guilty as charged (or not charged – the police stayed clear) but was re-enacting a very similar scenario at the time of his apologia.

Many leopards need a professional spot-changer or watcher in their employ. As a generalization, a master is only as good as his best servant: the quality of a man's nearest and dearest associate is an excellent guide to his own true stature. If the deputy, partner or sidekick is made of clay, so, more often than not, are the master's feet.

This is an uncommonly useful fact; so long as the master can maintain objectivity about those around him, he can, by applying this test, derive an objective judgement about himself. Unfortunately, the self-deceptive mechanism comes into play. Surrounded by ninnies, the maestro convinces himself that his staff is made up of every genius known to the business world. They naturally demonstrate that true and fine talent by hanging on to his every word and behest.

The ultra-rich can be excused for living in a dream world, since so much of their life story is in itself of dreamlike quality. The billionaire H. L. Hunt once said that 'there are times when I wish I would wake up stone-broke. It would be a great adventure to see how good I was, to see if I could create lots of wealth again.' This, of course, was wishful thinking of the woolliest kind: the process that took him from fifty bucks in 1921 to a couple of billion three decades later proved nothing about his 'goodness' in any context other than oil.

But the story, like all get-rich tales, is a true adventure, and a true-life one. You could excuse the old cuss for saying, in effect, that he wanted to live so rewarding a life all over again. And, in his use of the word 'good', he put his oil-stained finger on a vital clue: that, in addition to human decency, the rich can afford high professional standards.

By and large, the millionaire has some professional talent that is incomparably superior to those of his fellows. This talent is the horse he rides to the winning post. To develop this star talent fully, and surround it with the most able supporting cast money can buy, is a relatively dignified pastime, and one that has the concomitant virtue of defending a man's fortune. It's not asking much to demand that the man be good at his job and insist that others be equally proficient at theirs.

In this he will differ from one not untypical monster who, in addition to forcing an audience of 140 to listen to a two-day masterly monologue, would sabotage anybody else's ideas as soon as he heard about them – in order to prove that he was indispensable. Very few fortune-makers are: but even those who are possessed of rare genius must recognize that, if man doesn't dispense with them, God certainly will – at least from this earth

Until that event, certain moral precepts will guide the feet more safely to their destination, material as well as spiritual. If you are happy being private, count your blessings – not your hypothetical unmade public millions. If you can't manage by yourself, buy somebody who can. If you've made money by fooling all of the people, stop it before some of them find out. If you're telling lies to others, tell the truth to yourself. If you succeed by doing less badly than others, don't kid yourself that you've triumphed by doing much better. If you must buy other businesses, run the many as carefully as the few or the one. If you maintain a complex structure, for tax, divorce or other reasons, make sure that at least you understand it. If you diversify, keep your eye on the real ball and the main chance. If you must bet, pick certainties. If you back others, don't pick a simulacrum of your younger self, or anybody else, if your choice is not governed by expertise and experience.

If you borrow, borrow big – and with security. If you lend, lend proportionately small – and with double security. If you work for a company, remember that feathering the corporate nest is the honest way of feathering your own. If dealing, don't steal. If you start small, preserve your little virtues. If you put your hand in the public purse, do so legitimately: graft is criminal. If you are lucky, light a candle. If you are dealing with a fat corporation, light two candles.

If you are paying too much tax, change your tax adviser. If you have an invention, sell it reluctantly – and dearly. If you are selling, don't cheat. If you can make things better, go on doing it. If you know what people want, give it to them. If your personal life is complex, put plenty in the piggybank: two Humble Oil beneficiaries, Mrs Cecil Blaffer Hudson and Bobo Rockefeller, collected nearly $13 million between them as they competed for the world-record divorce settlement.

All these are laws of the obvious. But making gigantic fortunes is mostly nothing but the exploitation of the obvious – an obvious so glaring that nobody else has noticed, or known how to exploit it. The discovery must be obvious because, unless the truth is large, it will never yield the gains that will add up to a net worth of suitable size. Countless big fortunes have arisen through standing self-evident propositions, received truths, on their heads – including the ancient saw, 'If your idea's so good, why isn't anybody else doing it?'

The answer is that one reason why the idea is so good is exactly because nobody else has caught on. What the financially blind use as an excuse for their lack of vision, the long-sighted employ as a radio telescope. There are, true, examples of fortunes made by indulging in some general, obvious passion. All that proves is that making money proves nothing.

The fact adds to the questions asked down the centuries by religious leaders and philosophers, by political thinkers like Veblen and, above all, Marx: questions that will never go away, because they have no answer. To put them at their simplest, these permanent doubts, partly moral, partly rational, partly egalitarian, can be expressed in one huge query: Why does one man possess so much, while another has so little?

Because the unanswerable questions of ownership, inheritance, control, accountability and so on are never tackled (and perhaps never can be), society is uneasily divided between fascination by fortunes and guilty resentment of the rich. But any student of the wealthy, and of the means by which they acquired their wealth, must conclude that there is no rational relationship between their riches and their achievement: the one is wildly disproportionate to the other. This statement of fact carries inevitable connotations of disapproval. It is also the reason (as a few of the rich have had the grace to recognize) behind the powerful truth that 'from him to whom much is given, much shall be required'. For it is equally true that, to him to whom much is given, too much is given.

# 17 The well-dressed executive

from *The New Naked Manager*

Next to being told how good they are individually, executives best love to hear how bad they are as a bunch. Any course of myth-destruction serves this therapeutic purpose, but at a price: that of building another myth, which is that all executives, being foolish and foible-ridden, make a bad job worse. All that I know about management was learnt from executives, some of whom are my friends, many of whom I admire, most of whom deserve respect – clever people who work hard according to their best lights in circumstances that are often against them. This chapter is for them. As for the idle, selfish, stupid self-deceivers, this is how to beat them and enjoy it.

The myths keep on coming, and from all directions: from the consultants and the professors, the gurus and the goops, the vain autobiographers and the eager army of business journalists. One grand myth in particular became firmly entrenched in the 1980s with the aid of all the above interested parties: the idea, akin to the Big Bang theory of the creation of the universe, that there is One Big Solution. Whether it's the One-Minute Manager or the Eight Attributes of Corporate Excellence, the fundamental fiction is the same: that Highest Common Factors exist, which you can derive from study of the Highest Uncommon Companies or their executives.

Since you can find out what happens in corporations only by observing their activities, past and present, and drawing conclusions from what you see, it's impossible for any writer about management, including this one, to avoid perpetuating the myth.

But the evidence, as savants in other fields would see at once, is purely anecdotal. Parables are marvellous teaching tools. But don't forget that the only thing winning companies have in common is their success – which may well not last: merely look at the loss-making agonies of Caterpillar Tractor, one of the top stars of *In Search of Excellence* and for decades among everybody's top marketing companies. To get anywhere in understanding management, you have to move from the particular to the general, but don't be led beyond the general to the universal.

The temptation to follow those misleading footsteps, though, is wellnigh irresistible. Just imagine finding the secret of successful innovation, the key to market survival, let alone triumph in the 1980s: surely the key lies among the successful innovators? That's what *Fortune* magazine thought, anyway. It looked at 'Eight Big Masters of Innovation', selected by an exhaustive process, and sought to discover what American Airlines, Apple, Campbell Soup, GE, Intel, Merck, 3M and Philip Morris could teach the sluggards. So what's the Holy Grail of innovation?

Surprise, surprise: 'The management of each of the eight is convinced of the *need* to innovate, regarding new ideas as the essence of long-term survival.' That discovery is about as original, and as useful, as announcing that water is wet. Then, 'No matter how dependent the companies are on purely technological advances, they are uniformly devoted to marketing' – again, what else is new? Other glimpses of the obvious are duly sanctified: 'Listening carefully to their customers . . . clearly defined cultures . . . such mom-and-flag values as product quality, market leadership and [naturally] the necessity of invention.' It's more valuable (but not much) to know that the Eight 'ruthlessly limit the search for new ideas to areas they are competent to exploit'.

This meagre result is par for the course. What lends the executive his peculiar charm and weakness, though, is less his readiness to swallow other men's myths than his inability to recognize his own nakedness – his impotence, incompetence and error. So do recognize it: the shock of recognition will improve your performance and give you a lasting start on unshocked competitors. Make things easier for yourself by simplifying everything you can, wherever and whenever you can.

William Blackie, when chief executive of Caterpillar Tractor, never said wiser words than these: 'I deride the idea that an executive's function is problem-solving – it is the bad executive who is up to his neck in problems.' Blackie wasn't thinking of the real, monster anxieties, like those of his own successors as they wrestled with recession in key markets, deadly competition from Komatsu and excessive costs in their own plants. He referred to the fact that, in the standard big-company bureaucracy, executives stalk new problems with the eagerness of the hunters of the snark. As if ordinary life threw up too few troubles, they invent and invite extra complexity. Any business situation can be reduced to simple terms. If it is, the solution usually appears from the reduction, and the 'problem' evaporates.

The surest way to simplify is to concentrate. Don't, if you are brilliant at making executive jets, reckon that you will be an expert hand at autos (especially steam ones). If the company can find one lucrative activity or market in which it functions well, sufficient unto the day be the profit thereof. Concentration also means that the single-minded company must be single-minded about its overriding objective, which is to be the best at everything from production costs (the lowest) and efficiency (the highest) in serving the consumer. If you can supply more effectively on a lower cost base than anybody else, you must win.

The more a business concentrates, the less time its executives need to waste. The single-minded company, alas, tends to become monomaniacal as well; its executives are expected to live only for power tools or whatever, and they don't like to buck the system. So every last detail of the business is regurgitated to fill long days of discussion. Even in average circumstances, discussions take up half an executive's time, and interruptions do the rest of the damage.

According to a Swedish study, fourteen minutes is the maximum for which an executive is left on his own; and nine minutes is his top time without interruption. No wonder he can't think straight. Resist this vice strenuously. The object, as in management generally, is to get the most with the least, the maximum effective management thought and follow-up with the minimum expenditure of hours. Ask of every activity, and especially of every meeting, whether it serves any purpose directly related to the company's profit. Organize the company so that a normal working day will cover normal tasks. And pack executives (including yourself) off home at decent times (that is, unless they don't want to go). Never disturb them after hours without grave cause, and humble apologies.

A dangerously narrow line divides a company that wastes no time from a stagnant bunch of idle corporate loafers. The best way to avoid stagnation is to manage young. That is, give men high responsibility as soon as you know that they won't stuff your bank (Penn Square) with so many duff energy loans, and pass them on to so many big bank suckers, that not only does your own bank crumble, but the once-great Continental Illinois is saved from collapse (and with it the entire US banking system) only by a $4.5 billion bail-out. Mozart was dead at thirty-five. So are many living executives. The one great idea that, if Freud was right, is all any man is given, comes early rather than late. If you wait until men are over forty, let alone fifty, to give them their most important job, you will miss their prime – and so will they. Young executives are no more all brilliant balls of energy than old ones are all sputtered-out volcanoes. But the good oldsters were better when they were younger, or would have been, if somebody had given them a chance.

And don't kid yourself that you've rejuvenated the company by lowering the average age of the executives from fifty-seven to fifty-three. That is different in degree, but not in kind, from the octogenarian British chairman who decided to retire to make way for a younger man. He meant his son, a stripling in his sixties. Somebody, preferably that son, should long before have told the old roadblock to clear himself away. But the circumstances of the people almost certainly made serious criticism impossible. Don't let it happen in your company, and don't stay where it has happened. If an executive can't be frank with his colleagues and seniors, he won't be frank with himself either; both sins are equally dangerous.

Never take frankness as far as boasting. The Canadian press tycoon Lord Thomson should have bitterly regretted the day when he described his Scottish television franchise as 'a licence to print money'. So it was; but it didn't take long before the government, alerted and offended, altered the licence drastically in its own favour. Remember, as a better example, the Swiss of Hoffman-La Roche, who have the world's most profitable drug company. For years nobody, except possibly its bankers, knew how much money Roche coined. When the facts began to emerge, under the pressure of government investigations, the reasons for Roche's secrecy became even more apparent: it was charging $10 a gram for tranquillizers that cost 56 cents to produce. Such conduct is extreme and not to be imitated. But 'speak only when spoken to and avoid vainglory' is a sounder course than hiring a public relations army and missing no opportunity to extol your own merits. You may not have any.

For salutary proof of your demerits, follow up a few complaints. No criticism that has reached me in my game, however rude or ignorant, has been without a valuable grain of truth, and your game is no different. In some cases, it isn't just a grain of truth, but a whole Sahara Desert. To be specific, if a car company delivers to a customer (probably several weeks late) a model that comes to pieces in his hands, and then takes several months of acrimonious correspondence, and several returns of the machine, before its offence is put right, then that firm is rotten from top to bottom and needs total overhaul fast.

Don't skate around complaints on the grounds that detail is not your business. The argument that board-level executives, or any executives, should look at the wood and forget about the trees is an incitement to, and an excuse for, unforgivable slackness. The good executive at any level can distinguish between a vital detail and rubbish, and a detail a day keeps the liquidator away. Sometimes, spotting even a beam in your own eye, let alone a few motes, is psychologically difficult. Overcoming this repression is where outside critics come in – so don't be like General Motors and try to wish your own private Ralph Naders away. Like Nader's Raiders, they will, more often than not, be right.

That, true, was in another era, and, besides, the car Nader complained of (the Corvair) is dead. But GM's harassing of Nader's private life fell into the same pattern as the blind eye for its own faults that culminated in dreadful reverses at the hands of the Japanese. The great corporation today is greatly changed, and not before time: but it deserved its great punishment for infringing a creakingly ancient moral rule. Do unto others as you would be done by: in other words, behave yourself. Few sights in world business are more unattractive than that of large companies seeking credit and praise for progressive labour policies, or for their anti-pollution, anti-racialism, and anti-poverty programmes – as if they had some right, which they were generously waiving, to foul the environment, or exacerbate social tensions, or grind the workers' faces in the dust.

After Walter Reuther forced the guaranteed annual wage on GM, the company took credit for the innovation. Executives whose firms have ignored their social responsibilities for decades applaud themselves for doing so no longer. But in fact, the environment is still being polluted, and you will still find only slightly more Jews on the boards of US blue chips than non-white men in any executive role in any European company: and you will still find disgracefully few women in senior executive positions anywhere in the western world (and you can just forget about Japan). The tide of women emerging from the business schools will change this sorry situation – but too slowly for the tastes of many able women. Like the Jewish immigrants before them, or the Asians in Britain today, they are creating their own opportunities as entrepreneurs. But corporate America will be poorer without them – and serve it right. If prejudice restricts a company's hiring policy, it will miss able people. In many mediocre giants, careers are still not really open to all talents. Change that, and you will change the giants, and possibly their mediocrity.

The company's social obligations begin at home. 'In many auto companies life is like a jungle,' said one escapee. 'Among executives, it is dog eat dog.' That is no less barbaric than it sounds, and an uncivilized company is no more worth living in than a cannibal country. Even decent companies such as General Foods were in danger of forgetting that people are not pawns. 'That place is much like being in the army,' an observer once said. 'They rotate people terrifically.'

Don't let your company be like either a jungle or the services. Executives are neither animals nor conscripts; they can be made to behave like both, but at dreadful loss in both effectiveness and ordinary humanity. Employees are not 'Honeywellers' and 'IBM-ers', as companies like to call them: and it's fortunate for companies, as well as individuals, that changing social norms, the high pressures of high technology and the work of the Theory $\Upsilon$ enthusiasts have dispelled much of the aura of the old Organization Man. Employees produce their best work if they are treated as what they are, individuals. Their loyalty to the corporation is worthwhile only if it is voluntary, non-conformist and, like undercarriages, easily retractable.

The only excuse for being displeased when a good executive retracts himself is if the move is a genuine mistake. If the manager is moving to a better job, and you can't outbid the opposition, be happy. After all, the man is supposed to be your friend; and nobody is indispensable (especially you). Huge turnover of executives is a bad sign; someone is either managing or hiring badly. But nil turnover is possibly even worse. The company can't be hiring and developing the ambitious, able, and energetic people it desperately needs; otherwise some of them would inevitably energize themselves out of the place. Moreover, if holes don't open up, you can't fill some of them with new talent, and that is fatal.

Fresh talent need not be imported; it can very often be dredged up from the company's own depths. But only these regular transfusions can save a corporation from the major surgery to which most eventually come. Unfortunately, the surgery only rearranges the same parts. The most effective shake-ups are cataclysmic, not kaleidoscopic. The best thing that ever happened to I. G. Farben, the pre-war German chemical giant, was the break-up by the Allied occupiers of a lumbering, cartel-ridden mammoth into three aggressive and distinct component parts. The worst thing that happened to Krupp after the Nazi defeat was its preservation intact by a wily owner: that signed the company's death-warrant as a leading European industrial force. 'The first billion-dollar giant that deliberately hives off a few hundred million dollars of superfluous, profitable sales will make history and a fortune for its stockholders.'

The last sentence is in quotes because I wrote it a long time ago – years before company after company proved my point by unloading division after division, including some mistakes that had only recently been purchased. In some cases the grounds were grand strategy (like Gould selling off boring base businesses to concentrate on gee-whiz electronics): in others, management was repairing past errors (like Coca-Cola abandoning its attempt to lord it over Californian wine): in others still, the pressures were financial (like the need to reduce vast debts after Du Pont's purchase of Conoco, or after the mega-buy of Esmark by the now largely disbanded Beatrice Foods). Whatever the motive, the consequences are the same: a business worth more to the stockholders and in a position, like any tree, to grow more strongly for being pruned.

Size, apart from its other drawbacks, kills homeliness. One common factor of unusually successful firms is their hick quality. They don't have plush metropolitan offices, or, so.netimes, plush offices at all. Their heart is in some undistinguished locale such as Goole, Yorkshire. Their bosses know New York and London, but can't wait to get home. Homespun companies such as the boys from Hartford, Connecticut (Emhart: shoe machinery and materials, etc.) have built world interests in their concentrated specialities without succumbing to the tempting passion for sophistication and complication.

Simple principles sound laughably naïve; one modern tycoon built his fortune on an old-fashioned platform of paying for everything in cash, neither giving nor receiving credit, and never borrowing – but note that he made a fortune. Non-tycoons, lacking the intuitive quality of business genius, can't afford the same luxury of sticking to principles at all costs. The common-or-garden executive needs flexibility, readiness to change course, even in midstream, willingness to look acidly even at success.

The Apollo programme, hailed as a triumph of 'good' professional management, is a caution in itself. Because you have landed a man on the moon by 1970 for a mere $50 billion, don't assume you've managed brilliantly – maybe it should have been done for $30 billion. Worry more about the worms inside the apple. Then, maybe, astronauts won't be fried alive, and Apollo 13 won't be sent on a hazardous fool's errand to the moon; both through major procedural defects. The real lesson of Apollo is that, if the objective is attainable and there is no limit to the resources available, executives can achieve almost any task. That is not news. But don't manage (and many companies do) as if you are NASA. There are always limits to the resources of a corporation – first, that it isn't the executives' money; second, that behind the stockholders, the money belongs to the community.

Executives are highly privileged individuals. They receive sweeping power over society's economic resources – far more than that of politicians, but entirely in a private capacity – to do with what they will, under conditions of low accountability and virtual permanence. Few executives feel this burden of national responsibility. But they won't do their duty by the country's wealth until they see their work stripped of its mythological trappings and in its true, unflattering light – and thus do it better.

One persistent myth, which the Europeans used to believe about America, is that some other national economy holds the antidote to whatever ails your own country. Americans have now fallen for this comforting idea themselves – the comfort lying in the fact that, if there truly were some magic ingredient that could be imported, a sort of managerial ginseng, economic ailments would be easily curable. The Japanese management model has proved unsurprisingly attractive to US businessmen wondering and worrying about how these ace competitors from the East have captured so many home and overseas markets. It's true that, just as any sensible company constantly studies its competitors, and even counterparts in other businesses, to find ways of improving its performance, much can always be learnt from other countries. But there are no panaceas available, from Japan or anywhere else.

The reality of Japan is that its magic consists of little more (though that's a lot) than dedicated application to clearly defined tasks, founded on the belief that constant improvement (in products, processes, efficiency) is always possible: built around the conviction that a corporation worth working for is worth fighting for; sustained by a tradition of mutual respect, and animated by a non-stop competitive drive. Nothing in Japanese management success should be strange to any American manager who has read the realities of lasting American success – as the Japanese certainly have.

The Ten Truths of Management given in these pages form a

simple anti-myth kit. A wise reader of the manuscript objected that hardly any of the truths apply to executives only, but are common to almost all humanity. He had holed in one. Management is precisely that, a general human activity, to which the best guides are not the management textbooks, but history, sociology, and psychology. The first myth of management – that it exists – seeks to take management away from where it belongs and to put it on a pedestal of pseudo-science. Executives placed on pedestals fall from a great height. If the Ten Truths (see p. 103) keep you off the pedestal, at least the drop will be much shorter.

Another truth lies behind all ten. One of the least attractive myths of management holds that nobody can get rich without at some point being a crook, a con-man, or a mobster. Many crooks, con-men, and mobsters have made great wealth. It does not follow that crookedness is the path to business success, nor that executives can throw private morality overboard as they plunge into corporate vice. Ponder, rather, how it is that the Quakers and similar deeply religious gentry made so much worldly lucre. It was because they treated their people honestly and decently, worked hard and honestly themselves, spent honestly and saved pennies, honestly put more back into the company than they took out, made honestly good products, gave honest value for money and, being honest, told no lies. The naked manager can never find better clothes.

# Index

The names of companies are in small capitals and are referred to in the same familiar form as is used in the text.

Abegglen, James, 159
accounting methods, 17, 27–9, 51, 56–7, 78
Adams, Robert M., 150
*Advanced Management Report*, 198
*Age of the Common Millionaire, The*, 231
Agnelli, Giovanni, 48
Amdahl, Gene, 142
AMERICAN AIRLINES, 243
AMERICAN CYANAMID, 175
AMERICAN HOME PRODUCTS, 204
APPLE, 5, 132–3, 139–40, 143, 145, 181, 212, 214, 243
Appleby, Robert, 193
ARMOUR, 35
Ash, Roy, 9, 116
AT & T, 39–40, 161, 162, 181
ATARI, 7, 181, 184
AUHEUSER-BUSCH, 209
AUTOMATIC SPRINKLER, 6
AVIS, 8, 227
AVON, 7

BALL CORPORATION, 171–2
BAT, 182, 184
BAYER, 51

BEATRICE FOODS, 249
BEECHAM, 206–7
Bell, David, 85
de Benedetti, Carlo, 200–201
Bergerac, Jacques, 173
Berndtson, Per, 41
BLACK AND DECKER, 193
Blackie, William, 244
Bludhorn, Charles, 12
BMW, 204
BOCA-RATON, 145
Bonoma, Thomas V., 188–9
books on business, 219–29
Bosch, Robert, 202
BOEING, 13
Breech, Ernest R., 48
BRITISH LEYLAND, 32
Bryan, John H., Jr, 169–70
Bray, John, 110–11
BTR, 206–7
BURMAH OIL, 72, 84–5
*Business Week*, 7, 28, 30, 72, 138, 210–11
*Business of Success, The* (Heller), xi, 80
*Business of Winning, The* (Heller), xi, 80, 93
buy-outs, 112–14

Caldwell, Philip, 96
Calloway, D. Wayne, 210
CAMPBELL SOUP, 243
CANON, 136, 151, 152–3, 155–7, 159, 160, 162
Cascade, Bois, 14
Carter, Jimmy, 100
Cary, Frank, 207
cash liquidity, 27, 30, 57, 79, 85, 103, 207
CATERPILLAR TRACTOR, 214, 243, 244
Caulkin, Simon, 134
CHICAGO PACIFIC, 194
CHRYSLER, 35, 223
CIBA-GEIGY, 51
CITROËN, 200
Clark, Thomas B., 171–2
COCA-COLA, 173–4, 204, 209, 249
Cohen, Sir Jack, 176
COLOROLL, 111
Colston, Sir Charles, 193
COMET, 183
*Common Millionaire, The*, 230
CONOCO, 249
Conran, Sir Terence, 177–8
CONSOLIDATED FOODS, 169–70
CONTINENTAL ILLINOIS, 3, 9, 245
Cornfield, Bernie, 12, 235, 237
Couch, John, 154
Coverdale, Ralph, 131

DAIMLER-BENZ, 10, 49, 77, 200–201
Danforth, T. R., 235
DANFOSS, 201
DART, 167–8
DELUXE CHECK PRINTERS, 204, 206
Denning, Frederick W., 160
DESIGN AND MANUFACTURING, 88
DIGITAL EQUIPMENT CORPORATION, 109, 136–8, 213
discounted cash flow, 57
DISNEY, 7
diversification, 165–72
DOVER, 204, 206
DOW JONES, 204–5

Dreyfus, Pierre, 48
Drucker, Peter, xii, xiii, 93, 139, 196, 228
DU PONT, 9, 13, 34, 42, 47, 51, 88, 146, 167, 249
DURACELL, 167
Duttweiler, Gottlieb, 233

earnings per share, 21–30
Eisenhower, Dwight, 53
ELECTROLUX, 194, 202
EMHART, 249
EQUITY FINANCING, 3
Ericsson, L. M., 162, 204
Estridge, Philip, 144–5
executive stress, 244–5
EXPRESS DAIRIES, 176
EXXON, 150

FAIRCHILD, 135
FIAT, 33, 48, 49, 77, 200
Figgie, Harry, 6
*Financial Times*, ix, 11, 168, 194
Ford, Henry, 135
Ford, Henry, II, 96, 221, 224, 229
FORD MOTORS, 33, 87, 88, 199, 223–5, 229
Forte, Sir Charles, 109–10, 176
*Fortune* magazine, 7, 30, 38, 87, 88, 99, 137, 174, 176, 180–81, 184, 202, 204–6, 208, 209, 243
Foster, William K., 198
FUJI, 89, 91
Fujisawa, Takeo, 125–7
*Further Up the Organisation* (Townsend), 8

Galbraith, John Kenneth, 230
Geneen, Harold, 48, 221, 225–6
GENERAL ELECTRIC COMPANY (GEC), x, 9, 42, 46, 48, 49, 88, 109–10, 151–2, 161, 243
GENERAL MOTORS (GM), 9, 13, 33, 38, 49, 54, 58, 77, 88, 246–7
Giannini, A. P., 233

giant companies, 13–14, 91–2, 200
Goizueta, Robert, 173–4
Gould, Jay, 23
GOULD INC., 152, 249
government interference, 52–3, 99
GRAND METROPOLITAN, 176–7
Green, Sir Owen, 207
GUEST KEEN & NETTLEFOLD, 37
Gulbenkian, Calouste, 237
GULF OIL, 166–7

HABITAT, 179
HANES, 169–70
*Harvard Business Review*, 185, 188
Harvard Business School, 44
Hawthorne experiments, 61–3
Hayes, Robert, 151
Heath, Edward, 53
Hefner, Hugh M., 39
HEIDELBERGER DRUCKMASCHINEN, 201
HEUBLEIN, 175
HEWLETT-PACKARD, 7, 127, 136–8, 150, 180
HOFFMAN LA ROCHE, 78, 246
Hollingbery, Michael, 183–4
Honda, Soichiro, 109, 125–7
HONDA, 90
HONEYWELL, 16, 162
HOOVER, 192–5
Hoover, Herbert, Jr, 193
Hunt, H. L., 238

Iacocca, Lee, 220–21, 223–5, 228
IBM, 5, 10, 88, 132, 140–48, 154, 161–2, 180, 187, 201, 204, 207, 212–14, 216
ICI, 9, 51, 77
I. G. FARBEN, 37, 248
IMPERIAL GROUP, 168
IMPERIAL TOBACCO, 182
*In Search of Excellence* (Iacocca), 7, 219–21, 243
inflation, 51–2, 56–8, 98–9
Insull, Samuel, 3

INTEL, 145, 161, 243
INTERNATIONAL HARVESTER, 9
INTERNATIONAL NICKEL, 31
IOS, 3
ITT, 3, 9, 48, 88, 173, 225–7

Japanese industry, xi, xiii, 49, 76, 89–90, 125–6, 136, 146, 151, 155–63, 187, 206, 214, 221, 250
Jobs, Steven, 132–5, 139, 141, 154
JOHNSON, S. C., AND SON, 208
Joseph, Sir Maxwell, 108–9, 176–7

KAISER ALUMINIUM, 31
Kaku, Ryuzaburo, 152–3, 155–7, 159
KELLOGG, 204–5
KENTUCKY FRIED CHICKEN, 175
Kettering, Charles, 135
KING RESOURCES, 3
KOCKUMS shipyard, 101
KOMATSU, 214, 244
KRAFT, 167–8
Krenger, Ivan, 3
Krumm, Daniel J., 206
KRUPP, 72, 248

Land, Edwin, 158
Lehr, Lewis, 149
LEITZ, 90
leverage, 112–13, 205
LEVI-STRAUSS, 7–8
Lewis, John Spedan, 232
LIP, 74
Little, Royal D., 109–10, 112, 114
LITTON INDUSTRIES, 3, 9, 42–4, 72, 116
LOCKHEED, 35, 37, 72
LOUIS VUITTON, 202
LTV, 88

*Management Today*, 38, 95, 169–70, 183, 191, 200–201, 206–7
managers
  accessibility of, 162
  achievement, criterion of, 3

age of, 69, 75, 97, 104
ambition of, 107–8, 207
blurring of functions of, 77
cash, appreciation of need for, 57
competitiveness of, 83
costs, duty to minimize, 59, 99–100
expertise of, myth of, 14
failings of, 5–6
failure, effect of, on, 49
fraud by, 23
freedom of, 69
immigrants as, 86–7
independence of, 147–8
inertia of, 116
innovation, necessity of, for, 243
insecurity of, 67
insight of, 84
judged by results, 14
knowledge
    of industry, 170–71
    of markets, 180–81
largest companies, of, 33, 49
leaders, as, 93–5
military chain of command of, 49
motivation of, 42–3, 61–8,
    115–16, 159
myth-builders, as, 43
outside commitments of, 95–6
outsight of, 84
promotion of, 117, 162
selection of, 61
short-term decisions of, 19
staff, relations with, 51, 76
stock options of, 12, 21
technology, and, 139
training of, 77, 162
*Managing* (Geneen), 221, 225–6
Margerison, Charles, 130
marketing, 135, 142–4, 157, 161,
    170, 180, 184–5, 188–9, 192,
    204, 207, 211, 215–17
Markhula, Mike, 133, 135
Marks, Simon, 1st Baron, 48
MARKS & SPENCER, 189–92
Massaro, Donald, 137

Matsushita, Konosuke, 101–3
MATTEL, 181–2, 184
MAYTAG, 204, 206
MAZDA, 128–9, 199
McCormack, Mark, 220–23
McDONALDS, 203
McGregor, Douglas, 62
McKenna, Regis, 132
McSwinney, James W., 30
MEAD CORPORATION, 30
MERCK, 204, 243
MERCEDES, 204
mergers, 36–7, 47–8, 165–77, 215,
    246
MICHELIN, 154
MICROSOFT, 145
MIGROS, 233
MITCHELL ENERGY, 204–5
MMM, 149–50, 154, 243
Moda, Mitz, 125
MOËT-HENNESSY, 201
MONTECATINI, 51
Montgomery, F.-M. Bernard, 1st
    Viscount, 118–21
Morgan, J. P., 23
MOTHERCARE, 177–9
motivation, 42–3, 61–8, 115–16, 159
*My Years with General Motors* (Sloan),
    228

NABISCO, 168
Nader, Ralph, 246
*Naked Investor, The* (Heller), 11, 165
*Naked Manager, The*, x, xi, 1–2, 81,
    102, 219
*Naked Market, The* (Heller), 1, 165,
    173, 180
NALCO CHEMICAL, 204
NATIONAL SEMICONDUCTOR, 135
NATIONAL STUDENT MARKETING, 3
NATIONAL CASH REGISTER (NCR),
    154, 237
NESTLÉ, 168
*New Naked Manager, The* (Heller), x,
    1, 219, 230, 242

Nixdorf, Heinz, 201–2
Nixon, Richard, 53
Nordhoff, Heinz, 48
NORTON, 90

OCCIDENTAL, 167
OGILVY AND MATHER, 209
oil price fluctuation, 77, 98–9, 164, 213
OLIVETTI, 162, 181, 199, 200–201
Olsen, Ken, 109–10, 138
*Once and Future Manager, The* (Heller), 41, 51, 61, 71
Opel, John, 141–3, 146

Palmer, Arnold, 221–2
Patterson, John H., 237
PECHINEY, 77
PENN CENTRAL, 19
PENN SQUARE, 3
PEPSI-COLA, 173, 209–11
Pereira, Cesar L., 198
Perot, Ross, 12
*Peter Principle, The* (Peter), 220
PEUGEOT, 33, 200
PHILCO, 87
PHILIP MORRIS, 166–7, 209, 243
PHILIPS, 162
PLAYBOY ENTERPRISES, 38–9
PLOUGH, 175
POLAROID, 42, 158
price-cutting, 183–4, 216
price/earnings ratio, 16, 20–24
PROCTER & GAMBLE, 209
profits, 3, 18–19, 24–5, 27, 58, 68–9, 78, 85, 215

Quaker businessmen, 102
quality of products, 101–2

Ramsay, Bill, 184–5
RANK ORGANIZATION, 31
Rayner, Derek, 1st Baron, 190
RCA, 37, 42, 151
Reagan, Ronald, 199

Regensbrief, Samuel, 87–8
RENAULT, 48
Reuther, Walter, 247
REVLON, 7, 173
RHONE-POULENC, 51
Ringoen, Richard M., 171–2
Rock, Art, 133
ROHM, 162
ROLLS-ROYCE, 3, 19
ROTHMANS INTERNATIONAL, 166
ROWNTREE-MACKINTOSH, 36

SAINSBURY, 190
SAKURA, 89, 91
sales, 111, 114–15, 128–9, 142–4
scale, dis-economies of, 33–4, 38, 90
SCHERING, 175
Sculley, John, 135
SEARS ROEBUCK, 191–2
SEQUOIA CAPITAL FUND, 135
shares, 20–22, 26–9, 32
SHELL, 13, 31, 33–4, 49, 67
SHULTON, 175
SIEMENS, 201–2
Simpson, David, 152
Singleton, Henry, 133
Sloan, Alfred P., 228
small companies, 38–9, 86–91, 110
SMITHKLINE BECKMAN, 204, 207
'social audit', 55, 78
SONY, 153–4, 196
SQUIBB, 175
STANDARD OIL TRUST, 37
stock market collapses, 11, 16, 45, 51, 98, 231
stock options, 12, 21–2, 27, 135
*Supermanagers, The*, (Heller), xi, 106, 122
*Supermarketers, The*, xii, 187
Sutton, Thomas C., 206

Talley, Truman, 106–7, 219
Tatas family, 233
Taylor, Max, 131

technology in management, 139–41,
    149–50, 152–4
*Technology Review*, 125
TENNECO, 88
TESCO, 183–4
Tessler, Andrew, 104
TETRA PAK, 201
TEXAS INSTRUMENTS, 180, 182,
    188–9
TEXTRON, 109
Thackray, John, 150, 169–70
Thatcher, Margaret, 194
Thomson, Roy, 1st Baron, 245
Thornton, Tex, 43, 116
*Time* magazine, 141–2, 181, 200
TOJO RAYON, 51
Townsend, Robert, 8, 220, 227
TOYOTA, 77, 90, 199
Trade unions, 1, 47, 54–5
Tse, K. K., 189–90
TUBE INVESTMENTS, 37, 184
TUPPERWARE, 7, 167

UNILEVER, 49, 167–8
United States of America
    accounting practices, 27–8
    balance of payments deficit, 11
    dollar instability, 45
    European industry
        penetration by, 202–3
        views of, 201
    management methods, xi, 158–63
        adopted in Europe, 44
UNITED TECHNOLOGIES, 194
UNIVAC, 148

*Up The Organisation* (Townsend), 103,
    220, 227–8
US STEEL, 31, 88, 167

Valentine, Don, 132–3, 135, 136
VENESTA, 38
VOLKSWAGEN, 33, 42, 46, 48, 58,
    198–200
VOLVO, 33

*Wall Street Journal*, 205
Watson, Thomas, Sr, 141, 143, 148
Weinstock, Sir Arnold, 48, 109–10
Werthen, Hans, 202
WESTERN ELECTRIC, 88
WESTINGHOUSE, 88
WESTLAND, 194–5, 197
*What They Don't Teach You at Harvard
    Business School* (McCormack),
    221–2
WHITE CONSOLIDATED, 202
women in business, 104–5, 247
workforce, 54, 64–5, 73–6, 118–19,
    143, 159, 247–8
WORTHINGTON INDUSTRIES, 204
Wozniak, Stephen, 132, 150

XEROX, 37, 42, 84, 136, 154, 159

Young, Arthur, 198
Young, John, 137–8

ZANUSSI, 202
ZEISS, 90
Zilkha, Selim, 177–8